From Comrade to Citizen

From Comrade to Citizen

*The Struggle for Political Rights
in China*

Merle Goldman

Harvard University Press
Cambridge, Massachusetts
London, England

First Harvard University Press paperback edition, 2007

Library of Congress Cataloging-in-Publication Data

Goldman, Merle.
From comrade to citizen : the struggle for political rights in China / Merle Goldman.
p. cm.
Includes bibliographical references and index.
ISBN-13 978-0-674-01890-7 (cloth: alk. paper)
ISBN-10 0-674-01890-7 (cloth: alk. paper)
ISBN-13 978-0-674-02544-8 (pbk.)
ISBN-10 0-674-02544-X (pbk.)
1. Democratization—China.   2. China—Politics and government—1976–
3. Human rights—China.   4. Political culture—China.   I. Title.

JQ1516.G63 2005
320.651—dc22   2005040287

Dedicated to my grandchildren

Jessica, Todd, Jake, Sam, Jonah, David, Elie,
Nathan, Lauren, and Isaac

Acknowledgments

Like my other books, this one has taken a long time in coming to fruition. It differs from the other books, however, in that I had the title before I wrote the book. But even the title changed on the advice of my colleague Ellis Joffe of Hebrew University in Jerusalem. Originally the book was to be entitled from "From Subject to Citizen." Immediately on hearing the title, Ellis objected, explaining that a "subject" in the context of the Mao Zedong era (1949–1976) was called "comrade." As usual, he was right.

Many others have contributed to this book. I am most grateful to the readers—Joseph Fewsmith, Elizabeth Perry, and Paul Cohen—who, as in the past, have read my books with great care and given wise counsel. My colleagues at the Fairbank Center for East Asian Research of Harvard University, with which I have been affiliated since my graduate school days, have contributed in so many different ways to my work. Chief among them are Roderick MacFarquhar, Steven Goldstein, Robert Ross, Ezra Vogel, and Lucian Pye. In addition, I have benefited greatly from visiting scholars to the Center, including Robert Culp, who wrote on citizenship in China in an earlier period, and Wang Juntao and Liu Junning, who attempted to act as citizens in China. The Fairbank Center not only has provided intellectual inspiration and stimulation but also has made it possible for me to interact with distinguished scholars and participants in the important events in Chinese history.

This book could not have been written without the computer assistance of Jorge Espada and especially the editorial assistance of Nancy Hearst, the Fairbank Center Librarian, who, as with my past books, not only rechecked all the footnotes but also offered editorial assistance and advice that has been invaluable. I am so fortunate to live and work in an environment that offers so much scholarly sustenance.

Finally, but of course not least, once again I must thank my wonderful family—my late parents, my children, my grandchildren, and especially my husband, Marshall—who, throughout the slow, tedious process of my producing a book, have never faltered in their faith that it would be done and never resented the time it took away from other activities. I feel blessed to have such a family.

Contents

Abbreviations

ACFTU	All-China Federation of Trade Unions
ALL	Administrative Litigation Law
BWAF	Beijing Workers Autonomous Federation
CAS	Chinese Academy of Sciences
CASS	Chinese Academy of Social Sciences
CCP	Chinese Communist Party
CDP	China Democracy Party
CPPCC	Chinese People's Political Consultative Conference
CYL	Communist Youth League
GLF	Great Leap Forward
LGLR	League to Guarantee Labor Rights
MFN	most-favored nation
NGO	nongovernmental organization
NPC	National People's Congress
PLA	People's Liberation Army
SERI	Beijing Social and Economic Sciences Research Institute
SEZ	special economic zone
SOE	state-owned enterprise
VOA	Voice of America

From Comrade to Citizen

Introduction

From Comrades to Citizens in the Post-Mao Era

The conventional Western view of China in the last two decades of the twentieth century, as having experienced extraordinary economic reforms but few political reforms, is not altogether accurate. Indeed, China's economy was transformed as China moved from a state-controlled economy to a market economy involved in international trade, while its political system remained a Leninist party-state. But a number of significant grassroots political reforms took place as well. In 1987 China began elections for village head and village council; by the late 1990s these elections were held in nearly 80 percent of China's almost one million rural villages.[1] Also by the early twenty-first century several of China's townships held multicandidate elections for township head, and a few townships held direct competitive elections for the township party committee, including the party secretary. Hitherto, the party committees in the townships had been appointed by a higher-level party committee.[2] Because the party committee has the ultimate power in the township area, this innovation introduced a degree of party accountability at the basic level of China's government. In some cities, members of neighborhood committees, which carry out civic administrative matters, were elected through competitive elections.[3] In addition, the media in local areas, particularly in Guangdong Province, ran exposés of official corruption and cover-ups, despite the party's periodic efforts to censor them and punish their editors.[4]

China's formerly rubber-stamp congress, the National People's Congress (NPC), became more assertive and no longer unanimously approved all legislation sent to it by the State Council.[5] The NPC also became a platform for expressing dissent, as in 1992 when 30 percent of delegates either voted no or abstained on the vote to build the Three Gorges Dam. And

1

one-tenth of the NPC delegates in March 2003 voted against former party secretary and president Jiang Zemin's staying on as chair of the state Central Military Commission after his retirement as head of the party.[6] In a few cases, the NPC sent back measures for revision, though it did not initiate any legislation on its own. Moreover, local people's congresses became more open to popular input. China also experienced expanding public space and the beginnings of a civil society with the establishment of thousands of nongovernmental organizations (NGOs), though they still had to be registered with the Ministry of Civil Affairs and under the auspices of a government agency.[7]

Although the party sanctioned these grassroots political changes in order to enhance its authority and maintain stability in the post-Mao era, other political changes were going on at the same time that were conducted without the party's imprimatur. One of the major changes in the last two decades of the twentieth century was a growing sense of rights consciousness, particularly of political rights. Initially articulated by intellectuals, this rights consciousness gradually spread to the population in general—workers, peasants, the growing middle class, and religious believers.

Thus, in the post-Mao era a number of individuals began to act as citizens. And at times, through their words and actions, they forced the leaders of China's party-state to reconsider their policies. In addition to a handful of party elders who spoke out on critical political issues, there are other individual examples, such as Gao Yaojie, an elderly female doctor who despite persistent harassment drew attention to the fact that the sale of contaminated blood was the major source of the AIDS epidemic in Henan Province; by late 2003, party leaders, who had previously ignored or covered up the problem, began to take the spread of AIDS seriously. Another example is Cao Siyuan, an independent consultant who in June 2003 convened a conference in Qingdao of leading academics and a number of officials to propose revisions to China's 1982 constitution—such as expunging Marxist ideology from the opening clause of the preamble and setting up a constitutional commission in the NPC to ensure that the constitutional stipulations are implemented.[8] Though Cao was put under surveillance and harassed by the authorities for convening the conference without party permission, his actions accelerated existing official discussions on revisions to the constitution; for instance, it was decided at the NPC meeting in March 2004 to insert into China's constitution a commitment to "protect private property" and to "respect and protect human rights."

The most prominent example of an individual speaking out on controversial issues in the post-Mao era is Jiang Yanyong, a retired army doctor in a Beijing military hospital. In reaction to the minister of health's claim on April 3, 2003, that the SARS (severe acute respiratory syndrome) epidemic had been brought under control, Jiang sent letters to the Western and Hong Kong media on April 8 contradicting the government's claim and calling for immediate action to contain the spreading disease. His efforts forced China's leaders at least to acknowledge publicly the seriousness of the disease, dismiss the minister of health and vice mayor of Beijing, who had claimed that the disease was under control, and begin efforts to control SARS. On February 24, 2004, Jiang brought up an even more sensitive issue—the military crackdown on June 4, 1989, on unarmed student demonstrators—in a letter to China's leaders, in which he described what he witnessed on the night of June 3, 1989, when scores of people who had been killed or wounded by the People's Liberation Army (PLA) were brought to his hospital. He urged China's leaders to admit the wrongs committed during the June 4 military crackdown and change the official designation of the 1989 demonstrations that had provoked the crackdown from "counterrevolutionary" to "patriotic." On this issue, which was politically sensitive, there was no rethinking of the party's policy. Rather, Jiang was detained on June 1, 2004, on the eve of the fifteenth anniversary of the June 4 crackdown. He was released seven weeks later, primarily thanks to internal and external pressures, including petitions on the Internet, but he remained under surveillance.

More significant than individual acts of citizenship is the group articulation and assertion of political rights in the post-Mao era. Periodically throughout Chinese history, including the People's Republic, individuals have dissented from government policies; most were repressed, a few were not. But groups that dissented were considered an organized threat to the regime and were usually harshly repressed. Nevertheless, group articulation of political rights in the post-Mao period began with two types of intellectuals. One group was the "establishment intellectuals," to use the term coined by Carol Hamrin and Timothy Cheek.[9] They were in the research institutes, media, and official commissions associated with the top party leaders in the 1980s, particularly with Hu Yaobang, general secretary from 1980 to 1987, and his successor, Zhao Ziyang, 1987 to 1989.[10] They sometimes expressed ideas that diverged from the leadership, but generally they expanded on the views of their official patrons, who sought to achieve reforms of the economic and political systems within the prevailing Leninist party-state. In the 1990s a small number of establishment intellectuals broke away from or disregarded party patronage and expressed a broad range of ideological views that not only diverged from the party's ideology but at times openly criticized the party's policies. They had become "critical intellectuals" within the establishment. In Western parlance, they would be called public intellectuals, intellectuals who spoke out publicly on political issues.[11]

The other group that articulated and at times attempted to assert their political rights could be called the "disestablished intellectuals." They had been on their way to becoming intellectuals in the establishment, but the suspension of higher education during the Cultural Revolution (1966–1976) interrupted their education and Mao ordered them to rebel against authority, turning them into Red Guards. When they provoked chaos, Mao then sent them to the countryside to learn from the peasants. Soon after Mao's death in September 1976, they returned to the cities, where a small number of them became involved in political activities—in particular the Democracy Wall movement (1978–1979), which demanded political as well as economic reforms. Others who became disestablished intellectuals were the student leaders of the 1989 Tiananmen demonstrations. Participation in these two movements prevented these intellectuals from becoming part of the establishment. A number of them became political activists, working outside the prevailing political system to bring about change.

At times the two groups worked together in critical political actions, blurring the distinctions between the establishment intellectuals and the disestablished intellectuals. They could be called cohorts (tong chai) within their generations, in that they shared a specific common experience—such as Red Guards and "sent-down youth" in the Cultural Revolution, and leadership of the 1989 Tiananmen movement. Their relationship was determined not so much by their age as by the unusual experiences they had gone through together.[12]

In the post-Mao period, these two groups were transformed from comrades into citizens. Ezra Vogel, in his classic article "From Friendship to Comradeship," points out that during the revolutionary struggle and in the early days of the People's Republic, the term comrade (tongzhi) connoted loyal, faithful, and trusted followers, including most intellectuals, with a small number of well-known exceptions.[13] But as the party and Mao Zedong launched ever-expanding political campaigns against supposed "enemies," starting in the mid-1950s, the term *comrade* came to identify those who unquestioningly obeyed party orders and subscribed to party policies. Any intellectual who dared to express a view that diverged from the party leadership, specifically from Mao, was persecuted and silenced. At great personal risk, a small number of intellectuals, some responding to Mao's relaxation of controls and encouragement of criticism of the bureaucracy during the Hundred Flowers period (1956–June 1957), criticized party officials and their policies and urged the leadership to live up to its professed ideals. In the subsequent anti-rightist campaign of 1957–1958, they and their families, colleagues, and friends were silenced, jailed, or worse. Some 550,000 intellectuals were labeled "rightists" and purged from their positions.[14] During the Cultural Revolution, millions more were persecuted, along with the once-honored skilled workers and party cadres.

After Mao's death, virtually all intellectuals were rehabilitated, and a significant number were appointed to important political positions as members of the intellectual networks of party general secretary Hu Yaobang and his successor Zhao Ziyang in the 1980s. Through their personal ties to senior leaders, they became the leaders of institutes, newspapers, and professional associations, as well as government officials, while at the same time they acted in the Confucian tradition as moral spokesmen addressing the leadership on behalf of the people. Though indoctrinated in Marxism-Leninism, they were influenced by the ideological debates in Eastern Europe in the 1970s and 1980s, which emphasized the humanistic aspects of Marxism and challenged the Leninist party-state. Some of them lost their positions during the campaigns against spiritual pollution in 1983–1984 and against bourgeois liberalization in 1987, but most remained in their posts until the purge of Zhao Ziyang in May 1989 and the military crackdown on demonstrators in Tiananmen Square on June 4, 1989. In the aftermath of these events, they were deprived of their official positions and were virtually silenced or went abroad into exile.

Despite the purge of the Marxist humanists from their official positions, a small number of intellectuals in the establishment who criticized party policies, and some outside it who had been blocked from positions in the establishment because of past political activities, attempted in the last two decades of the twentieth century to bring about political change without the permission or acquiescence of the party. Their actions resembled what

T. H. Marshall, in his classic study of citizenship in Western Europe in the nineteenth century, describes as "political citizenship"—the assertion of the right to participate in the exercise of political power.[16]

In the post-Mao era, groups as well as individuals challenged the party's policies through their actions as well as their ideas. They not only expressed views that directly challenged the party's policies, they also joined with others in actions to try to bring about fundamental political changes in the prevailing Leninist party-state. They helped move politics from the exclusive domain of the party and the intellectual elite into the public realm by at times including other social groups in their political activities and calling for political reforms that would allow political engagement beyond elite circles. Although they were continually persecuted, detained, and even imprisoned for their actions, they and new adherents persisted in attempting to achieve political rights in the last two decades of the twentieth century.

Critical Establishment Intellectuals Act as Citizens

During the Mao period (1949–1976), including the brief periods of political relaxation, such as the Hundred Flowers months, intellectuals could publicly express only ideas that Mao had enunciated. In the post-Mao era, particularly in the 1990s, groups of establishment intellectuals expressed a variety of ideological views—neo-Maoism, neoconservatism, neonationalism, new left, and liberalism. Furthermore, they participated in political discourse and debates in which at times they not only disagreed with one another but, more significantly, dissented from the views of the party leadership. Equally unprecedented in the People's Republic was the relatively independent role of politically oriented intellectuals in the establishment. Whereas in the 1980s most of the intellectuals who dominated ideological and political discourse were members of networks associated with China's reformist party leaders, in the 1990s they spoke and acted more as independent actors and participated in relatively independent ideological groups. They debated, organized, and published books and articles that challenged party views and policies, as well as one another.

The neo-Maoists and a few of the liberals were of the older generation active in the 1950s, but most of the other participants in the political discourse and debates were the generations of the Cultural Revolution and the 1989 demonstrations. Unlike the Marxist humanists of the 1980s, who did not want to risk severing themselves from the establishment even when they thought the political system was bankrupt, as many did after the Cultural Revolution, small cohorts of the Cultural Revolution and 1989 generations were willing to risk becoming marginalized or even disestablished. The role of loyal dissenters and upright literati who, in the Confucian tradition, spoke the truth to power and sought to transform the government from within, which was typical of establishment intellectuals during the Mao era and even the 1980s, no longer characterized the establishment intellectuals of the 1990s. In the last decade of the twentieth century, a small number of critical intellectuals in the establishment and those operating on its margins became increasingly conscious of their political rights and at times were willing to join with other groups to fight for them. They were transformed from faithful courtiers into a loyal opposition—or in modern parlance, from "comrades" into "citizens."

Disestablished Intellectuals: The Democracy Wall and 1989 Tiananmen Generations

While most Marxist humanists and critical intellectuals in the establishment sought to bring about political change through their positions in the political, economic, and cultural hierarchies, a small number of intellectuals worked outside the establishment or outside the official channels to bring about political change. They came from the generation of educated urban youth who most likely would have been in the establishment, had their education not been suspended during the Cultural Revolution and had they not responded to Mao's summons to rebel against authority. When these former Red Guards returned to the cities after their exile to the countryside to learn from the peasants, a number of them maintained ties with the groups they had formed during the Cultural Revolution and in late 1978 and 1979 participated in the Democracy Wall movement, in which some called publicly for political as well as economic reforms. The other major group of disestablished intellectuals consisted of the leaders of the 1989 demonstrations, who also called for political reforms along with an end to the spreading corruption and skyrocketing inflation of the late 1980s. Although the Democracy Wall and 1989 demonstrations had a variety of goals, ultimately both movements sought political reforms that would move China in a more democratic direction.

The party regarded both movements as challenges to its authority and suppressed them and arrested their leaders. When those leaders were released from prison or labor reform camps in the 1980s and early 1990s, most members of their generations were going into business *(xiahai)* or were becoming increasingly professionalized.[17] But because of their past political activities, the leaders of the Democracy Wall and 1989 demonstrations had difficulty entering the professions. Yet, in spite of the party's repression, some of them continued to act as citizens, by speaking out and organizing on issues of political consequence in the 1980s and 1990s.

Ironically, it was during the destructive, chaotic Cultural Revolution, when Mao summoned the youth to rebel against authority and the party bureaucracy was paralyzed, that the participants of the Democracy Wall movement learned to engage freely in public debates, publish leaflets, mobilize support, and organize political actions with others without the permission of the authorities. The leaders of the 1989 demonstrations used similar methods in their six weeks of political action, beginning with Hu Yaobang's death on April 15, 1989, and ending with the military crackdown on June 3–4. Because their participation in these movements had deprived them of the opportunity to become members of the establishment, many of them had no choice but to become freelance intellectuals, workers, or individual entrepreneurs *(getihu)*. At times they made common cause with ordinary workers and other social groups. As a result, they turned increasingly to grassroots political efforts to bring about political change. Unlike during the Mao period, when everyone was employed by the state, China's move to the market in the post-Mao period made it possible for them to survive economically and to support their political activities. Despite the party's repression of their movements and the arrest of their leaders, a significant number of the participants in these two movements persisted in trying to assert their political rights.

Although the political activists came mainly from these two movements, in the late 1990s they were joined by a small number of computer experts, mostly from the post–June 4 generation, who used the new telecommunications technologies—computers, the Internet, cell phones, pagers, and instant messaging—to express political views that diverged from the party's.[18] The Democracy Wall activists had used wall posters, mimeographed pamphlets, and debates in public spaces in front of city walls and in parks, and the 1989 demonstrators had used access to public squares, the foreign media, telephones, copy machines, fax machines, and travel to spread their ideas and elicit support. By the late 1990s the new telecommunications technologies provided cyber-dissidents and others with the potential to break down the separation between intellectuals and ordinary citizens and to coordinate and organize a movement on a national scale. These various coalitions resonated with the May 4 movement, when students sought to engage in joint efforts with workers and other social groups, and as Elizabeth Perry points out, only then did their combined quest to assert their political rights become a significant political force.[19] Equally as important, the new technologies made possible much greater interaction with the international community, which provided support for those seeking to assert their political rights and at times exerted pressure on the Chinese government to moderate its repression of those demanding political rights.

Although some leaders of the Democracy Wall movement were arrested in 1979–1980, others continued to engage in grassroots, nonofficial activities to bring about political change. One such effort was participation in competitive elections to local people's congresses in 1980 from the university districts in Beijing. Also, some of the Democracy Wall leaders attempted to establish politically oriented, nongovernmental think tanks in the 1980s. One of the most successful was the Beijing Social and Economic Sciences Research Institute (English acronym: SERI), established by two Democracy Wall veterans, Chen Ziming and Wang Juntao. SERI was dismantled in the crackdown after June 4, 1989. After a lull, some grassroots political organizations reemerged in the mid-1990s. They organized petitions, staged demonstrations, published independent publications, and formed new coalitions, culminating with the effort to establish an opposition political party, the China Democracy Party (CDP), in 1998.[20] Many of the leaders of the CDP were workers or individual entrepreneurs who, but for their participation in the 1978–1979 Democracy Wall movement and the 1989 Tiananmen demonstrations, would have been intellectuals. The CDP represented what party leaders had feared most since 1980—a coalition of intellectuals, small business owners, and workers engaged in political activity, reminiscent of Poland's Solidarity movement, which had brought down the Communist Party in Poland.

As other classes joined in the intellectuals' political activities toward the end of the twentieth century, consciousness of political rights began to spread beyond intellectual circles to workers, peasants, home owners evicted from their homes to make way for modernization projects, and religious believers who worshipped without official approval. Elizabeth Perry points out that the protests of ordinary citizens are based more on "rules consciousness" than on "rights consciousness." As she explains, since ancient times peasants as well as literati have taken actions to ensure that the state upholds the rules that it has established.[21] Nevertheless, in the late twentieth century there was an overlap between "rules consciousness" and "rights consciousness," as ordinary people as well as intellectuals used the language of rights and appealed to China's laws and stipulations in China's constitution to check or correct the party's policies. They also urged the party to respect the rights it recognized when it signed on to the two U.N. covenants on human rights in 1997–1998. They did it through a variety of methods, such as bringing suit against repressive officials, organizing petitions, or participating in demonstrations. The separation between the political consciousness and actions of the intellectuals and those of the rest of the population was no longer so distinct and on a number of occasions, as we shall see, intellectuals and other groups joined together in political actions.

The Historical Roots of an Active Citizenry

There were precedents for the various efforts to assert political rights during the last two decades of the twentieth century. An active citizenry may have been rare in the People's Republic, but it was not unprecedented in the late nineteenth century and early decades of the twentieth century. The concept of citizenship, as identified with political rights, was introduced from the West by way of Japan in the late Qing dynasty (1644–1911).[22] But as Andrew Nathan explains in his book *Chinese Democracy*, unlike in the West, the governments of the late Qing and the Republican period, as well as the People's Republic, considered rights not as inherent natural rights, but as given by the state.[23] Governments granted political rights, they did not recognize them. Moreover, political rights existed to enable citizens to contribute to the state rather than to protect the citizens from the state. The late Qing government, for example, allowed the establishment of county and subcounty councils, as well as provincial legislatures, with a limited suffrage, in order to imbue the population with the idea of citizenship as linking the individual to the state in the expectation of creating a more stable political order.[24]

The late nineteenth-century reformers Kang Youwei and Liang Qichao, who launched the 1898 Hundred Days of Reform that sought to reform China's traditional political system, both spoke of *citizens*. They used the terms *gongmin* (public persons) and *guomin* (nation's people) to define a citizen. The historians Joshua Fogel and Peter Zarrow explain that the two terms had similar meanings. They both implied popular sovereignty and participation.[25] Kang wrote in 1902, "Since all the people have the right to participate in assemblies and they all have the responsibility to be concerned about their country, they are called citizens *(gongmin)*." Both Kang and Liang saw the scholar-official elite as leading the reforms to create a new nation, but they regarded the nation's foundation as based on "renovated citizens" who not only were aware of their responsibilities but also participated in politics. Thus, the 1898 reformers' definition of citizenship included the notion of participation in the political life of the nation.[26]

The May 4 movement further promoted the idea of active citizen participation. In the early decades of the twentieth century, students, workers, and merchants established autonomous groups, encouraged the expression of independent opinions, and founded political associations. They also used the term *shimin* (city people) to define citizens in an urban setting. But as China became convulsed by warlordism in the 1920s, war with Japan in the 1930s, and open military conflict between the Kuomintang and the Chinese Communist Party (CCP) in the 1940s and earlier, the inclination to assert political rights and establish an autonomous citizenry declined in favor of building a strong state.[27] The overwhelming majority of intellectuals, like the political leaders, gradually became less concerned with citizen participation and more concerned with enhancing the power of the state so that China once again could become united, rich, and powerful. In fact, the Nationalist government (1928–1945) under the Kuomintang and Chiang Kai-shek's leadership equated citizen participation with support of the state.[28] It feared that individual or group assertions of political rights would weaken the state in its confrontation with Japan and the Chinese Communists, further destabilizing Chinese society. Overriding nationalist concerns, therefore, led to pervasive intellectual support for statism and weakening of the desire for autonomy and citizens' rights.[29]

Reinforced by the traditional Confucian belief in intellectual service to the state, this statist view continued into the post-Mao period. Despite their persecution during the Mao era, when Deng Xiaoping and his fellow reformers welcomed the intellectuals who had been purged by Mao back into the establishment to help reform the economy and open China to the outside world in the post-Mao period, most intellectuals enthusiastically gave their services to the state and were drawn into government service through political patronage as intellectuals had been since ancient times.

The over-fifty generation of intellectuals had been among the most se-
verely persecuted by Mao; nevertheless, when the Deng leadership asked
for their help and advice at the start of the reform era in the late 1970s and
early 1980s, they responded quickly and sought to work once again in the
official establishment.

Thus, the Confucian practices of government consulting with scholars
and utilizing their skills, and intellectuals providing their services to the
government, were revived in the post-Mao era. The ensuing patron–client
relationship between officialdom and intellectuals was not only a way
to get information and expertise from the intellectuals; as in Confucian
times, it was also a way to exert control and co-opt the intellectuals into the
establishment. Like their predecessors in traditional China and during the
Mao era, post-Mao intellectuals complied and initially sought to bring
about reform by remonstrating with the leadership rather than by asserting their political rights. With a Confucian sense of moral mission, they
sought to reform China by working in the establishment and reminding its
leaders of their highest ideals. They also saw themselves as acting on behalf
of the people vis-à-vis the state.

The "cultural fever" that gripped the intellectual community in the mid-
1980s involved reappraisals of China's history and culture, particularly
Confucianism, and comparisons with the West. This fever resembled past
literati attempts to deal with China's problems by reinterpreting history
and revising ideology. Like the Confucian literati, establishment intellectuals in the 1980s regarded themselves as responsible for defining and maintaining moral and ideological norms, not only for the general population
at large but also for the political leadership. Also, by reinterpreting Marxism in a humanistic context, establishment intellectuals sought to exert
moral and ideological constraints on the political leadership. Intellectuals
once again tried to act as the conscience of society, as their predecessors
had done before 1949 and as they had been unable to do under Mao.

Under the auspices of various political patrons, most notably the reformist party leaders Hu Yaobang and Zhao Ziyang, intellectuals not only
assumed the leadership of important government policy-making institutes
and think tanks, published in official newspapers and journals, participated in policy deliberations, and were put in charge of professional federations in place of the party hacks of the Mao era, they also organized
associations and societies that had more autonomy than the official professional federations, though still under the patronage of the party. Only

gradually, as their efforts failed to limit the persistent repression of dissidents and recurring political campaigns, did they move toward the idea of trying to limit political power by developing laws and establishing institutions to circumscribe political power and prevent political abuses. But they still sought to achieve these goals by working within the establishment and through their political patrons.[30]

Nevertheless, in the late 1980s a few establishment intellectuals began to criticize publicly the traditional close relationship between intellectuals and the state, which they denounced as a means of co-opting the intellectuals. They also provided the ideological justification for intellectuals to work outside the prevailing political system to bring about change. One of the first to state these views publicly was literary critic and Beijing Normal University professor Liu Xiaobo. He had gone abroad in 1988 and returned to Beijing at the height of the 1989 protests and joined three other intellectuals on June 3–4, 1989, to try to evacuate Tiananmen Square peacefully. In late 1989 and 1990, Liu published in a Hong Kong journal a series of essays in which he berated his fellow intellectuals for their subservience to the political leadership and castigated them for not having "broken free from the classic mold unchanged for thousands of years." He compared them to the idealized Confucian scholar-bureaucrat, Qu Yuan, who, though abused by the emperor, "never wavered in his loyalty to the emperor." Liu then asked: "Why is it that intellectuals in the end always remained the 'prostitutes' and 'tools' of emperors? Why have intellectuals always tried their best to undermine one another instead of forming a cohesive force?"[31] His answer was that they opposed only corrupt officials and "fatuous" rulers," but not the despotism of the autocratic system "because . . . [they have] traditionally been given power and have been bureaucratized"; when they are listened to and given political position and fame, their "opposition . . . soon becomes obedience for the purpose of achieving their own vested interest."[32] During the dynastic period, Liu explained, Chinese intellectuals staked their lives on open-minded monarchs and considered "becoming an outstanding scholar and then an official."[33]

Instead, Liu asserted, "one must rely on a class or group with independent political power and stake his life on a social force to achieve political success."[34] Otherwise, because of the patron–client relationship, China's "intellectuals cannot openly express their dissatisfaction with the people in power and the status quo through regular channels and can give vent to it only secretly."[35] They may privately denounce the Chinese autocracy, but publicly "they either sing its praises, contrary to their convictions or remain silent. Silence has become the common tool with which modern Chinese intellectuals resist evil." Consequently, "they cannot do a thing to weaken evil forces even if they are seething with discontent." They are "steeped in the ancient intellectual-cum-bureaucrat tradition that holds that a 'good scholar will make an official.'"[36] Liu lamented, China's intellectuals "have always chosen to follow the politicians." Consequently, he charged, "Mao stripped the people of all actual power over their lives."[37]

Because he defended the students in the negotiations that led to the peaceful exit of many students from the square, Liu spent eighteen months in prison and was expelled from the intellectual establishment. Thus, through his actions as well as through his words, Liu's close relationship with the state had been broken, as was also true of a small number of his former fellow establishment intellectuals in the 1990s. They separated themselves, or were separated, from the official establishment; and like their forbears in the late nineteenth century, they sought to assert their political rights.

The Role of the Emerging Middle Class in Political Change

As China moved toward a market economy and integration into the international economy in the post-Mao era, there developed a growing and prospering middle class. Its market practices helped establish the preconditions for a public sphere and a civil society, though few members of the new middle class became directly involved in political issues. Only a small number of them played a role in the independent political activities of the critical and disestablished intellectuals. Western political scientists and social theorists have assumed a link between the emergence of a middle class and the assertion of political rights.[38] In the West, democracy is regarded as arising from the urban middle class—the bourgeoisie— which has an interest in limiting the powers of the state and gaining a degree of independence. But China's growing urban middle class in the last decades of the twentieth century had not yet become independent.[39] Moreover, Jiang Zemin's "three represents" proposal, presented formally on July 1, 2001, the eightieth anniversary of the CCP, listed three aspects of Chinese life that the party should embody—the most advanced elements, advanced culture, and masses of the people—implying that the party sought to include private businesspeople in its ranks. The slogan reflected both the leadership's recognition of their growing economic power and its ongoing effort to co-opt them into the party.

The role of China's emerging middle class in the last decades of the twentieth century was fragmented. Unlike in the West, China's business-people were not protected by property rights, the rule of law, or the support of a strong middle class, and therefore they were dependent on party connections for their opportunities and survival. Furthermore, after June 4, 1989, as most intellectuals and students turned away from political action and became more professionalized, business-oriented, and absorbed into China's expanding market economy, they intentionally sought to avoid the perils of political action. Nevertheless, a small number of former intellectuals and officials who turned to business were willing to fund some efforts at political reform in the 1980s and 1990s. They helped establish independent think tanks and sponsor independent publications and even political groups, which gave the critical and disestablished intellectuals opportunities to engage in independent political activities.

A few of these businesspeople had emerged during the 1989 demonstrations. Wan Runnan, head of the high-tech Stone Group, is an example of a member of the Cultural Revolution generation who made the transition from revolutionary to entrepreneur. During the Tiananmen Square demonstrations, he donated money, communications networks, photocopiers, fax machines, and printing equipment to the demonstrators in the square. In addition, a group of small-scale entrepreneurs—such as the Flying Tiger Corps, an association of motorcycle owners—spread news, messages, and handbills during the Tiananmen demonstrations. In fact, the neo-Maoist Wang Renzhi, who assumed authority in the Propaganda Department after June 4, warned that the private entrepreneurs who supported the students during the demonstration revealed "a natural tie between a private economy and democracy."[40]

The few private businesspeople who supported independent political activities, however, were the exception and not the rule in the post-Mao era. Unlike in the West, China's rising urban middle class in the late twentieth century was not yet a force for change. The efforts for political change were led instead by the small number of critical and disestablished intellectuals. Moreover, it was not so much what these intellectuals said as what they did, sometimes in coalition with other social groups, that made them different from their intellectual predecessors in the People's Republic. They published their own books, set up new organizations, organized petitions, and took political actions on their own initiatives. They formed nonofficial groups and with other social groups worked using a variety of methods to assert their political rights and bring about political change in China.

The Development of Citizenship in Expanding "Public Space"

Although the Leninist party-state continued, China's move to the market, and the accompanying decentralization of political power, increasing involvement with the international community, relaxation of controls over personal activities, and Deng Xiaoping's pragmatic leadership produced a more open intellectual environment than at any time since the 1949 Communist revolution. These developments also expanded the public space, which helped increase intellectual and political autonomy in the 1980s and especially the 1990s. As in most of China's pre-1949 history, de facto intellectual autonomy developed in academia, the arts, and popular culture. But if anyone or any group in these areas dared to challenge the leadership politically or confront the party's authority directly, the government, as during the imperial period, had the will and the capacity to intervene forcefully and suppress them. As long as the intellectuals' interests remained within the limits of their discipline and outside the realm of politics, they were left pretty much alone. Moreover, because college graduates and intellectuals in the 1990s were no longer assigned jobs by the government, they were not totally dependent on the party-state for their livelihood and could conduct their lives less deterred by political considerations.

These developments bore some similarities to what Jürgen Habermas describes as a "public sphere" in Western Europe.[41] Even if the details do not exactly fit Chinese history, historians Mary Backus Rankin and William Rowe have described such a sphere in China in the eighteenth and nineteenth centuries. Citing Habermas, Rankin explains that "the Chinese term *gong*, or public, independently acquired a range of meanings that partially overlap with Western usage."[42] The term *gong* refers to the extra-bureaucratic activities of ordinary people as well as officials who undertook open, public initiatives that were "distinguished both from direct state administration or coercive control and from private spheres, particularly of family or other kin groups but also of individual businesses, apolitical friendship networks, and other activities that do not concern matters of common interest."[43] Rankin traces the development of this public sphere back to the late Ming and the late Qing dynasties when local elites ran local affairs outside the bureaucratic frameworks.

However, the late Ming spheres of public activities, as Rankin points out, were primarily local and had little direct impact on national policy. Those engaged in public activities were not connected to a bourgeoisie, unlike in the West, but were a hybrid of gentry-merchant elites active in local public spheres.[44] William Rowe, in his book on Hankow in the eighteenth century,[45] argues that in late imperial China these activities evolved into an elite tradition of local activism. David Strand's study of city politics in Beijing in the 1920s describes the expansion of the public sphere to teahouses, restaurants, and parks, which became places for political discussion. And during the Republican era these venues opened up in small towns as well as in other urban settings.[46] As these scholars suggest, what Rowe calls "a 'critical' public sphere of extrabureaucratic political debate" existed in China before 1949.[47] Therefore, they assert that *gong* can be interpreted as the Chinese counterpart to the Habermasian "public sphere."

Political scientist Edward Gu, however, counters that the use of the term *public sphere* is "too value laden" to be applied to China.[48] He also quotes Habermas to support his argument: "Citizens act as a public when they deal with the guarantee that they may assemble and unite freely, and express and publicize their opinions freely."[49] Such a guarantee, Gu explains, did not yet exist in China at the end of the twentieth century. Whereas the public sphere in the West, Gu asserts, was based on a bourgeoisie and a civil society, such phenomena were just beginning to emerge in China at the end of the twentieth century. Moreover, China's more relaxed, but still unlimited, Leninist party-state was much more interventionist than the traditional Confucian state, the European states of the eighteenth and nineteenth centuries, or for that matter the Eastern European Communist states of the 1970s and 1980s. Without institutional and legal protections in China, open political debate or association could be easily suppressed. Therefore Gu suggests that the less delimited term *public space*, denoting an area between the state and the family, is more appropriate than *public sphere* to describe what was happening in China at the end of the twentieth century. The term has a fluidity, connoting a capacity to contract just as quickly as it can open up, depending on the political leadership's whim, tolerance, or policy at any given time. Yet within this fluid public space, critical and disestablished intellectuals as well as others periodically attempted to act as citizens in the 1980s and 1990s.

Another new factor in the last two decades of the twentieth century that helped the critical and disestablished intellectuals organize under unofficial auspices and use unorthodox means to make their views known was China's growing contact with the outside world. This contact opened China up to foreign pressure politically as well as intellectually. Through access to the international media and publics, participants in the Democracy Wall movement of the late 1970s and the 1989 Tiananmen movement, as well as the disestablished intellectuals and political activists in the 1990s, were able to make their views and activities known to the international community and human rights organizations. More important, the Voice of America (VOA), Radio Free Asia, the BBC, Hong Kong news outlets, and the Internet relayed this news back to the Chinese public, circumventing the domestic censorship that attempted to prevent these views and activities from becoming public knowledge. At the same time, greater international interaction not only exerted pressure on the Chinese government to reform, but also protected those involved in independent political activities against too harsh punishment. Unlike Mao, who did not care what the outside world thought of his actions, the governments of Deng Xiaoping and his successors, Jiang Zemin and Hu Jintao, did and do care about China's outside image, because they wanted China to be accepted as a respectable member of the international community. Therefore, international pressure could act as a restraint on the government's repressive actions and help expand public space for brief periods.

In addition, in the post-Mao period China participated in the deliberations of the U.N. Commission on Human Rights in Geneva, where it initially asserted that the Western interpretation of human rights as political and civil rights was alien to Chinese culture, which emphasized economic concerns and national sovereignty. Yet, although Chinese traditional thought did not have the concept of rights, it did have the ideal of the Confucian scholar-official who criticized the government's abuses of power and called for fair treatment of the population. Ideally, a Confucian official was to express and maintain his moral values no matter what the political consequences might be for himself. In the early decades of the twentieth century, a number of prominent Chinese intellectuals, influenced also by Western human rights discussions, formed human rights groups and published articles in which they viewed human rights as political rights, which were inalienable and a check on political power.[50] These groups and views were suppressed after 1949, but in reaction to the destructiveness and persecutions of the Cultural Revolution these issues re-emerged in the post-Mao period in discussions among officials as well as intellectuals on the relevance of political rights to China.

Consequently, internal and external pressures led China to sign the U.N. Covenant on Economic, Social, and Cultural Rights in 1997 and the U.N. Covenant on Civil and Political Rights in 1998. The Covenant on Economic, Social, and Cultural Rights was ratified by the NPC, but the clause on the right to form unofficial labor unions was removed. China had not yet ratified the Covenant on Civil and Political Rights by the end of the twentieth century. Nevertheless, although China's formal acceptance of the two covenants did not necessarily limit the leadership's actions, China's public commitment to them was used to justify the political actions of those seeking political and economic rights.

Another new phenomenon in the post-Mao era that expanded the public space for political discourse and activity was, as mentioned, the spread of the new telecommunications technology. Private citizens and cyber-dissidents, primarily of the post-1989 generation, increasingly used the Internet and other new telecommunications technologies, which became widespread by the late 1990s. These gave the Chinese people more access not only to uncensored, independent information, but also to one another. Again, their access was made possible by the party's contradictory policies. Because of the party's drive to compete economically and technologically in the international arena, China's leaders in the mid-1990s promoted and built the advanced infrastructures required for large-scale Internet access, joined global computer networks, and opened up the Internet to the Chinese public. By the end of 2004, the number of Internet users in China had reached 94 million, up 18.2 percent from the year before. In 2003 the number of users had increased 34.5 percent.[51] At the same time, the party was acutely aware of the Internet's potential to undermine its authority and introduced a variety of methods to control Internet content and prevent access to "undesirable" sites, through censorship, surveillance, firewalls, and filtering. Even so, the more sophisticated users found ways to evade official controls and access the sites they desired through a variety of methods, including foreign proxy servers.[52]

China's embrace of the new global telecommunications technologies provided new communication mechanisms that enabled new kinds of interactions—among various groups, and with groups beyond the Chinese people's own immediate circles—that were less easy for the government to control than the print and television media. Not only critical intellectuals in the establishment, but disestablished intellectuals, political activists, cyber-dissidents, and ordinary citizens used the Internet to carry on debates, coordinate meetings, write petitions, and organize activities, allowing for freer discourse and more widespread interaction among groups and individuals than perhaps at any other time in twentieth-century China. The new methods for communicating and disseminating information made possible a large potential audience and greatly expanded the public space. Whereas the political movements in the 1980s had relatively limited outreach, by the late 1990s, as political scientist Teresa Wright notes, the new communications technologies enabled news of nonofficial political actions to be communicated to a national constituency and a worldwide audience almost instantaneously.[53]

Nevertheless, faced with a still coercive, intrusive party-state, and without effective institutions and laws to protect political debate and association, public efforts to assert political rights in an expanding space were inevitably short-lived, particularly when carried out by groups rather than by single individuals. A small number of critical and disestablished intellectuals acted as citizens nevertheless, in spite of the potential penalties, and assumed their political rights without waiting for the state to grant them. For brief periods they were able to open up enough public space—through publications, at meetings, in petition drives, in group actions, and on the Internet—to express views that dissented from those in authority. Not surprisingly, one of their overriding demands was for freedom of expression and association, which would give them the opportunity to continue their political activities.

Perhaps the greatest change in the role of politically oriented intellectuals in the post-Mao era was a blurring of the separation between intellectuals and ordinary people. This blurring had already begun in the Cultural Revolution when educated youth were sent to the countryside and factories to work with the masses, but it became increasingly apparent in the last two decades of the twentieth century. By the mid-1990s, critical intellectuals in the establishment and disestablished intellectuals formed shifting coalitions, as seen in such actions as organizing petitions to the government, signed by people inside and outside the establishment, or collective protests, such as those carried out by the families and associates of those killed in the June 4 military crackdown. The most significant blurring of class lines was seen in the joint efforts by disestablished intellectuals, individual entrepreneurs, workers, and even a small number of peasants to found an alternative political party, the China Democracy Party (CDP), in 1998.

Organized demonstrations and movements of civil disobedience by various social groups—workers, peasants, pensioners, home owners, and religious believers—also accelerated in the 1990s.[54] Whereas the coalitions of critical and disestablished intellectuals demanded political rights, these social groups demanded a variety of rights. Religious and meditation groups that were not recognized by the state, such as the house-church Christians and the Buddhist-Daoist Falungong, demanded religious and meditation rights; the workers, who had lost their guaranteed wages, pensions, and health care because of privatization of the state-owned enterprises (SOEs), and migrant workers who had not been paid for their work, demanded economic rights; peasants demanded an end to corrupt officials and fewer taxes and fees; and home owners who had been evicted to make way for modernization projects demanded the right to more economic compensation. By the late 1990s a small number of individuals from these social groups, particularly the workers, had some contact with the disestablished intellectuals and were beginning to express a sense of rights consciousness and to demand their rights, not just through their actions, but also with their words.

Emergent Civil Society

The expansion of public space in post-Mao China was accompanied by the beginning of civil society. This was another factor facilitating the organization of groups and networks that took political initiatives without state approval. Unlike the ideological dissent of individual intellectuals during the Mao era, a distinguishing feature of the 1980s and particularly the 1990s was that a number of critical and disestablished intellectuals formed their own groups without high-level political patronage or permission. Their activities fit David Strand's definition of civil society as "the autonomy of individuals and groups in relation to the state."[55]

Yet, unlike the development of civil society in Eastern Europe in the 1970s and 1980s, China's emergent civil society in the late twentieth century did not establish political alternatives to the party-state or confront the state directly, with the possible exception of the CDP. As in premodern times, elites organized themselves and founded associations that offered public services that the state did not provide.[56] The historian Timothy Brook points out that throughout Chinese history the process of group formation was independent of the central government; he cites the private academies formed in Ming times that hosted discussions among scholars on important moral and political issues. One of the most famous, the Donglin Academy, which sought to revitalize Confucianism in the early seventeenth century, became a base for challenging the bureaucracy and eunuch factions at court. Similarly, Ming literary clubs formed alliances that also challenged the court.[57] Mostly, however, civil society in premodern China, as in post-Mao China, was, as B. Michael Frolic explains, state-led, an "adjunct to state power . . . to help it manage . . . a changing society" or what is called today state corporatism.[58] During the late Qing and the Republican eras, urban residents, professional associations, student groups, labor unions, chambers of commerce, and advocacy groups were able to organize themselves and influence national affairs. But the emergence of a truly civil society, as would exist in a public sphere, was limited in these eras by the absence of laws and institutions to protect such associations. Furthermore, even in the Republican era, when such laws and a middle class were beginning to develop, associations generally sought to complement and influence state policies rather than to act as counterweights to government.[59] Despite the fact that in the imperial and post-Mao periods civil organizations were not protected by laws, during both periods there was still considerable room for maneuver. Although these organizations in the post-Mao period had to be registered with the state under sponsorship of an official agency, some of them were organized from below with a voluntary membership, as was the case with SERI. After June 4, 1989, groups that formed around economic, technical, humanitarian, educational, gender, environmental, legal, and professional concerns continued to have some degree of autonomy because their agendas were in the interests of the state. They may have been organized by private initiatives, but the state allowed them into spaces that the state had vacated. Their numbers grew astronomically in the 1990s. By early 1996, more than two hundred thousand groups had registered with the Ministry of Civil Affairs, and thousands more operated informally.[60] Instead of functioning merely as instruments of the party, these groups began to represent the interests of their members. As long as they stayed out of the political arena, they were allowed to continue to function.

The more politically oriented organizations, however, were quickly suppressed for fear that they would link up with other social groups and challenge the party. Nevertheless, such politically oriented groups continued to pop up throughout the last two decades of the century. Even though some of the groups that participated in the Democracy Wall movement of 1978–1979 as a carryover of the groups formed during the Cultural Revolution were repressed, others escaped the suppression and continued to function throughout the 1980s. The fact that during the spring 1989 demonstrations so many autonomous organizations suddenly appeared suggests that there already were established groups with a potent organizational force.[61] In the aftermath of June 4, groups formed by the relatives of those killed on June 3–4, such as the Tiananmen Mothers movement, became a strong political force demanding a truthful accounting of what had happened on that day and a change in its designation from "counterrevolutionary movement" to "patriotic movement."

In the mid-1990s a number of independent groups emerged, focused on a variety of political issues. Among the various groups, those formed during the Democracy Wall movement of 1978–1979 and the CDP, formed in 1998, were closer to the Eastern European model of civil society that developed in the 1970s and 1980s in Czechoslovakia and Poland, though they were unable to sustain strong autonomous organizations like Solidarity in Poland and Charter 77 in Czechoslovakia. A number of the originators of these organizations, such as the participants in the Democracy Wall movement and China's Marxist humanists of the 1980s, were influenced by their Eastern European counterparts. They had learned about these movements through internal Chinese publications, which they had access to through their families and friends. In the 1980s they echoed the Eastern European demands for human rights. But unlike their counterparts in Eastern Europe, who had developed a strong civil society in opposition to the state, in the last decades of the twentieth century such efforts by these groups in China were thwarted by the still-powerful party-state.

Most of China's politically oriented groups followed the more traditional pattern, as exemplified by SERI in the 1980s, of trying to influence the political leadership to change rather than seeking to establish alternative structures. Yet even their efforts that emphasized mutually supportive relations between the state and society instead of confrontation were not tolerated by the party. Nevertheless, in one respect such groups in China were moving in the same direction as those in Eastern Europe, in that they were beginning to link up with other classes. SERI, for example, differed from other intellectual NGOs in the 1980s in that it not only allied with other intellectuals but also invited managers and individual entrepreneurs, some from the countryside, to participate in its discussions and activities. This invitation was not extended to the workers until the declaration of martial law on May 19 during the 1989 demonstrations, when SERI's leaders tried to form a united front of the various autonomous organizations formed during the demonstrations, including the Beijing Workers Autonomous Federation. Yet most Chinese intellectuals, including the critical and disestablished intellectuals, continued to try to persuade the state to change itself through the nonconfrontational approaches of petitions, debates, and publications, rather than challenge the state directly. When in 1998 a small number took the first steps toward establishing a different political system by creating the CDP as an opposition party, this coalition of disestablished intellectuals, individual entrepreneurs, and workers provided for the first time a new political model in the People's Republic.

All such independent organized efforts, however, whether complementary or confrontational, were short-lived. In addition to the lack of a tradition of direct confrontation, China did not have a strong independent religious organization, such as the Roman Catholic Church, or an organized worker–intellectual coalition, such as the Solidarity movement, to confront the state.[62] Nor was there a large, organized independent group of intellectuals, like Czechoslovakia's Charter 77, led by a person of the stature of playwright Vaclav Havel. Furthermore, during the premarket era China had not developed a second economy like that in Hungary during its Communist period, where participants established effective organizations with other social groups, including the critical Marxists, to act as a force for political change. In China, the major independent activities of the critical and disestablished intellectuals consisted of publishing articles and books, forming associations, debating ideas, signing petitions, mobilizing groups, and staging demonstrations. Toward the end of the century, there was a sprouting of brief alliances between intellectuals and workers, and an effort to organize an opposition party—as detailed in the following chapters. But it is clear that China was following its own path toward political change. While the developments in China in the 1980s and 1990s differ from the path taken by Eastern European countries, they also have the potential to produce in China changes as profound as those that occurred earlier in Eastern Europe.

— 1 —

Democracy Wall

The First Assertion of Political Rights in the Post-Mao Era

The participants in the 1978–1979 Democracy Wall movement were the first group to assert their rights in the post-Mao era. Not surprisingly, most of the leaders of this movement were members of the Cultural Revolution generation—many were former Red Guards. In some respects these educated youth were unique in the People's Republic. In their formative years, they were fervent followers of Mao, who ordered them to rebel against authority—their families, teachers, elders, and party officials. At the same time, as Martin Whyte points out, with the bureaucratic structure under attack and the party's grassroots controls immobilized, this generation had opportunities to engage in unsupervised activities and uncensored debates.[1] Moreover, the "four big freedoms" Mao introduced in the Cultural Revolution—freedom to speak freely, to air one's views fully, to write big-character posters, and to hold great debates—which were to be used against authority and Mao's critics, provided the youth with a degree of liberty they had never experienced before. Students were allowed to form their own groups, post their own wall posters, and set up their own newspapers to attack the authorities.

The Legacy of the Cultural Revolution

By the summer of 1968 Mao realized he was losing control of the students, who in some areas were engaging in armed battles against one another, as well as against the party and even the army, and he ordered them to the countryside and to the factories to learn from the peasants and workers. In the countryside in particular, they were shocked by the poverty and harsh existence of China's supposedly "revolutionary" peasants.[2] These experi-

25

ences, plus their subsequent disillusionment when they found that the Cultural Revolution had not created the new world they had expected, led them to question Mao's authority as well as the party's.

Their Cultural Revolution experiences also disposed some of them to work outside predetermined frameworks and to initiate changes on their own. As sociologist Guobin Yang explains, taken away from their families, placed in new environments, and provided with opportunities to roam the country they experienced a sense of freedom to create new rules.³ When they returned to the cities at the end of the Cultural Revolution after Mao's death, a number of them maintained or reestablished the common bonds they had developed as Red Guards or sent-down youth. Guobin Yang observes that compared with both their predecessors and the post–Cultural Revolution generation, they were relatively independent and self-motivated. Most important, their Cultural Revolution experiences and disenchantment with the political system had engendered a questioning spirit and a search for new ideas and values akin to those of the May 4 generation. A small number of them also had a sense of social responsibility for the fate of society.⁴ Like their predecessors among the literati and the May 4 participants, they believed they were embarked on a historic mission as agents of national salvation in charge of the people's moral well-being and destined to enlighten the leadership and their intellectual contemporaries.

An article in the *China Youth Daily (Beijing qingnian bao)* written almost twenty years after the Cultural Revolution summarizes the general view held of this generation: "The image the Cultural Revolution generation presents to the public so far has been one of seething anger and volatile emotion." It quotes a former Red Guard who complained, "We were sent to the countryside, when we should be going to school. We are unemployed when we should be working. We are passed over, when we should be promoted." Yet this article emphasizes that this generation also projected "a sense of mission, and a belief·that it is one's responsibility to take care of the world and the nation." It points out that with "materialism sweeping across the land . . . the Cultural Revolution generation has only grown more steadfast in its idealism, the product of the age of heroism, and with the passage of time, is demonstrating a purity and nobility that has never been seen before."⁵

In addition to the uniqueness of the Cultural Revolution generation in the People's Republic, there were precedents during the Cultural Revolution period that inspired later citizens' movements, such as the posters by

Li-Yi-Zhe, a collective pseudonym for a group of disaffected youth who hung wall posters in Guangzhou in November 1974 denouncing the government as dictatorial and calling for legal guarantees of democratic and individual rights. The largest protest, which occurred on April 5, 1976, toward the end of the Cultural Revolution, was a precedent for the 1978–1979 Democracy Wall and the 1989 Tiananmen movements. The demonstration took place in Tiananmen Square, the symbolic center not only of the government but also of people taking control over their lives, as students and workers did during the May 4 movement. It occurred during the Qingming festival to honor the dead, when Beijing's ostensibly passive citizens suddenly marched to the square to pay their respects to Zhou Enlai, whose death in January 1976 had been barely acknowledged officially. The demonstration was partially premeditated because the demonstrators marched to the square holding elaborate wreaths made by their work units and they recited poems prepared in advance to honor Zhou's memory. As thousands of others joined the demonstration, it quickly turned into a spontaneous public outcry by ordinary citizens against the violence and injustices of the Cultural Revolution and its instigators.

Whereas Zhou was honored, Mao was implicitly denounced. Large portraits of Zhou were placed in a row directly opposite the huge picture of Mao above the entrance to the Forbidden City. Indirect criticisms of Mao were voiced in poems, with such lines as "gone for good is Qin Shihuang's feudal society."[6] Since the 1950s, and especially in the "Criticize Lin Biao and Confucius" campaign of 1974, Mao had compared himself to Qin Shihuang, the innovative but despotic and repressive first emperor of the Qin dynasty (202–221 BC). Clearly, Mao was the target of the participants' denunciation of the first emperor. This particular quotation was repeatedly recited aloud and copied down by the demonstrators. The April 5 attack on Mao, albeit indirect, broke the taboo against publicly criticizing this leader who had previously been held sacrosanct.

A small number of the demonstrators also called for political rights. One young worker declared, "Let the people themselves choose . . . these leaders!"[7] Another criticized the party for treating the people like children, servants, or "docile tools." However, the overall message of the April 5 demonstration was a call to return to the pre–Cultural Revolution era, particularly the supposedly "golden" age of the early 1950s when the party apparatus was in control and the leaders emulated the Soviet model. Only a few demonstrators talked of alternatives or of asserting their political rights. And none of the writings prepared for this demonstration openly questioned the leading role of the party. The goal was to turn back rather than to move in a different direction.

The Cultural Revolution, therefore, left contradictory legacies. Both the post-Mao leadership and the population in general agreed about the destructive nature of the Cultural Revolution and its persecutions. As the famous May 4 writer Ba Jin explained: "Never before in the history of man nor in any other country have people had such a fearful and ridiculous, weird and tragic experience as we had during the Cultural Revolution." He criticized Mao and the political system that had given Mao unlimited power to unleash such a tragedy. Yet despite this destructiveness, even some of its victims, including Ba Jin himself, also stressed a positive impact. Although Ba Jin attributed his wife's death to the persecution he had suffered, he wrote: "Those ten bitter years were far from being a complete waste; I gained something, I cannot put it in so many words, but it is something intense, shining and growing."[8]

One legacy of the Cultural Revolution was a willingness to question the Leninist political structure and the party leadership. Some of the victims among the party cadres, intellectuals, and skilled workers, who were the major targets of the Cultural Revolution, saw it not just as an aberration of the Leninist-Maoist political system, but as the culmination of the political campaigns that Mao had begun in Yan'an in the early 1940s. With few exceptions, virtually the entire nation, including those who were persecuted and ostracized, had accepted Mao's authority. They did whatever Mao and the party ordered them to do, even attacking their colleagues and friends and members of their families, in the belief that they were helping to modernize and strengthen the country. They equated service to the party-state and Mao with service to China.

It was not until the Cultural Revolution, however, when, as Ba Jin observed, "No one in China was spared, many narrowly escaped death, and everyone was pushed to the extremes of endurance," that some finally realized the enormity of unquestioning obedience to whatever the party leadership dictated. As Ba Jin explained, "To let one person or even a handful of people decide your fate and do all of the thinking for you is a very dangerous thing." In addition to blaming Mao and the political system, he also blamed himself and his colleagues for what had happened. "It has taken me a long time but I am now able to admit to myself that the responsibility for all of this does not lie solely with Lin [Biao] and the Gang . . . they could not have done it if we had not let ourselves be taken in."[9] Thus, for a segment of China's intellectuals, party officials, and educated youth, an indirect consequence of the Cultural Revolution was a determination not to allow others to control their lives.("Never again," some asserted, would they blindly follow orders and unquestioningly accept the authority of political leaders.)

Consequently, for a small number of participants the Cultural Revolution experience had been an education in citizenship. The Democracy Wall movement of the late 1970s revealed that instead of rearing a generation of revolutionary successors, as he had planned,(Mao had bred among the Cultural Revolution generation a small, but important, minority of questioners and political activists.)They now saw their first loyalty as being not to the party-state, but to the nation, and sought to achieve their political rights as citizens of the nation. Although most youth in the aftermath of the Cultural Revolution turned away from politics, this segment, particularly the "sent-down" (xiafang) youth whose education had been cut short and who had been sent to the countryside to work with the peasants, emerged from that experience politically awakened, skeptical, and relatively independent.[10] Unlike the members of the intellectual establishment who had been purged during Mao's campaigns but returned to relatively high positions—in government, the media, and academia—after being rehabilitated in the late 1970s, most of the sent-down youth remained on the fringes of society. Because their formal education had been interrupted, many became menial laborers. These were the people who led the Democracy Wall movement, the first effort to assert political rights in the post-Mao era.

Democracy Wall, 1978–1979

The movement that came to be called Democracy Wall began in front of Beijing's Xidan Wall and quickly spread to other walls in Beijing and then to other cities—Shanghai, Guangzhou, Wuhan, Hangzhou, Xi'an, and Qingdao—throughout the country. As former Red Guards gradually returned to the cities after Mao's death, some of them maintained or reestablished contacts with their associates in the countryside or the factories where they had been sent during the Cultural Revolution. Although most returnees went back to school and worked within the system, a small number, inspired by their Cultural Revolution experience, sought new directions. In addition to using the skills and strategies they had acquired in the Cultural Revolution—printing and distributing pamphlets, delivering speeches, engaging in debates, organizing groups, and putting up wall posters—some former Red Guards were determined that never again would they, their families, their colleagues, or the Chinese people be subjected to the manipulation and persecution they had suffered during the Cultural Revolution.

Consequently, these activists launched the first mass movement in the People's Republic in which participants sought to protect and enlarge their own individual and collective political rights. Unlike most Chinese intellectuals in the early decades of the twentieth century, participants in the Democracy Wall movement did not regard rights—which they variously referred to as human, civil, and political rights—as a gift from the state or as a means of increasing state power. Rather, they regarded these rights as inalienable and demanded the rights to be heard on political issues and to express views that differed from those propagated by the government.

Because they knew little of Chinese efforts during the early decades of the twentieth century to acquire political and individual rights and were not aware of the establishment of human rights groups before 1949, the Democracy Wall activists expressed their views in the Marxist terminology in which they had been educated.[11] Moreover, they knew more about the dissident and human rights movements in Eastern Europe and the Soviet Union than their own pre-1949 history. They learned about these movements in the newspapers for the party elite, to which several of the Democracy Wall leaders had access as children of the elite. Another change from previous movements was that their activism spread beyond students and intellectuals to include other social classes, such as workers, because some of the Democracy Wall leaders had become workers during the Cultural Revolution.

An even more radical departure from previous practices in the People's Republic was that the Democracy Wall participants spoke out on political issues not as individuals but as members of groups formed independently during the Cultural Revolution and its aftermath. These groups became the core political activists in the Democracy Wall movement and thereafter. Although most of the participants focused on economic issues and Cultural Revolution grievances, a small number emphasized political issues. Initially coordinating their actions within a city, and by mid-1979 sometimes among cities, the activists were beginning to develop loose networks across regions. The activists numbered only several hundred to a few thousand at any one time, but their posters, debates, ideas, and journals attracted tens of thousands of readers and listeners. Both officials and ordinary people who shared a revulsion over Mao's use of terror and chaos in the Cultural Revolution and who wanted a change were among the readers and discussants at the city walls.

The Democracy Wall activists made their appearance during the uncertainty in the months preceding and following the December 12–22, 1978, Third Plenum of the Eleventh Central Committee, which many believed would initiate major changes in party policy. Around this time, the party relaxed political controls but provided few guidelines on the permissible limits of criticism and debate. Just one month before the plenum, the party officially removed the "rightist" designation from virtually all those who had been so labeled in previous campaigns. It also nullified the "counter-revolutionary" verdict on the April 5, 1976, demonstration and released hundreds of the participants who had been imprisoned. The poems recited during the demonstration, including the one comparing Mao to the despotic first emperor of the Qin dynasty, were officially published. In addition, Deng Xiaoping called for "socialist democracy and rule of law." He and most of his Long March revolutionary colleagues took these initiatives in order to reinforce their efforts to discredit the Maoists still in the leadership, consolidate their own power, and reject Mao's utopian visions in favor of pragmatic economic policies. The impact of these measures appeared to legitimize open criticism of political repression.

Unlike the brief April 5 demonstration and the later Tiananmen Square demonstrations in the spring of 1989, which lasted about six weeks, the Democracy Wall movement continued erratically for more than a year. It was allowed to go on for so long because it was used in the leadership power struggle and it was helpful to Deng Xiaoping in his search for new approaches. Deng took advantage of this dissent from below—the demands of the Democracy Wall activists for political and economic reforms—to help oust the Maoists still remaining in power. Like Mao during the Cultural Revolution, he used spontaneous demonstrations in the streets as leverage against his opponents in the party and as a means to consolidate his own position. The Democracy Wall movement helped make Deng Xiaoping China's paramount political leader.

Therefore, when wall posters appeared on Xidan Wall in the fall of 1978 denouncing Mao and other officials associated with the Gang of Four and demanding political and economic reforms, Deng, in interviews with foreign journalists in late November 1978, expressed approval of the posters.[12] As these journalists then relayed Deng's approval to the demonstrators at the wall, their numbers swelled into the thousands and wall posters spread to other walls in Beijing and to other cities. People visited the walls daily, from daybreak until late at night, to read and copy the wall posters and to listen to the speeches. In addition to memorializing Zhou Enlai and criticizing the Gang of Four, a number of the posters talked about building institutions necessary for a functioning democracy. Some proposed competitive elections, from the local level to the national; others called for legal guarantees of freedom of speech, assembly, procession, and demonstration, and punishment for those who suppressed these freedoms.

Whereas purged party officials, factory managers, and workers had planned and led the April 5, 1976, demonstration, the Democracy Wall movement appears to have begun somewhat spontaneously among youth on the margins of society. Although some were children of party cadres or professionals, in the aftermath of the Cultural Revolution they were unable to get the government jobs or engage in the intellectual pursuits to which they aspired. A small number had passed the exams and entered the universities, but after graduation most were unable to obtain positions commensurate with their skills because of their political pasts.

The groups of young people who put up the wall posters, engaged in public debates, and distributed a wide variety of pamphlets in front of Beijing's Xidan Wall, along Chang'an Street leading to Tiananmen Square, in late 1978 and 1979 were continuing the activities they had engaged in during the Cultural Revolution. The author of the first wall poster to be put up on Xidan Wall, on November 19, for example, was a Beijing garage mechanic, the son of a veteran party cadre. For the first time in a public space, a poster directly attacked Mao Zedong by name and criticized Mao's "mistaken judgment" in carrying out class struggle during the Cultural Revolution.[14] Subsequently, some of the posters, speeches, meetings, and pamphlets that were distributed there not only denounced Mao and called for the return of Deng Xiaoping to power, but also called for far-reaching political and economic reforms. Shortly thereafter, posters went up almost daily until December 1979, when the wall was closed down.

Yet it was not so much what the participants said at Xidan Wall, but what they did there, that indicated that some of them had become "citizens." Mostly young workers, who might have been students or intellectuals had the Cultural Revolution not interrupted their educations, organized activities in front of the wall without permission from the party authorities. As in the Cultural Revolution, they engaged in unprecedented political debates, distributed unofficial journals, and organized groups to carry out political activities. Their overriding common theme was a critique of the Cultural Revolution and Mao's policies and a demand for a reversal of the unjust verdicts of the Mao period. But in what was a first in the People's Republic, several of the groups also publicly called for individual, political, and human rights in an effort to prevent another Cultural Revolution.

Although the rights of freedom of expression, association, and assembly had been spelled out in all of China's various constitutions from the late nineteenth century into the post-Mao era, they had not been implemented or enforced with laws and institutions.[15] Like human rights activists in China before 1949 and in Eastern Europe in the 1970s and 1980s, the Democracy Wall participants cited these constitutional rights to justify their efforts to act as citizens rather than as the subjects they had been relegated to being under Mao. As one of their journals explained, "People must rely on their own struggle to get and to protect their democratic rights and not rely on any supernatural beings or emperors to bestow them. Things bestowed cannot be depended upon. . . . If democracy is something that can be bestowed by a bestower, it can also be taken back by the bestower."[16]

The first unofficial journal to appear was *April 5 Forum (Siwu luntan)*. The experiences of its editors, Xu Wenli and Liu Qing, during the Cultural Revolution, as students-turned-workers, were typical for other Democracy Wall activists as well. Xu was born in 1944 in Anhui Province, the son of a doctor.[17] His great grandfather had been a local official in the Qing dynasty. During the Cultural Revolution, Xu was a soldier in the PLA, and after demobilization he joined the construction division of the Beijing Railways Bureau where he worked as an electrician. The co-founder of *April 5 Forum*, Liu Qing, had finished high school, was sent to the countryside in 1965, studied at Nanjing University from 1973 to 1977, then worked in a factory, and later moved back to Beijing.[18]

In later interviews, Xu Wenli explained why he became a leader of the Democracy Wall movement. In one interview, he described his dismay when during the April 5 demonstration, where he had been a bystander, the police violently cracked down on the demonstrators.[19] On that day, Xu vowed to oppose such violent responses to peaceful protests. In an interview with a Hong Kong journal, Xu explained his motivation for setting up a journal. Because China had not had privately run newspapers since 1949, Xu believed that it was "necessary to allow the masses to run some newspapers themselves so as to reflect the people's demands and wishes . . . [and] to reflect the demands for democracy, rule of law and reform."[20] Xu declared in his article "A Reform Program for the Eighties" that "the management of our affairs can no longer be left to a tiny minority. Government must hand power back to the people."[21]

Thus, on November 26, 1978, Xu started *April 5 News (Siwu bao)*. When he was joined shortly thereafter by four friends, they changed the name to *April 5 Forum*, commemorating the April 5, 1976, movement against Mao and the Gang of Four. Of the twenty or so people who became associated with the journal, the majority were factory workers, a few were young teachers, and several were members of the Communist Youth League. Xu edited all but a few of the nineteen issues of *April 5 Forum*, which carried a mixture of political analysis, commentary, short stories, and poetry and expressed a broad socialist stance.[22] Although Xu acknowledged that Marx's original doctrine had been distorted by decades of totalitarianism and the Leninist party-state, he believed that it could still lead to democracy, which he defined as a multiparty system with separation of powers.

As other journals that may have initially been underground suddenly emerged in the more open atmosphere of 1978–1979, their founders described their publications as "run by the people" *(minban kanwu)* and included the names and addresses of the publishers on the mastheads. Among the influential journals appearing in late November and December 1978 were *Reference News for the Masses (Qunzhong cankao xiaoxi)* and *Tribune of the People (Renmin luntan)*, and in January and February 1979, *Today (Jintian)*, *Beijing Spring (Beijing zhichun)*, *Fertile Soil (Wotu)*, the *Human Rights Journal (Renquan bao)*, *Seek Truth Journal (Qiushi bao)*, and *Explorations (Tansuo)*.[23] In Beijing alone there were several dozen unofficial journals. Operating out of their editors' living quarters, almost all of them were mimeographed, with print runs of just a few hundred copies because supplies of paper and ink were limited. *Beijing Spring*, which sought political reform within the prevailing political system, was able to print ten thousand copies of one issue through its connections to reform party officials. But this was an exception. The publishers of these journals usually wrote, edited, mimeographed, distributed, sold, and posted their publications at Xidan Wall.

Most of the journals, like *April 5 Forum*, continued to critique the Cultural Revolution, seek redress for Cultural Revolution abuses, urge economic reforms, and support the agenda of the reformist party leaders under Deng Xiaoping. But there were some important exceptions. *Explorations* and the *Human Rights Journal*, along with *Enlightenment (Qimeng)*, criticized Deng and the Leninist party-state and advocated alternative political ideologies and systems. Several of the journals had evolved from wall posters, such as the poster put up by Wei Jingsheng on December 5, 1978, the famous "Fifth Modernization" wall poster—"Without democracy, there can be no four modernizations," referring to the party's policy of economic modernization. It attracted many spectators. Wei wrote his name and address on the poster, and sympathetic readers contacted him directly. This marked the beginning of *Explorations*, with Wei as editor in chief. Even though most of the founders of *Explorations* believed in Marxism, one of Wei's fellow editors explained that they did not state publicly that Marxism was its underlying principle because they disagreed over how to interpret Marxism. They all agreed, however, on the guiding principles of freedom of speech, press, assembly, and association stipulated in China's constitution.[24] The first issue, dated January 8, 1979, numbering about 150 copies and sold around Xidan Wall and Tiananmen Square, carried three articles, one of which was the text of Wei's "Fifth Modernization" poster.

The various groups formed around these journals also organized coalitions among themselves to carry out common political agendas. Although they advocated different views and approaches, most shared the desire to reform the Leninist political structure and to express themselves more freely. They may not have had a clear understanding of democracy, but they knew they wanted to make the existing political system more open and accountable. Their views overlapped with those of the Marxist humanists in the intellectual establishment, but they expressed themselves more directly and specifically.[25] The Marxist humanists criticized Mao indirectly through code words; the Democracy Wall activists criticized Mao openly by name. Several journal groups held weekly "joint conferences" where they debated and argued about politics in an intense but civil manner. They created public spaces not only in front of Democracy Wall, but also in their rooms, at public parks, and in other public areas where they exchanged ideas on a diverse range of political, economic, and cultural issues. Early on, they attempted to coordinate activities in Beijing, and by mid-1979 they began to make contacts with their counterparts in other cities.

Although the members of the journal groups behaved as citizens in their actions, they were limited ideologically and intellectually because they had had little exposure to ideas other than those of Marxism-Leninism and Mao Zedong Thought, in which they had been educated and in whose idiom they continued to express themselves. Most of the journals adopted a Marxist-Leninist framework of analysis; their editors identified themselves as Marxists and socialists, as well as supporters of the party's post-Mao policies and leadership. Even the Democracy Wall activists with a non–Marxist-Leninist view of democracy, such as Wei Jingsheng, editor of *Explorations*, and Ren Wanding, editor of the *Human Rights Journal*, called themselves Marxists. They were aware of some classic Western political thinkers, but when asked what they had read, they named only a few foreign books, and those were in translation. They knew no Western languages.[26]

Although Wei Jingsheng was the most anti-Leninist of the journal editors, his background and experience were typical for most Democracy Wall participants. His parents had joined the revolution before 1949 and had worked in the People's Liberation Army. Wei attended the elite high school attached to People's University, where the Red Guards had been active early in the Cultural Revolution. He was imprisoned for three months at the end of 1967 and then spent four years in the army, traveling throughout the country, where he was shocked to see great poverty, especially in the northwest, twenty years after the revolution. At the end of the Cultural Revolution, Wei became an electrician at the Beijing Zoo.

Most of the journals contained a broad mixture of political, social, and economic commentaries and analyses and were concerned primarily with issues of freedom of speech, publication, association, and rule of law. A few were devoted to literary commentaries, short stories, and poetry, which exposed the dark side of life and explored inner emotions, another deviation from the Maoist period, which was dominated by optimistic socialist realist literature. The literary journals, particularly *Today*, cultivated a unique literary and artistic flowering that spread to the artistic establishment. Poems in *Today*, for example, were published in the official *Poetry Journal (Shikan)*. *Today* also published the works of a number of writers and poets—Bei Dao, Mang Ke, Gu Cheng, Duo Duo, and Shu Ting—who were to become prominent in China and abroad and who made popular a new literary genre, called "misty poetry" *(menglong shi)*, a supposedly apolitical form of poetry that expressed individual emotions. By rejecting politics, they too were making a political statement in a society where virtually all aspects of life had been politicized. They acted as citizens in asserting their right to be apolitical.

The Issue of Rights

The pre-1949 definition of citizenship as the assertion of political rights was revived and played an unprecedented role in the Democracy Wall movement. Although the concept of rights had been fervently debated in intellectual circles during the early decades of the twentieth century and was briefly discussed during the Hundred Flowers movement of 1956 through June 1957, since the 1949 Communist revolution it had been denigrated as a Western bourgeois concept.[27] Nevertheless, a number of the Democracy Wall journals—*April 5 Forum, Explorations, Beijing Spring, Human Rights Journal,* and *Seek Truth Journal*—though of differing political persuasions, went beyond supporting the policies of the reform leadership to explore new avenues of political action and dialogue, specifically on the question of political, civil, and human rights.

As with other issues, their discussions of these rights also took place within a Marxist-Leninist ideological framework. Like the Soviet and Eastern European dissidents, whom they learned about particularly in the party's internal news bulletin, *Reference News (Cankao xiaoxi),* the Democracy Wall participants referred to these rights as the basis for their actions. They repeatedly emphasized the importance of the rights of freedom of expression, association, and political participation, as guaranteed in China's constitution, plus the "four big freedoms" that Mao had inserted into the 1975 constitution, as the basis for their actions.

The introductory issues of a number of their journals stressed their founders' commitment to political rights as stipulated in China's constitutions. *April 5 Forum* stated that its purpose was "to exercise the right to supervise and administer the state, a right the Constitution has vested in the people, so as to turn the Constitution from provisions written on paper into a basis for the existence and development of our society." Each person, it pointed out "has a share of responsibility for the fate of his country."[28] *Seek Truth Journal* on January 1, 1979, stated: "All that conforms to the constitution is legal, and all that runs counter to the constitution is illegal. . . . In accordance with the Constitution's provisions concerning the citizens' right to enjoy the freedom of speech, correspondence, and press, our journal publishes its first issue today." Moreover, "in keeping with the

Constitution's provision that the citizens' freedom of person and their homes are inviolable, the journal is committed to resolutely defending the civil rights of its staff members as well as those who are associated with and contribute to the journal."[29] *Beijing Spring* described itself as "a comprehensive periodical, run by the masses, that fully exercises the democratic rights of speech and press as stipulated in the Constitution. It will publish the appeals of the people and various kinds of articles of an exploratory nature."[30]

Another journal, *China Human Rights (Zhongguo renquan)*, on March 22, 1979, declared that its purpose was to "expose the various crimes of trampling on democracy and human rights and of violating the current Constitution."[31] Its editor, Ren Wanding, a former Red Guard, had been criticized in the Cultural Revolution because his parents reportedly had been members of the Kuomintang and belonged to the educated elite. A graduate of Beijing Institute of Architecture and Engineering, Ren had earlier established the China Human Rights League, the first human rights organization in China since 1949, and issued a document, "Nineteen Point Human Rights Declaration," that was hung up on Democracy Wall as an eight-page wall poster on January 25, 1979. It was jointly signed by seven groups and unofficial journals. Calling the April 5 demonstration "a human rights movement," the declaration stated that "the significance of human rights is more far-reaching, profound and lasting than anything else. This is a new mark of the political consciousness of the Chinese people and is a natural trend in contemporary history."[32] The declaration addressed the Chinese people as "citizens" *(gongmin)*, which in the context of the declaration meant participants in the political process.[33]

In addition to freedom of speech and association, the declaration also called for the release of ideological and political prisoners; the right to criticize and reassess the party and the nation's leaders and representation of political parties in the legislature because "without many parties, the party is the government and is not separated from the government." In addition, it called for direct voting to elect national and local leaders and the delegates to the legislature, which was to act as a watchdog over the leadership.[34] Moreover, it called for the right of citizens to observe the discussions of the delegates to the legislature and leadership. The declaration concluded with an appeal "[to] the governments of all countries in the world, to human rights organizations, and to the public for support."[35]

Clearly, the actions of dissidents in the Soviet Union and Eastern Europe in the late 1970s, particularly their use of human rights discourse, greatly influenced the Democracy Wall activists. Intellectuals in the People's Republic had been fascinated by events in those regions, beginning with the Hungarian and Polish uprisings in 1956, and knew about the writings of Eastern European and Russian dissident intellectuals. An open letter to President Carter posted on Democracy Wall on December 8, 1978, described President Carter's concern for Soviet dissidents as "very moving." Then, addressing President Carter directly, it declared: "We would like to ask you to pay attention to the state of human rights in China. The Chinese people do not want to repeat the tragic life of the Soviet people in the Gulag Archipelago."[36] Several Democracy Wall activists also cited references to Marx on human rights to substantiate their arguments. For example, Xu Wenli asserted that, based on his understanding of Marx, "it is only proper that a progressive society should protect the most fundamental rights of man."[37]

Wei Jingsheng lacked Western-language skills and direct knowledge of Western writings; nevertheless, several articles in his journal, *Explorations,* revealed some understanding of Western democratic concepts. Commenting on Deng's statement to a foreign reporter that China had no human rights problems, one of the editors of *Explorations* asked: "What would be the danger to the interests of Chinese citizens if they were granted the same individual rights now being enjoyed by U.S. citizens?"[38] Another article in *Explorations* asked: "If we cannot even be ensured of the kind of civil rights long guaranteed in capitalist society, then the so-called rule by law and socialist democracy will be nothing but empty talk." Paraphrasing Wei's wall poster on the "Fifth Modernization," the author asserted that "Without achieving the first modernization, namely, the democratization of our politics, the 'four modernizations' we have been advocating all along can only remain a moon in the water forever."[39]

Despite these foreign references and the emulation of Eastern European dissidents, the major impetus for the Democracy Wall focus on human, civil, and political rights originated in the authors' own political awakening during their formative years in the Cultural Revolution, as revealed in interviews and articles. In an interview with a Hong Kong journal, Xu Wenli explained that he and his associates based their demand for civil rights on their experiences during the Cultural Revolution, when "rights were trampled upon seriously." Furthermore, Xu elaborated, "the right of freedom of speech and press that citizens are entitled to in all of China's constitutions has yet to be regularized institutionally and judicially." When Lin Biao and the Gang of Four held power, Xu explained, "The people could present no legal case against them in the struggle for freedom of speech and press." This was because they had no "legal safeguards."[40]

The group that formed around *Beijing Spring* was at the opposite end of the political spectrum from Wei Jingsheng's *Explorations.* Seeking gradual political reform within the existing political system, they believed the party could reform itself under Deng's leadership. Yet its members were also concerned with rights. Two of its leaders, university students Chen Ziming and Wang Juntao, saw themselves as successors to the literati, carrying on the Confucian tradition of participating in politics and urging those in power to reform. Though they were more moderate ideologically than most of their Democracy Wall colleagues, their experiences in the Cultural Revolution had also ignited their political activism.[41]

Chen Ziming was the son of several generations that had been educated at Peking University. In 1968, at age sixteen, he was appointed leader of Beijing's No. 8 Middle School and was sent to a remote production brigade in Inner Mongolia. There, like Wei Jingsheng in the northwest, he and his classmates were shocked to find that most of China's peasants still lived in abject poverty and were subjected to the tyranny of local party cadres. Furthermore, the native Mongol population was discriminated against and their region was neglected. The popular image of revolutionary peasants and dedicated leaders working for the cause of the people was replaced in Chen's and his classmates' minds by a deepening sense of distrust of the party, reinforcing the distrust that already had been engendered by Mao's summons to the youth to rebel against authority and their subsequent dispersal to the countryside for doing what they had been ordered to do.

Chen formed a group among the sent-down youth in Inner Mongolia that met regularly in late-night sessions to discuss the injustices and shortcomings of the political system. Based on the group's readings of the Marxist classics in Chinese translation, including *Das Kapital* and the works of Engels, the participants fervently debated a wide range of political issues. Moreover, in this less-controlled political environment, cut off from party authority, teachers, and family, Chen and his friends had more freedom to interpret Marxism however they wished and to read whatever they could find. Chen read a few Western classics of the French Enlightenment, such as Montesquieu's *The Spirit of Laws,* and books on economics, math, and animal husbandry. He became a "barefoot doctor," and in 1970 he was appointed chair of the brigade's Revolutionary Command. In 1971 he was made a member of the Communist Youth League (CYL), and through independent study he began to prepare for college. He returned to Beijing in 1974 and was admitted to Beijing Chemical Industry College. But shortly after his return, he sent a letter to one of his friends in Inner Mongolia criticizing the Gang of Four; this letter was intercepted by the authorities and as a result Chen was imprisoned in 1975. Before being transferred to a labor reform camp, he was allowed to visit his family in Beijing—just as the April 5, 1976, demonstration was getting under way. He joined the demonstrators and quickly assumed a leadership role when the crowds pushed him forward to negotiate with the authorities for the release of the protesters who had been arrested.[42]

Chen's future political partner, Wang Juntao, was the son of an official at the PLA Political Academy who had served in the Red Army in the 1930s and 1940s.[43] Wang grew up in a military compound, where his father and other military officers often debated political issues, and he assumed it was natural to question authority. He made his political debut during the April 5 demonstration when he led his high school class to the square and composed a poem in honor of Zhou Enlai. After the demonstration, Chen was sent to labor reform camp and Wang was imprisoned for seven months and then sent to a collective farm for a year and a half. After Mao's death, Chen took a position at the Chinese Academy of Sciences and Wang took the nationwide test in 1978 for college entrance and was accepted in Peking University's physics department.

Most of the people Chen gathered together as an editorial board for *Beijing Spring*, which he set up in early 1979, had also been members of his group in Inner Mongolia, imprisoned for their actions during the Cultural Revolution, or participants in the April 5 movement. Such shared ordeals made the board members a fairly close-knit group. Chen and several other board members also held seats on the Central Committee of the CYL; Wang Juntao was an alternate member.

Despite their relatively moderate stance, *Beijing Spring* was one of the first journals to advocate the radical strategy of using unofficial strikes to achieve one's rights. Its February 1979 issue hailed a student strike at the No. 1 Branch School of Beijing Teachers' College. Because this college required only three years of schooling and the students there were older, the government refused to remunerate them as it did students at four-year universities. As a result, the students went on strike to demand their rights;

after a month, their demands were met. Even though some people referred to their strike as "ultra-democracy" and "anarchism," *Beijing Spring* supported it, saying that "a strike with good reason serves as an impetus to institutionalizing democracy and strengthening the government" and "going on strike is a democratic right prescribed by the Constitution." *Beijing Spring* recommended that when the NPC formulated a civil code, it should include specific regulations regarding strikes, such as the constitutional right to strike.[44]

Independent groups outside of Beijing also contributed to the freer political climate in Beijing in the late 1970s. One of the most influential was a group in Guiyang, Guizhou, called the Enlightenment Society *(Qimeng She)*, which included more than a hundred ex–Red Guards who were workers or grade school teachers. Using their own money, a number of them traveled to Beijing, where they distributed their journal, made speeches, and hung wall posters. Among them was the poet Huang Xiang, who, though registered in Guiyang, lived in an independent artists' community established near the old summer palace. Huang had been harshly persecuted for the poems he wrote during the Cultural Revolution, which described the repression of the times and expressed a profound sense of disillusionment. On November 24, 1978, members of the Enlightenment Society posted Huang Xiang's poems along seventy yards of an embankment in Beijing, attracting hundreds of readers. One of Huang's colleagues, Li Jiahua, wrote an introduction to the poems, declaring, "We must free ourselves from the patriarchal rule of the past thousands of years," and that they could secure this freedom by insisting on the constitutional rights of citizens. They also posted a newspaper-size page at the History Museum calling for democracy and human rights. In January a Beijing branch of the society was publicly inaugurated and posted "An Open Letter to President Carter," urging the United States and other Western countries to pay attention to the state of human rights in China. They also translated the U.N. Universal Declaration of Human Rights and other Western treatises on democracy and posted them on Xidan Wall.

At the same time that the Guiyang group and activists from other cities joined the Beijing groups, other groups carried out similar activities in their own cities. In late November 1978, thousands began gathering daily at People's Square in Shanghai, where a significant number of wall posters also focused on the issue of political rights. In December 1978, one such poster reprinted the preamble to the American Declaration of Independence, with its resounding "We hold these truths to be self-evident, that all men are created equal, that they are endowed by their Creator with certain inalienable rights." Unofficial journals were also published in Shanghai. One of the most famous was *Voice of Democracy (Minzhu zhi sheng)*, edited by Fu Shenqi, a repairman at the Shanghai Generator Factory. Fu's background resembled that of his Beijing counterparts. Born in 1954 into a working-class family in Shanghai, he completed middle school and was sent to work in a Shanghai factory. In 1977 he entered Shanghai No. 4 Normal College, but he returned to the factory the following year and became a member of the CYL.[46] In Shanghai another form of grassroots movement coalesced around demonstrations by families demanding the return of sent-down urban youth who had been dispatched to remote rural areas and had not yet been allowed to return to the cities.

The experience of He Qiu, also known as He Fang, one of the editors of the Guangdong journal *Voice of the People (Renmin zhisheng)*, also resonated with that of the Beijing Democracy Wall activists. He Qiu was born in 1948. His father, a dentist, was a member of one of the small "democratic" parties, the Democracy Party of Farmers and Workers, and was a local party representative. In 1965 He Qiu graduated from junior high school and entered Canton Shipbuilding Academy. During the Cultural Revolution he became a worker at a shipbuilding factory. At that time, he criticized the Cultural Revolution and Mao's policies in a letter to his brother; as a result he was sent to a prison camp. After his rehabilitation, He Qiu joined the journal *Voice of the People,* where he wrote that China "must first realize the four great freedoms granted to the people in our constitution."[47]

Thus, in the late 1970s, members of the Cultural Revolution generation acted as citizens by demanding political rights, publishing unofficial journals, organizing their own groups, posting wall posters, and engaging in debates on political issues in China's major cities.

Repression Evokes Coordinated Action

As Deng solidified his political position in the months following the Third Plenum, he no longer needed the grassroots support of the Democracy Wall movement. More important, as the leadership became aware of the anti-Leninist views and independent actions of some of the participants in that movement, it began to suppress the more radical Democracy Wall leaders. In response, various other Democracy Wall groups joined together to defend their associates. Despite their wide range of views and internal factionalism, these disparate groups were impelled by the party's repression to form a united front to defend those under attack.

(Such a coordinated defense was also unprecedented in the People's Republic.)Few people during the Mao era dared to defend even members of their own families, let alone their associates, for fear of endangering themselves and other family members. However, the leaders of the Democracy Wall movement came to the defense of their colleagues, even though they may have disagreed with the views or tactics of those under attack. Their coalition building and organized resistance might be attributed to a loosening of party controls, but their Cultural Revolution experience of joining together to challenge authority may have also contributed to their willingness to stand up for their colleagues.

The first event to galvanize the various disparate groups into coordinated action was the arrest of Fu Yuehua, one of the few women activists in the movement. As petitioners from all over the country came to Beijing in early January 1979 to seek redress for abuses inflicted by local officials during the Cultural Revolution, they marched with placards calling for an end to oppression and demanding human rights. Fu took the lead in helping the petitioners organize their collective action.[48] When she was detained for her activities on January 18, 1979, her family contacted the Democracy Wall groups, which then sent a delegation to the police demanding to know the reasons for her arrest.[49]

The unofficial journals, led by *Explorations* and *April 5 Forum,* rallied to Fu's defense and their staffs gathered together weekly to plan coordinated action. Seven groups issued a "Joint Statement" on January 25, 1979, declaring that "if the various mass organizations, civilian publications and their affiliated citizens are victimized because of their involvement in activities stipulated in the Constitution, the mass organizations and publications have the responsibility to publicize the news both at home and abroad in order to rally the support of public opinion." They "should carry on sustained efforts to rescue citizens subjected to persecution and demand to visit the prisoners."[50]

Forging an organizational solidarity among themselves, the various groups jointly staged demonstrations, posted a series of posters, and published articles protesting Fu's detention and demanding her release. On January 29, 1979, they held a forum in front of Xidan Wall, urging an appeal to the higher courts against the detention of human rights activists. On February 8, 1979, another delegation of unofficial editors, led by Wei Jingsheng, went to the police station to inquire about Fu. Moreover, the cause of the petitioners, which Fu had championed, became the battle cry of the journals. On March 11, 1979, the third issue of *Explorations* published an article by Wei Jingsheng, entitled "The 20th-Century Bastille, Qincheng No. 1 Prison," exposing the brutal methods and torture used in the prison in which Fu was imprisoned. Although Soviet dissidents had been writing about conditions in the Gulag and in their *samizdat* (underground journals) for years, this was the first time such an exposé of the treatment of political prisoners had been published in the People's Republic.

The coalition to defend those under attack held together even when Deng Xiaoping personally moved to arrest Wei Jingsheng in late March 1979. Wei had denounced China's invasion of Vietnam in February 1979, and in the March issue of *Explorations* he published an article titled "Do We Want Democracy or a New Dictatorship?" in which he warned that Deng would turn into a new dictator if the existing political system continued. Such boldness infuriated Deng, who on March 29 ordered Wei arrested. Six months later, at a sham trial from which his family and friends were excluded, Wei was sentenced to fifteen years in prison and placed in solitary confinement in Qincheng No. 1 Prison, whose terrible conditions he had written about in his journal.

As revealed in Deng's speech to the Theory Conference on March 30, 1979, party leaders were increasingly worried that the activities of the Democracy Wall participants and their allies would spark social unrest and threaten the party. Deng charged that a small number of persons, "instead of accepting guidance . . . of leading officials of the party . . . have raised sundry demands . . . [that] are altogether unreasonable. They have provoked or tricked some of the masses . . . holding sit-downs and hunger strikes, and obstructing traffic." Deng was particularly infuriated about their demands for human rights. "They have raised some sensational slogans . . . [such] as 'give us human rights'. . . . There is a 'China Human Rights Group' which has gone so far as to . . . [request] the President of United States to 'show concern' for human rights in China. Can we permit such an open call for intervention in China's internal affairs? . . . Can we tolerate this kind of freedom of speech which flagrantly contravenes the principles of our Constitution?"

Deng specifically criticized the "troublemakers" who "speak in the name of democracy, a claim by which people are easily misled, . . . [who] have begun to form all kinds of secret . . . organizations which seek to establish contact with each other on a nationwide scale. . . . We must . . . [endeavor] to clear up the ideological confusion among a small section of the people, especially young people." He then enunciated the "four cardinal principles"—uphold the socialist road, the dictatorship of the proletariat, party leadership, and Marxism-Leninism and Mao Zedong Thought—which came to mean upholding the Leninist party-state. He said in conclusion, "We practice democratic centralism . . . not bourgeois . . . individualist democracy."[51]

Despite Deng's blistering attack, Wei's *Explorations* colleagues came to Wei's defense. On March 31 they drafted a leaflet entitled "*Explorations* Declaration to Citizens of the World," protesting Wei's arrest. Even though Xu Wenli and Liu Qing, the editors of *April 5 Forum*, did not agree with Wei's criticisms and tactics, they put up a wall poster on October 20, 1979, stating that Wei may have been mistaken in his ideology, but that did not mean that he had broken the law, nor was he guilty of being a "counterrevolutionary" as charged. *April 5 Forum* then pieced together secret recordings made of Wei's defense at his trial and sold transcripts at Xidan Wall on November 11, 1979. When the police detained those selling the transcripts, Liu Qing and several others went to the police station to find out the legal grounds on which their colleagues had been detained. For this, Liu Qing was arrested.

Liu Qing's family sought to defend Liu by citing the constitution's stipulation of freedom of speech, publication, association, demonstration, and strike:

> This is the most basic of all civil rights. . . . It also guarantees the right of every citizen to supervise and address inquiries to the state, government, and officials at all levels. . . . Nothing Liu Qing did went beyond the limits set by the Constitution. He merely exercised his constitutional right to propagate the need for democracy and legality. Law . . . should place the same constraints on the heads of state as on ordinary citizens. . . . By collaborating with Fu Yuehua and publishing the transcript of Wei Jingsheng's trial, Liu Qing did not violate Article 45 of the Constitution.[52]

In October 1980, sixteen unofficial journals from all over the country established the National Committee to Save Liu Qing. In an account of his detention that was smuggled out of a labor reform camp, Liu compared his case to the Dreyfus Affair and reminded his colleagues, "Our democratic system cannot develop from the benevolence of an emperor but depends on the efforts of society itself."[53]

Though the phenomenon of families and like-minded colleagues coming to the defense of their loved ones and colleagues was unusual in the People's Republic, even more unprecedented was the resistance to the party's crackdown by those with opposing views and strategies. The Democracy Wall participants formed a genuine citizens' movement to protest the treatment of their Democracy Wall colleagues. Even the most moderate and best-connected of the unofficial groups—the *Beijing Spring* group—eventually joined the coordinated efforts to defend their colleagues. Initially, the editors of *Beijing Spring* had refused to join the organized protest against Fu Yuehua's arrest or to sign an agreement calling on all unofficial groups to defend their comrades. But as the party intensified its suppression of the movement, the April and May issues of *Beijing Spring* expressed some concern and the June issue printed a protest for the first time against the arrests and repression, but without mentioning the names of those who had been arrested. In its August 10 issue, *Beijing Spring* reprinted Wei Jingsheng's article "The 20th-Century Bastille, Qincheng No. 1 Prison," as did other unofficial magazines all over the country.

By its September issue, *Beijing Spring* openly defended Wei Jingsheng and Fu Yuehua. Paraphrasing Patrick Henry, it declared that it did not agree with Wei's views, but it defended his right to express them.[54] After Wei was sentenced, Wang Juntao was summoned to the CYL offices and ordered to cease publication. But *Beijing Spring* published another, final, issue with a plea on Wei's behalf: "What had Wei been guilty of opposing?" the editors asked. "Certainly not public ownership, but privilege, injustice and dictatorship."[55] In November 1979, *Beijing Spring* was closed down.

The End of Democracy Wall

Democracy Wall at Xidan was likewise closed down in December 1979. Even though Deng Xiaoping had briefly expressed interest in political reform in the late 1970s, the Democracy Wall activists' demands for political rights went much further than Deng intended to go. Their demands for limited terms of office for government officials, more regularized party procedures, an increase in younger party members, and the introduction of some rule of law were in accord with Deng's political goals, but their calls for civil, political, and human rights, and their demands for freedom of the press and association, challenged the Leninist party-state, a basic tenet of Deng's thinking. Moreover, events in Eastern Europe—the Charter 77 movement in Czechoslovakia and Solidarity in Poland—influenced not only the Democracy Wall activists, but also the party leadership. Perhaps what worried China's leaders, even more than Democracy Wall and the protests of the petitioners in Beijing, Shanghai, and other cities, was the impact of the Eastern European dissident organizations and an independent labor movement on the Cultural Revolution generation, a generation that was ready, in terms of both outlook and actions, to challenge the political system from below. To a leadership already fearful of its legitimacy, Democracy Wall's grassroots coalition of workers and intellectuals appeared to be a burgeoning Solidarity movement, even though in actuality these two movements were quite different. Solidarity not only had the support of large numbers of workers and intellectuals, it also had the support of the Roman Catholic church and represented a much broader multiclass movement than Democracy Wall.

There is evidence that the Democracy Wall activists were well aware of the Solidarity movement. Though Liu Qing was arrested in November 1979, his co-editor, Xu Wenli, was not arrested until 1981 and he continued to publish several more issues of *April 5 Forum*. In its September 1980 issue, Xu published an open letter to Lech Walesa, the leader of Solidarity, which said, "My friends and I learned with great joy that your independent and autonomous trade union Solidarity has successfully accomplished the legal formalities for registration." He heralded Solidarity as "a shining model for working classes in socialist countries the world over." The editorial board of *April 5 Forum* also called attention to Solidarity's worldwide impact. It "breaks through national boundaries and achieves a wide international significance."[56] The Shanghai journal *Voice of Democracy* likewise declared its support for the "strikes of Polish workers fighting for democracy and against bureaucratic tyranny."[57]

When in the winter of 1980 three thousand steelworkers in Taiyuan, Shanxi Province, organized to protest against their poor living conditions and were supported by the local unofficial journal, *Wind against the Waves*, the leaders of the protest were arrested. In 1981 the party moved against the leaders of the remaining unofficial publications and groups. Liu Qing's co-editor Xu Wenli of *April 5 Forum*, for example, was sentenced to fifteen years in prison. Though *Beijing Spring* had spoken in moderate tones, it still had engaged in political activities similar to those of the editors of *April 5 Forum*. Nevertheless, whereas the latter, who were mostly workers, received long prison terms, *Beijing Spring*'s editors continued on with their university educations—Chen Ziming at the Chinese Academy of Sciences (CAS), and Wang Juntao in the physics department at Peking University.

At the same time, the party repudiated some of the laws that the Democracy Wall activists had cited to justify their activities. On February 29, 1980, the Fifth Plenum of the Eleventh Central Committee proposed eliminating the "four big freedoms" that Mao had inserted into the 1975 constitution. On July 26, 1980, the editorial boards of the remaining sixteen underground journals in twelve cities issued a joint statement that protested against the party's proposed abrogation of the four big freedoms and called for a publication law. But the Third Plenum of the Fifth NPC in September 1980 decreed that because the four big freedoms had never played a "positive" role, they should be eliminated. They were thus omitted from the 1982 constitution and could no longer be cited as justification for actions.

The Significance of the Democracy Wall Movement

Although the Democracy Wall activists employed the same methods of forming groups, putting up wall posters, printing pamphlets, conducting open debates, and networking that they had used after Mao summoned them to rebel against authority during the Cultural Revolution, their goals in 1978–1979 were quite different. They did not seek new leaders, but new political institutions and new ideas. Most continued to use the Marxist terminology in which they had been indoctrinated, but because of the suffering they and their families, friends, and colleagues had experienced during the Cultural Revolution, they called for political, civil, and human rights, protected by institutions and legal procedures, to prevent such repression and arbitrary treatment from happening again.

Despite the suppression of the Democracy Wall movement and its leaders, some of their proposals, such as the need to revise Marxism-Leninism and to carry out political reforms, continued to be echoed in the official media in the 1980s by establishment intellectuals connected to reformist party leaders Hu Yaobang and Zhao Ziyang. Several of these establishment intellectuals had personally observed the activities at Democracy Wall, and a few, such as political scientist Yan Jiaqi, had published in the movement's unofficial journals under pseudonyms. Most, however, stayed away, fearing that any connection to the Democracy Wall movement would deprive them of the status and public forum they had just recently been granted in the post-Mao era. Although sympathetic to the movement, Yan Jiaqi explained his reluctance to join it: In October 1978 he had been admitted into the party as a provisional member, and he did not want to do anything that might jeopardize his chances of becoming a full party member and working for reform from within the political system.[58]

A few establishment intellectuals protested the closure of Democracy Wall; these included Guo Luoji, a professor of philosophy at Peking University, who spoke out against the arrest of Wei Jingsheng. For this, Guo was sent to Nanjing University, where he was no longer allowed to teach. Most establishment intellectuals, however, remained silent and chose not to become associated with the Democracy Wall activists. Nevertheless, some of the activists' demands—for political, civil, and human rights and freedom of speech and association guaranteed by law—were heard in the revival of the discussion on political reform in 1986 and again during the 1989 Tiananmen Square demonstrations.

Yet it was not so much what the Democracy Wall activists said, but what they did, that defined them as citizens in the People's Republic. They sought to assert their political rights without seeking permission from the party and to establish their own groups and publications without official sanction. Though most of the Democracy Wall activists were silenced, scores of them, including some recently released from prison in the 1990s, would participate in the effort to establish an opposition party, the China Democracy Party, in 1998. The Cultural Revolution and the Democracy Wall movement not only imbued a segment of China's youth with a desire for political rights, they also provided training in organizing networks, speech making, writing wall posters, printing pamphlets, and mobilizing support for political actions. And, most important, they created a generation that periodically in the following decades continued the efforts to assert human, individual, and political rights as protection against the abuses of political power.

— 2 —

The Establishment of an Independent
Political Organization in the 1980s

Beijing Social and Economic Sciences Research Institute

Despite the crackdown on the Democracy Wall movement, the imprisonment of most of its leaders, and the suppression of its journals, the movement's precedent of forming relatively independent political groups with
their own political agendas continued. In the 1980s there emerged a number of intellectual groups that expressed a variety of political as well as
ideological views.[1] One such group, calling themselves Toward the Future (Zouxiang weilai), was organized by Jin Guantao and his wife, Lin
Qingfeng, former scientists who advocated applying a scientific approach
to social issues. Another group of younger intellectuals published articles
in *Reading (Dushu)*, a popular journal for China's intellectuals, and met
regularly in cultural salons. Although these groups were more independent
than the intellectual networks under political patronage, their predomi-
nant approach was the traditional one of educating both the leaders and
the people about the need for reform.

At the same time, however, the 1980s also saw the emergence of political
think tanks that continued the more activist political stance of the Democracy Wall movement. Although most of the Democracy Wall leaders were
sent to prison, a few, such as the leaders of the *Beijing Spring* group,
Chen Ziming and Wang Juntao, were able to continue their studies, while
maintaining their contacts with their Cultural Revolution colleagues. They
shared with other intellectual groups the Confucian view that the intellectual elite are responsible for the fate of society. Like their Confucian fore-
bears, they saw themselves as guiding the moral and intellectual enlightenment of the leadership as well as the populace in general, and they placed

51

their faith in a rationalist approach to problems. Initially, they also had the Confucian aspiration of the establishment intellectuals for positions in the official and intellectual hierarchies—the universities, institutes, and bureaucracy. They, too, wanted to publish articles in the official media, establish officially approved journals, advise the leadership on policy, and convene conferences as a means to spread their ideas.

What made the *Beijing Spring* group different from establishment intellectual groups in the 1980s was not so much what they wrote or said, but what they did. They shared with their elders and other intellectual groups the Confucian concern for education and moral improvement. But they also believed that bringing about an orderly society and good government required more than merely enlightening the leadership and educating the public. Despite espousing Confucian values, Chen Ziming rejected the Confucian ideal of the scholar-official. He criticized the concept of "appointing those excellent in academic work" and "everything being measured by one's status in the government hierarchy."[2] Like literary critic Liu Xiaobo, Chen urged intellectuals to separate themselves from officials and assert their independence, which up to that point had rarely happened in the People's Republic. He and his associates attempted to practice what they preached. They not only stressed the need to build new political institutions as a prerequisite for political reform, they themselves built an autonomous, politically engaged civic organization with its own independent financial base that was able to exert political influence without interference from political patrons or the state.

In the process, they also helped nurture a civil society in China. Their version, however, differed from that of their Eastern European counterparts, who saw civil society as being in opposition to the government. Chen Ziming and Wang Juntao still retained the traditional Chinese view of government and society as being not in opposition, but mutually interdependent and working together, though in their separate ways. The statement Chen wrote after he was sentenced to thirteen years in prison for his role in the 1989 Tiananmen demonstrations encapsulates this view: "I believe that the relationship between the government and the stratum of intellectuals needs to be radically changed. The two must develop independently, recognize the common areas in their goals, each shoulder particular responsibilities, each accord the other with sufficient respect, contend but not clash and cooperate but remain independent of each other."[3] Indeed, this view of civil society was one that had Chinese characteristics.

The Making of Independent Intellectuals

The desire of the *Beijing Spring* group for independence derived from their Cultural Revolution experience, when they had periodically engaged in independent activities. Most members of the *Beijing Spring* group had been Red Guards and sent-down youth who, like Chen, had been sent to the countryside during the Cultural Revolution, where they formed discussion groups. Some had participated in the April 5 demonstration and had been imprisoned together in labor reform camps. The experience of Min Qi was typical. Although Min did not come from an elite family like Chen or Wang, he had been imprisoned during the Cultural Revolution for criticizing Lin Biao, and, like Chen, he was sent to Inner Mongolia. He too, while visiting relatives in Beijing, had participated in the April 5, 1976, demonstration. In 1979 he joined the staff of *Beijing Spring* as its theory editor. Even after Min Qi was admitted by examination in 1985 to the Chinese Academy of Social Sciences (CASS) and became editor of its official journal, *Chinese Social Sciences (Zhongguo shehui kexue)*, he remained close to the *Beijing Spring* group. When in late 1986 the group set up its own independent think tank, the Beijing Social and Economic Sciences Research Institute, he became its general secretary.[4]

Like Min Qi, most members of the *Beijing Spring* group took the establishment route, while at the same time participating in actions outside the establishment. In the spring of 1980, Wang Juntao and one of the founding editors of *April 5 Forum* went to Hu Yaobang's home for an interview and, much to their surprise, Hu engaged them in a vigorous debate. Hu urged Wang to work within the official system. "Little brother," he said, "I recognize that you have done correct things, but you need to do them at the correct time and in the correct place. When I was young I too wanted to annihilate the reactionaries very quickly. . . . But later I came to realize how arduous and protracted a thing a revolution is. . . . Only then did I learn how to wait and how to compromise."[5] Wang was willing to compromise at certain points in his career, but despite Hu's advice, he was not willing to wait.

Participation in the 1980 Local Elections

After Deng Xiaoping suppressed the Democracy Wall movement in 1979, Chen and Wang sought to achieve their political goals by organizing and participating in relatively democratic elections to the local people's congresses, which were held for the first time in 1980. Students took the initiative to conduct multicandidate elections for delegates to the local congresses in the university areas, principally in Beijing, Shanghai, and a few other cities. Although the local congresses had little real power, former Red Guards and Democracy Wall activists who had been silenced by the closure of Democracy Wall seized the opportunity to work for reform by running in these elections. They conducted their election campaigns by again using the skills of speech making, pamphlet writing, organization building, and group mobilization that they had acquired during the Cultural Revolution and the Democracy Wall movement.

The first pilot election was held in April 1980 at Fudan University in Shanghai. Chen Ziming's brother, who attended Shanghai's Tongji University at the time, informed Chen about the elections at Fudan. The authorities were generally supportive of these local elections. But when one of the candidates at Hunan Teachers College in Changsha, Liang Heng, criticized the party directly during the election campaign there in October 1980, the party intervened, provoking a student hunger strike and a class boycott. The party subsequently annulled the vote in Changsha. Chen, Wang, and scores of other candidates nevertheless participated eagerly in the Beijing local elections held in November and December 1980. Although the party leadership did not directly affirm the election movement, the participants were encouraged by Deng's August 18, 1980, speech in which he attributed Mao's destructive policies to a political system that had given its leaders unlimited powers. Also, the Beijing Party Committee at that time was fairly open and supported the local elections, and the university administrations helped by providing duplicating materials, paper for posters, and space for debates.

The *Beijing Spring* group organized elections at a number of Beijing's universities—Peking University, Tsinghua University, People's University, and others. Of the fourteen universities in Beijing that held elections for delegates to local congresses, nine were organized by the *Beijing Spring* group, which also sponsored specific candidates.[6] Chen contested a seat to represent the Chinese Academy of Sciences, where he was chair of the graduate student association. In one of his campaign speeches, Chen admitted, "Some people warned me I will be in trouble and told me 'to forget it.' They asked how I can still believe in the party's promises?" Chen reasoned: "If a government respects the laws, follows the people's interests, governs according to the constitution, how can it cause chaos?"[7]

In another speech at CAS during the 1980 election campaign, Chen presented his political platform. He explained, "The Cultural Revolution did not take place overnight. It began with the anti-rightist campaign and the purge of Peng Dehuai for remonstrating . . . [We] must get rid of life-long tenure for cadres and we need an election system for cadres in which the cadres take exams." He also asserted: "Those officials who oppose citizens' rights should be punished and [we should] not allow the party to substitute for the nation's laws. . . . I believe only in representatives elected by the people." Chen offered an interpretation of Marxism that differed from Mao's and the party's. Marxism, he explained, does not mean "increasing class struggle and proletariat dictatorship. . . . This is a distorted Marxism . . . that has created so many wrongs and so many tragedies . . . over the last ten years."[8]

Chen called for competitive elections, which he defined as "freedom to nominate as is determined by election laws and freedom to publicize candidates, with multicandidate elections, secret ballots. . . . Only when we have democracy can people's freedom and good life improve. . . . Only when there is an election can people's indifference toward politics become active and only when we have competitive elections can people become conscious of their responsibility and power." He rejected China's system of democratic centralism, when he declared, "Our generation cannot blindly believe in any 'great leader's empty promises.' . . . High level leaders are too old and the tenure system cannot be continued." Therefore, he insisted that "the only way is to have elections at different levels from the bottom to the top. . . . only with elections can we create politicians who are close to the people and . . . only with elections can we check the role of officials who cheat. . . . [Those who believe] in the tradition of loyalty to the emperor suffocated themselves because of their loyalty. We must criticize this old system." Likewise, he pointed out that China's current political system, based on the Soviet model, "means that a small number of leaders can ignore the constitution, dismiss the NPC, and cultivate the bureaucracy and privileges." Chen concluded: "We must have a thorough structural reform."[9]

During the electoral campaign at Peking University, normal life on campus came to a virtual standstill for six weeks, from November 3 to December 18, 1980. There were twenty-nine candidates, the majority of whom organized their own election committees and publicity, conducted question-and-answer sessions, and held discussions in canteens, hallways, and classrooms. Big-character posters, pamphlets, and public opinion polls were posted all over the campus. At least ten student-run newspapers sprang up overnight to report on the election campaigns. At several large meetings with audiences of several hundred, the candidates presented their views according to procedures—on speaking order, time limits, and responses—agreed upon by the candidates and their staffs without official input. Even though party investigative commissions, the *People's Daily*, and journalists from other media came to observe and question the candidates, and the Ministry of Civil Affairs was in charge of the overall election, the campaigns and meetings were conducted in a relatively free and orderly atmosphere established by the participants.[10]

Wang Juntao was one of the candidates at Peking University, and his classmates in the physics department were members of his campaign committee. He ran on a platform calling for both political and economic reform. Like his fellow students, Wang knew little about liberal democracy, nor did he know much about Chinese reformers who had promoted democracy and human rights in the early decades of the twentieth century. Wang's knowledge came primarily from learning about the four big freedoms in the Cultural Revolution and reading texts by Marx in translation, especially the footnotes describing the works of Rousseau, Locke, and Adam Smith. Wang was fairly well informed, however, about the efforts of Confucian reformers, such as Wang Anshi, the prime minister during the Song dynasty, which made him aware of the difficulty of carrying out political reforms in China.[1]

In several campaign speeches, Wang stressed that economic reforms must be accompanied by political reforms in order to be successful: "If reform is one-sided, it will cause setbacks. . . . Political and economic reforms must proceed together and be mutually supportive. . . . Our political structure comes from feudal tradition, Stalinist doctrine, and the political experience in civil war."[12] Though he knew little about it, he called for the establishment of a system of separation of powers and checks and balances, because, as he explained, Our party-government lacks an effective monitor outside the party. Therefore, he recommended, "the party leadership organs should carry out a division of powers and eliminate the individual concentration of power." He suggested that the NPC system be strengthened and an independent judiciary be established, without interference from the party and government. He also called for the independent expression of public opinion to provide feedback and limits on government. As he explained, "Our nation's newspapers are completely controlled by the government. They neither comment on or criticize the government objectively. We should allow all kinds of democratic parties and mass organizations to run newspapers. . . . All mass organizations should be completely independent of the government."[13]

In addition, Wang called for democratic elections for representatives to the NPC in which "a minority be allowed to express their own ideas and the means to publicize them." He urged the elimination of life tenure for the leadership; and limitation of tenure for party and state leaders to one term of five years, or at most two terms. He also explained that although China's constitutions stipulated basic rights and freedom, they had not been realized because (1) there were no laws to carry them out, (2) certain laws opposed the constitution, and (3) "citizens (gongmin) do not have basic rights." Therefore, he declared, "It is urgent that our nation carry out freedom of speech and publication."[14]

Although Deng's August 18, 1980, speech had criticized China's prevailing political system for allowing the concentration of political power, Wang was the only candidate at Peking University to offer a sustained critique of the party's thirty-year rule and to criticize Mao directly and publicly before the party's official acknowledgment of Mao's mistakes in June 1981. At a meeting on November 29, 1980, Wang charged that Mao had been made into a "holy god" to the point that "he almost destroyed our party and nation and culture of 2,000 years." Wang declared: "A revolutionary who adopts the theories of Marxism is not necessarily a Marxist. A Marxist is not a saint. That Mao could not understand the basic content of Marxism was one of the theoretical roots for his making serious mistakes during the period of our socialist revolutionary construction."[15] Wang condemned the anti-rightist campaign as well as the Great Leap Forward and the Cultural Revolution and praised the victims of Mao's persecution, such as former president Liu Shaoqi and former minister of defense Peng Dehuai. Apparently Wang had an electrifying impact on the students. He was a charismatic speaker; when he spoke at a meeting on November 7, 1980, before an audience of fifteen hundred, the students cheered and jumped up on the stage.[16]

Among the thirteen candidates who ran for the local congress from

Peking University were Zhang Wei, chairman of the university's student union, who called first for economic reform and then for gradual change, and Hu Ping, an editor of *Fertile Soil* during the Democracy Wall movement, who had become a philosophy graduate student at the university and focused on the issue of freedom of speech. Another candidate was Fang Zhiyuan, who had run *Voice of the People* during the Democracy Wall movement.[17] They were all party members who were concerned that the participants in the election behave in an orderly manner and follow prearranged procedures in contrast to the disorder of the Cultural Revolution. The participants engaged in a "gentlemanly contest" *(junzi zheng)*, in which, for example, Zhang Wei and Wang Juntao, who represented two different factions, agreed not to attack each other. At the last meeting before the election, the thirteen candidates each spoke for ten minutes and responded to one another as well as to the audience according to the rules they had agreed upon.

In the first round of voting, in which more than six thousand Peking University students cast their votes in a secret ballot and in an orderly fashion, Wang and philosophy graduate student Hu Ping were the top votegetters. Because neither of them received 50 percent of the total vote, however, there was a run-off. Though Wang was an eloquent speaker, because of his public denunciation of Mao he narrowly lost the election to Hu Ping. Defeat, however, did not lessen Wang's efforts for political reform. In one of his election speeches, he had declared: "My reason for standing as a candidate is to try to promote the political democratization of China. Regardless of whether I am elected or not, I will continue to struggle towards this lofty goal for the rest of my life."[18]

Wang's colleague Chen Ziming easily won the seat from the Academy of Sciences. But Chen and the other elected representatives had only short-lived victories; they did not attend the local congress meetings, where they were made to feel unwelcome. Competitive elections for local urban congresses were discontinued shortly after the 1980 elections. Nevertheless, that participation in a democratic process, along with their experiences in the Cultural Revolution, had a profound impact on the candidates and their supporters. Without any party guidance, they had worked out among themselves procedures for conducting debates and campaigns, which virtually all of them had followed. They learned how to negotiate, compromise, and abide by a set of rules. A number of them, particularly Chen and Wang, were to put these skills to use in the future by building their own organizations and working for political reform with people in and out of the establishment.

Building an Independent Base

Even though his position in the Communist Youth League was a virtually sure channel to party leadership, Wang let his CYL membership lapse by not paying his dues, a rare act in those days.[19] Such a move was not even contemplated by the older establishment intellectuals, who sought to hold on to their party registrations at all costs, no matter how badly the party treated them. Most of them considered party membership and access to the leadership a means to gain information and influence policy. By contrast, as the party leaders continued to ignore their ideas for reform, Wang and Chen began searching for new ways to put their political ideas into practice at a grassroots level. Soon after graduation, both men left the positions to which they had been assigned and attempted to win support for the establishment of a civil service system based on merit to replace the prevailing *nomenklatura* system, which was based on political criteria.

Although a civil service was a traditional Chinese institution, in the People's Republic this was a revolutionary proposal. Chen, Wang, and their associates studied the personnel systems of China's imperial period, as well as those in Japan, Taiwan, and the West, and presented their proposals for a new civil service system to the authorities on a number of occasions. But they never received any response. Wang went to Wuhan in the mid-1980s to try to find a college administrator who would introduce their program to train civil servants. While there, Wang drew around him another circle of associates who sought similar aims. No administrator, however, was willing to carry out their ideas.

In the meantime, in response to the party's encouragement of market activities, Chen and his wife, Wang Zhihong, in the mid-1980s established two correspondence schools in Beijing to teach people administrative skills. These schools proved to be very lucrative.[20] But unlike some of their former Red Guard colleagues who also became rich in China's emerging market economy, Chen and his wife did not use their profits to enrich themselves. They continued to live frugally, and they put virtually all of their profits into establishing the first nonofficial social science think tank in Beijing, the Beijing Social and Economic Sciences Research Institute. Early on, Chen had realized that to be ideologically and politically independent, one had to be financially independent. His political goals may have been idealistic, but his methods were very pragmatic. He was not above using connections *(guanxi)* to get his think tank officially registered with a unit of the Beijing city government.

Nevertheless, Chen and his colleagues sought to maintain their autonomy at all costs. Because the authorities had repeatedly rebuffed their proposals, Chen concluded that his group "must work outside the party" to achieve its goals.[21] In addition to those who had endured the travails of the Cultural Revolution and imprisonment with him and had helped him publish *Beijing Spring,* Chen added Wang Juntao's Wuhan contacts to his SERI group. In 1988 Chen bought the *Economic Weekly (Jingjixue zhoubao)* from its semi-official sponsor, the Chinese Federation of Economic Associations. Because the periodical came with an official registration, Chen did not need to re-register it. He Jiadong, a former editor of the *Workers' Daily (Gongren ribao),* became its editor, and Wang was its major columnist. Together they transformed this journal from a pedestrian trade magazine into a forum for a broad range of topics that soon rivaled the highly regarded semi-independent *World Economic Herald (Shijie jingji daobao)* in Shanghai. Whereas the *World Economic Herald* was largely a mouthpiece for the reform views of Zhao Ziyang and his network, the *Economic Weekly* was unattached to any official faction or specific view of reform. It published articles by members of both Hu Yaobang's and Zhao Ziyang's networks as well as by disestablished intellectuals and included discussions on a broad range of topics, from Confucianism to the May 4 movement. Even more than the *World Economic Herald,* it presented opposing viewpoints in the same issue, still a rare occurrence in post-Mao China.

Even though their political stance was relatively moderate, Chen's and Wang's efforts to establish intellectual-political institutions outside the control of the state were radical, in both the traditional Chinese and the Chinese Communist contexts. In addition to running the *Economic Weekly,* SERI set up its own publishing house, which printed translations of Western books and original works by Chinese reformers. It also established a public opinion polling organization, utilizing experts trained in the newest methods, as an alternative to the party's official opinion polls. Its poll results, published also in the party's media, revealed a body of opinion that sometimes differed from that presented by the party. SERI also organized conferences and funded independent research projects on sensitive political subjects and established ties with researchers in Beijing's universities and institutes.

By the late 1980s, like their counterparts in Eastern Europe and the Soviet Union, Chen and Wang had built a network of independent organizations that attracted hundreds of professors, graduate students, and well-known intellectuals. SERI had achieved so much prominence that even intellectuals associated with Hu Yaobang's and Zhao Ziyang's intellectual networks, who had earlier kept their distance, wrote for the *Economic Weekly* and participated in SERI's seminars. More significantly, several asked Chen to help them set up their own publications, as they too began to seek more independence from the party in the late 1980s. Interaction between political activists in nonofficial think tanks and those in the intellectual establishment was another profound change in the intellectual community in the People's Republic. Although such joint activities were most prominent in Beijing and Shanghai, similar coalitions were forming all over the country.) Economic + Intellectual

Contacts with Workers and Other Classes

Initially Chen and Wang adopted the intellectuals' elitist stance toward workers. Even though by 1987 Chen had concluded that intellectuals could achieve political reforms only in coalition with other social groups, he specified allying with industrialists, rural entrepreneurs, and reform officials who were invited to SERI's seminars, but not with workers.[22] The student protesters in the 1989 Tiananmen demonstrations revealed a similar elitism when they literally locked arms to keep workers from participating in their protests. Although the students talked about sending delegations to factories to link up with workers as their May 4 predecessors had done, few did so. In addition to their elitism, Chen and his associates, like the 1989 students, were very much aware of the fact that since 1980 the leadership's greatest fear was the formation of a Solidarity-like coalition between intellectuals and workers. They did not want to do anything that would provoke the leadership's retaliation and put an end to their independent enterprises and activities.

When the 1989 Tiananmen demonstrations erupted following Hu Yaobang's death on April 15, several members of SERI, particularly Liu Gang, a graduate student in physics at Peking University, and Chen Xiaoping, a teacher of constitutional law at the Chinese University of Politics and Law, organized the student marches to Tiananmen Square and the student-led memorial commemoration for Hu on April 22.[23] A former student of the politically controversial astrophysicist Fang Lizhi, Liu Gang had helped Peking University students set up democratic salons in 1988 to discuss political issues. At that time he became acquainted with Wang Dan, who would become a co-leader of the 1989 demonstrations. Even though most intellectuals generally sympathized with the student protesters, and for the first time in the People's Republic establishment intellectuals marched in the square in support of the students, they still had little influence over the students.

Although several SERI associates organized and participated in the demonstrations, Chen and Wang played no visible role during the early stages of the demonstrations. They had come to doubt the efficacy of protests and feared that, as in the past, the 1989 protests would evoke a reaction from the party elders and a retreat from the reforms. Thus, initially they kept their distance. They were thrust directly into the events only when Zhao Ziyang's ally, Yan Mingfu, on May 13 asked them to try to persuade the student leaders to end their hunger strike and leave the square before the impending May 16 visit of Soviet party leader Mikhail Gorbachev. Chen and Wang agreed to help because they feared that if the situation were not soon defused, there would be a violent crackdown. And unlike most intellectuals, they had some influence over the student leaders in Beijing through their SERI colleagues. They had no contact, however, with the workers and the millions of ordinary Beijing residents and students from the provinces who had also joined the demonstrations by mid-May. In fact, at a conference of the government-sponsored All-China Federation of Trade Unions (ACFTU) on May 15, Chen opposed encouraging workers to join the student movement, saying, "I propose that at the present moment, it would be best for us not to play the ACFTU card. We should play our cards one by one, and not all at once. If you play all your cards, you have no deterrent left whatsoever. The best way is to use the deterrent skillfully and wield your power sparingly."[24]

Nevertheless, several of their SERI associates made contact with the workers in the square during the demonstrations and offered advice to the Beijing Workers Autonomous Federation (BWAF), which was organized in mid-May and led by worker Han Dongfang. The most helpful was Li Jinjin, the son of a Public Security Bureau official and a member of Wang Juntao's circle of Wuhan friends. Li had served in the army, and after the Cultural Revolution he earned an undergraduate law degree. He then enrolled in the graduate law program at Peking University, where he was elected chair of the graduate student association. He and a few other colleagues trained in law tried to ensure that the BWAF would adhere to the letter of the law so as to avoid provoking the authorities. Li drafted the BWAF's inaugural statement: "Our old unions were welfare organizations. But now we will create a union that is not a welfare organization but one concerned with workers rights."[25] When martial law was declared on May 19, the BWAF formally appointed Li as its legal counselor.

The imposition of martial law finally led Chen and Wang to make common cause with the workers for the first time. They urged students and Beijing residents to join with workers in "joint pickets" to put pressure on the leadership to find a peaceful resolution to the standoff between the demonstrators and the party. They supported the efforts of Hu Jiwei, an NPC Standing Committee member and former editor of the *People's Daily*, and Cao Siyuan, head of the Stone Group think tank, to convene an emergency meeting of the NPC Standing Committee to deal with the martial law order and find a peaceful way to resolve the standoff between the students and government. "This crisis cannot be resolved on the streets," Wang asserted at a meeting on May 19. "We need to bring democracy off the streets and into the Great Hall of the People." Chen added: "If the government is to be persuaded to enter into another round of dialogue and negotiations, it must talk to representatives of all social sectors."[26]

Beginning on May 20, Chen and Wang convened meetings with the leaders of the various autonomous federations that had been formed during the demonstrations, including the BWAF. On May 23 they linked these federations into a united group, called the Joint Liaison Group of All Circles in the Capital to Protect and Uphold the Constitution. On May 25 this group described itself as "a mass organization of the workers, intellectuals, cadres of the state apparatus, young students, patriotic-democratic elements, peasants and people engaged in business," whose immediate goal was "to mobilize the masses from all sections of the community to do everything possible to resist martial law."[27] For the first time in the People's Republic, a group of intellectuals had publicly overcome their exclusivity and fear of joining with workers and appeared to be moving toward forming a coalition with workers and other social groups for political action.

Chen and Wang even supported several BWAF initiatives. When its worker leader Han Dongfang called for a general strike in sympathy with the protesters, members of the *Beijing Spring* group sought to contact Zhu Houze, acting head of the ACFTU, to persuade him to join the strike. Although some of Zhu's aides appeared to support the idea, Zhu drew back at the last minute.[28] When three workers were arrested on May 29 and Han led a group of BWAF members to the offices of the Beijing Public Security Bureau to demand their release, hundreds of students rushed over from Tiananmen Square in an unprecedented show of support for the workers. As legal adviser to the BWAF, Li Jinjin asked the police for the legal justification for their detention.[29] That evening the student leaders allowed the BWAF to hold a press conference on the steps of their headquarters at the People's Monument to report on the arrests of the three workers, but the students allowed only Li to speak, not Han Dongfang. The three workers were released on May 31.

Despite increased contacts and cooperative efforts, however, there were tensions between Han Dongfang and the SERI intellectuals. At a May 26 meeting, Han had charged: "You theoreticians can go on acting as the brains of the movement, and students can give it its emotional spark. But unless the workers are the main force, the struggle for democracy will never succeed. . . . I hear you talking a lot about the 'citizens' [city people, *shimin*] who are out on the streets, when what I think you mean is 'workers' [*gongren*]. I don't know if that's a deliberate evasion on your part, but it's important to call these people by their true name." Han considered Chen's and Wang's efforts to resolve the standoff through constitutional means as not "grounded in reality."[30]

When Wang Dan and Wu'er Kaixi, the original student leaders of the Tiananmen demonstrations, went into hiding in late May, and Chen's and Wang's entreaties to the demonstrators to leave the square fell on deaf ears, the Joint Liaison Group gradually dwindled down to the core SERI people—Chen, Wang, Liu Gang, Chen Xiaoping, and a handful of others. The coalition failed to achieve any results. But its very existence, and the continuing stream of workers joining the demonstrations along with the students, perhaps more than any factor provoked the party leaders to launch the military crackdown on June 4. The specter of a Solidarity-like coalition of intellectuals and workers appeared to be materializing and was therefore crushed.

On June 10, police and soldiers burst into SERI's offices and seized manuscripts, files, and computer disks. Not surprisingly, the charges against Chen and Wang included their efforts to form a coalition with other social groups, specifically with the workers, and establish an organization outside of party control. They had become an anathema to the party, not because of their ideas—which were relatively moderate, compared to even those of some of the establishment intellectuals, not to mention those of the student leaders—but because of their actions in forming an independent political base that had established contacts with other social groups, including the workers. They were captured in 1990, put on trial in 1991, and labeled the "black hands" behind the 1989 Tiananmen demonstrations.

Wang Juntao's trial marked the appearance of another new phenomenon in the People's Republic—a public lawyer willing to defend someone accused of "subverting the state." Wang's lawyer was Zhang Sizhi. Born in 1927 in Zhengzhou, Henan, Zhang had joined the army at age sixteen, and in 1946, at age nineteen, he went to study at a missionary school in Xi'an. Because he became active in leading a student strike there, he was asked to withdraw. In 1947 he studied at Chaoyang Legal Studies College in Beijing and then in the legal studies department of People's University. He had a prestigious, yet checkered, career during the Mao era. In the summer of 1954 he attended Moscow Law School. After becoming a lawyer in 1956, he was the first director of the Beijing Legal Consultative Center and a founder and secretary-general of the Beijing Lawyers Association. He was also the first chief editor of the journal *Chinese Lawyer (Zhongguo lüshi)*. But in 1957 he was labeled a rightist and was subsequently sent to work in the countryside for fifteen years. During the Cultural Revolution, he taught in a rural high school.

When Zhang was allowed to return to the legal profession in Beijing in 1979, he was determined to fight for those who were treated unjustly—another example of the transformative nature of the Cultural Revolution experience. He was elected vice president of the Lawyers Association and also served as director of the Beijing Legal Advisory Office. In 1985 he became a professor at the Chinese University of Politics and Law and a lecturer at China TV Studies University. In the summer of 1987 Zhang defended three lawyers who had been jailed for defending others, and in the fall of 1987 he defended a hundred Guangdong peasants who had protested against official repression. He also headed the defense team for the Gang of Four. But Jiang Qing rejected him as her lawyer because he refused to plead not-guilty for her. When Wang Juntao had trouble finding a defense lawyer, Zhang stepped forth, also receiving help from a young lawyer from Luoyang, Sun Yachen. Together they presented a plea of not-guilty for Wang, who later described Zhang as "China's first great lawyer."[31] Regardless of how effective Zhang's defense of Wang was, however, it did not fend off the party's predetermined verdict of Wang's guilt. Both Chen and Wang were sentenced to thirteen years in prison.

The Significance of Politically Independent Intellectuals

Despite the final outcome and their small numbers, Chen, Wang, and the SERI group represented the beginnings of a genuine change in the relationship between Chinese intellectuals and the state in the post-Mao era. Unquestionably, in their behavior and their beliefs they had much in common with the Confucian literati and the establishment intellectuals in the People's Republic: they remonstrated with their leaders to change their political ways; they sought to join the political establishment and offered the leadership proposals for reform; and they continued to see themselves as members of a vanguard that speaks for others and tells the truth. Yet, unlike the Confucian literati and establishment intellectuals, they ultimately rejected political patronage and instead built an independent political organization, set up their own media outlets, and participated in political activities with people outside as well as inside the establishment. They had the makings of a protopolitical party.

Though they differed from their Eastern European counterparts in the 1980s in terms of the degree of their opposition to the prevailing political system, they exerted pressure from outside the party-state apparatus to challenge and influence an entrenched regime. Yet, unlike the Eastern Europeans, they were unable to bring down the party-state and help establish a new regime. A loosening up and devolution of party power accompanied the economic reforms, but China's party-state was much stronger than the Eastern European party-states in the 1980s. Moreover, unlike their Eastern European counterparts and even their May 4 predecessors, SERI and groups like it did not link up with the workers and other social groups in political action, except for that brief period before the June 4 crackdown. They lacked the sort of broad-based social support enjoyed by the Eastern European activists that might have helped them succeed.

What the American political scientist Tang Tsou characterized as a "zone of indifference" had begun to emerge with Deng's economic reforms; the devolution of central control, along with market practices, had made possible a bottom-up process of forming embryonic autonomous associations, as represented by SERI.[32] Although such associations multiplied and engaged in a myriad of activities in the post-Mao era, in the last decades of the twentieth century they had not developed into a community of citizens who could freely organize politically and establish legally recognized space for political activity outside the party-state. For semi-autonomous and even autonomous groups to survive in China in the last decades of the twentieth century, they had to be explicitly apolitical. Consequently, without any laws to protect them and without the backing of a broad social base or a civil society as existed in Eastern Europe, politically independent groups could not function openly for very long.

Nevertheless, Chen, Wang, and their SERI associates came closest to creating an autonomous political zone in the post-Mao era. Despite the arrests and repression they suffered, their assertion of relative independence in the 1980s had a profound influence on their politically engaged countrymen, both those who advocated liberal democracy and those who sought political reform. Overcoming institutional and political constraints, they were able to set up a political group outside of the establishment that for a short period of time in the late 1980s was able to create enough space in which to assert its political rights.

— 3 —

The Emergence of Unofficial
Political Movements in the 1990s

Despite the repression of groups such as SERI as well as members of Hu Yaobang's and Zhao Ziyang's intellectual networks in the aftermath of June 4, individuals continued to assert their political rights by organizing with like-minded colleagues into groups focused on specific political issues. Several kinds of unofficial grassroots political movements emerged in the 1990s.

Tiananmen Mothers' Struggle to Win Reassessment of June 4

One of the first and most prominent of these grassroots movements was the Tiananmen Mothers movement, which was organized in reaction to the party's effort to repress the memory of its military crackdown on the student demonstrators on June 4 and its depiction of the 1989 student demonstrations as "counterrevolutionary." The Mothers movement was initiated by the families of those killed during the crackdown and was conducted without official approval. Members of the families of those killed on June 4 not only became vociferous critics of the party's actions; more important, they organized and sustained a movement that publicly challenged the party's view of the event and called for some accountability. Again, these actions were unprecedented in the People's Republic. During the Mao era, when an individual or group was singled out for attack in a political campaign, with only a few exceptions their families, friends, and colleagues generally did not come to their defense, and some even denounced them for fear that if they did not, they too would be punished. Yet in the aftermath of June 4, despite threats of arrest and constant harassment, parents, wives, siblings, friends, and even individuals unacquainted with the mostly young people slain on June 4 campaigned and organized actions to get an official reassessment of the 1989 events.

They staged demonstrations, made public appeals to the NPC, the Chinese People's Political Consultative Conference (CPPCC), the judiciary, and the population at large, and opened up contacts with the international community, the foreign media, and the U.N. Commission on Human Rights. The ability of the Tiananmen Mothers to challenge the party was due not only to the party's loosening of controls, but also to the party's seeming reluctance to crack down too harshly on the families of those slain in the June 4 military crackdown, an event that had been beamed all over the world, because doing so would further shame China in the international community. At the same time, the Jiang Zemin leadership could not comply with families' demand for a reevaluation of the events of June 4, because the opposition of the previous party secretary, Zhao Ziyang, to the crackdown and his expulsion from the leadership had brought Jiang to power and gave him and his associates their legitimacy.

The Tiananmen Mothers movement was initiated and organized by Ding Zilin, with her husband, Jiang Peikun, both professors at People's University; their only son, Jiang Jielian, a junior at the high school attached to the university, was killed on June 3, 1989, on his way to Tiananmen Square. Defying government harassment, Ding launched a one-woman campaign to find out the names of those killed and wounded on June 4, onlookers as well as demonstrators, workers as well as students, and to establish the facts and determine who should be held responsible for what had happened. She also donated to the bereaved families money she had received from abroad. Even when she and her husband were put under close government surveillance, Ding continued her efforts. She was gradually joined in this endeavor by others who had also lost loved ones on June 4. Although her efforts came to be known as the Tiananmen Mothers movement, Ding described herself and her associates as a group of common citizens brought together by a shared fate and suffering. Despite escalating repression and the government's claim that the families did not really want an accounting of the dead and injured, members of Ding's group did not relent in their efforts. Over time, some of them also became public advocates of their loved ones' political causes.

With a few exceptions, most of the establishment intellectuals, including the humanist Marxists active in the 1980s, kept their distance from this movement, as they had from the Democracy Wall movement of the late

1970s. An outstanding exception was the famous playwright Wu Zuguang, who at a group meeting of the CPPCC Standing Committee in 1997 called for a reversal of the verdict on June 4 and blamed the violent event on Chen Xitong, former secretary of the Beijing Party Committee, and other officials, whom he charged with making false and misleading reports on the demonstrations to Deng Xiaoping and the party leadership.[2] Furthermore, in contrast to the party's depiction of the 1989 demonstrations as counterrevolutionary, Wu described them as patriotic protests against official corruption. Wu was prevented from speaking further at the meeting, but because of his stature and age he did not suffer any repercussions for his remarks.

Activated Citizens in the Post–June 4 Era

Prior to June 4, 1989, Ding Zilin, a professor in the philosophy department, and her husband Jiang Peikun, a professor of aesthetics at People's University, had epitomized loyal "comrades." Although she was a thirty-two-year veteran party member, because of her efforts to organize the Mothers movement and publicly challenge the party's interpretation of the events of June 4, Ding was expelled from the party in May 1992 and she and her husband were forced into retirement in 1993. Again, as with the *Beijing Spring* group, it was not so much what they said, as what they did, that the party found so threatening. In addition to organizing a movement on their own initiative, they coordinated public petitions, brought suit against the leadership for its actions, conducted yearly protests on June 4, and contacted the foreign media and human rights organizations to achieve their goals. In 1999, on the tenth anniversary of June 4, Ding explained why she organized and led the effort to name the victims and demand an official accounting. Criticizing herself and others who had remained silent during the persecutions of the Mao period—the anti-rightist campaign, the Great Leap Forward, and the Cultural Revolution—Ding observed that "if our fellow countrymen had squarely faced the successive onslaughts of death that occurred in China's past, perhaps we could have prevented this most recent tragedy."[3]

Initially, Ding gathered together various victims' families to talk about their pain and grief and weep together. But prior to the Qingming festival honoring the dead in April 1991, she decided to tell the story of her son's death to the outside world. She and Zhang Xianling, another mother who had lost her son, gave an interview to a Hong Kong newspaper in which they revealed for the first time the truth about their sons' deaths. In May 1991, in an interview with the American television network ABC, Ding not only condemned the government for the massacre on June 4, but denounced Premier Li Peng's explanation that the June 4 assault was necessary in order to maintain order. She demanded that the government reveal the total number of dead and provide a list of those who had been killed; she called on all people of conscience not to forget those who had lost their lives.

In 1994, on the fifth anniversary of June 4, with the help of her associates, Ding published a book entitled *The Factual Account of a Search for the June 4 Victims*, in which she made public a list of 96 individuals who had been killed. In the preface she wrote, "I cannot turn a blind eye to the pain of those who suffer my same fate. . . . As a group, they have been forgotten and forsaken by society. . . . I made the firm decision to continue in my mission of locating and helping June Fourth families, until the government itself actively takes up this project and there is no longer any need for our efforts."[4] By June 4, 1999, she reported the names of 155 individuals who had been killed and 65 who had been injured. She added, "these numbers are only the tip of the iceberg compared to the total number of people killed in the massacre. But, as one of our friends said, at least this tip is visible."[5]

The Tiananmen Mothers movement inspired other mothers to appeal for the release of their loved ones who were imprisoned for their political activities. Chen Ziming's sixty-eight-year-old mother applied for official permission to hold a demonstration in Beijing in support of her son, who had begun a fast to protest the halting of his medical treatment for cancer and the freezing of his and his wife's bank accounts, which he needed to pay for his medicine. Although she was denied permission to hold the protest, Chen's mother, accompanied by her husband, her daughter, and Chen's wife, holding a photo of Chen Ziming, went to a nearby park and read a statement calling for Chen's release.[6]

Despite the party's efforts to suppress their activities, a few dozen parents of those killed on June 4 met together annually on that date in the 1990s. On the eve of the seventh anniversary of June 4, in 1996, thirty-one relatives of the June 4 victims, mostly women, jointly wrote a petition to the Standing Committee of the NPC, demanding the formation of a special committee to conduct an independent investigation into the events of

June 4 and publication of the results, including the death tolls and the names of the victims.[8] They also called for compensation for those who had been killed. By 1998 the families not only demanded that those responsible for June 4 be held accountable, but Ding Zilin organized a petition to Jiang Zemin and the NPC, signed by fifty-six people, declaring that because of his leading role in the Tiananmen killings, Li Peng should not be appointed chair of the NPC. The petition declared: "We earnestly ask the National People's Congress membership review committee to disqualify him . . . we believe that incumbent Premier Li Peng bears the main responsibility in the June 4 incident that cannot be shirked."[9]

On September 28, 1998, Jiang Peikun had drafted two declarations, which went beyond demanding an accounting of what happened on June 4. They called for civil and economic rights and were signed by himself; his wife, Ding Zilin; Jiang Qisheng, a former PhD student at People's University; Lin Mu, Hu Yaobang's former secretary and a former party secretary of Northwestern University in Xi'an; and Wei Xiaotao, an engineer and brother of Wei Jingsheng. They circulated the two declarations as China was about to sign the U.N. Covenant on Civil and Political Rights in October 1998. They also translated their declarations into English and circulated them on the Internet so as to reach an international audience. One declaration, "On Civil Rights and Freedom," detailed how individual rights were suppressed in China; the other, "On Civil Rights and Social Justice," described the growing official corruption that was accompanying China's emerging market economy.

These declarations differed from their earlier efforts in that instead of just appealing to the authorities for redress as they had in the past they called on all Chinese citizens to take the initiative to realize their fundamental freedoms and rights. The declarations stated, "The primary basis of our appeal is the recognition that human rights are innate, everyone is born free," as enshrined in the U.N. Universal Declaration of Human Rights and the two U.N. human rights covenants. They explained that "as consciousness of citizens' rights has grown, increasingly Chinese people are aware that they must fight to protect their own rights and interests" and that "a pluralistic, modern society that is relatively independent of the existing system is beginning to take shape, and the dependence of the people upon state power has already weakened." Despite the government's talk about the rule of law, they asserted, "China's current legal system is in reality still a tool used by the ruling clique to maintain and safeguard its grip on power. Because under the existing legislative and judicial system the power of the CCP is still higher than the power of citizens, while the individual authority of leaders surpasses the authority of law, it is very difficult for ordinary citizen to protect their legitimate rights and interests effectively through the current legal process." Therefore, they urged their fellow citizens to "realize that it is not only the obligation of the government, but also the responsibility of each and every citizen, to change the current situation."[11]

The declaration "On Civil Rights and Social Justice" specifically criticized officials who took advantage of China's move to the market to expand their personal wealth. It described the growing alliance between power and money as extending "the power of the privileged from the political field into the economic field," where "all fairness and justice in the society were ruthlessly trampled underfoot."[12] It charged that this alliance was one of the principal causes of the demonstrations of 1989. The declaration acknowledged, "Even though these reforms have eliminated egalitarianism in the distribution of wealth in society and given people some economic freedom, they have also brought about an unprecedented polarization of rich and poor" in which "a sense of imminent crisis, social collapse and fear about the future pervades every corner of the whole society."[13]

While their concern about the growing social inequalities engendered by China's economic reforms was shared by party officials, their proposals to deal with them within the Chinese context were relatively radical. The declaration urged that China's current legal system be amended to bring it into compliance with the U.N. Universal Declaration of Human Rights and the two U.N. covenants. These amendments must guarantee the rights and freedom of citizens, in particular the rights to freedom of expression and association and to political participation. Furthermore, "In order to ensure that their legitimate rights and interests may not be infringed, workers should be allowed to organize and participate in independent unions and peasants should be allowed to organize and participate in independent peasants' unions." In addition, the government should end "media censorship and the ban on political parties, and . . . [implement] a system of direct elections by citizens, so as to establish effective checks and balances and supervision mechanisms to prevent the abuse of government power." It concluded that to realize "fairness and justice is the common desire of all Chinese people," which citizens have the right to pursue.[14] Thus, the events of June 4 had transformed Ding Zilin and her husband from loyal party comrades into activated citizens calling for fundamental political reforms.

Expansion of the Tiananmen Mothers Movement

In addition to the families of those killed, members of the 1989 generation who were also transformed by the events of June 4 participated in the Tiananmen Mothers movement.[15] The most prominent was People's University student Jiang Qisheng, originally from Jiangsu Province, who helped Ding document those killed and injured on June 4 and who acted as the spokesperson for the signers of the two declarations. His purge from the intellectual establishment after June 4 was typical of what happened to other student leaders who had participated in the 1989 demonstrations. A graduate of Beijing Institute of Aeronautics, he was a Ph.D. candidate in the philosophy department at People's University when the 1989 demonstrations began. He became deputy head of the Beijing Student Autonomous Federation, which had organized the students of Beijing's universities, and a member of the dialogue delegation that met with Li Peng in an effort to negotiate a peaceful end to the standoff. He was arrested in September 1989 and served eighteen months in Qincheng prison. When he was released in February 1991, he was expelled from the university and denied regular employment.

By the time of the tenth anniversary of June 4, memories of that event among the population at large were gradually fading.[16] Most college students were increasingly focused on finding lucrative jobs and establishing a profession. Even so, Jiang Qisheng with fifteen others from Beijing, Shaanxi, and Sichuan drafted an open letter that appealed for a collective quiet commemoration of June 4 by lighting candles on June 3–4 in honor of those killed.[17] Jiang played a major role in organizing the event by circulating an open letter and posting flyers on lampposts calling on Beijing's population to "light a myriad of candles to collectively commemorate the brave spirits of June Fourth" on the tenth anniversary.[18] Similar candlelight commemorations were attempted in other cities as well. A group of one hundred in Liaoning, for example, applied for official permission to hold a public candlelight commemoration to mark the tenth anniversary and called on the government to reveal the truth about June 4, compensate the victims' families, and release political prisoners. In Hangzhou, Zhejiang Province, fifty people submitted a similar application.[19] All of these applications were rejected.

Shortly before the tenth anniversary, on May 18, without legal documents, police took Jiang Qisheng from his home in Beijing and charged him with incitement to subvert state power.[20] He was also accused of circulating an essay that had called for peaceful political change and a multiparty system. At his trial, Jiang admitted to posting the flyers and showing the essay to friends, but he maintained that he was exercising freedom of expression and had committed no crime. In an eloquent defense statement on November 1, 1999, Jiang recalled the official reversal of the designation "counterrevolutionary" for the April 5, 1976, protest against the Gang of Four and the Cultural Revolution. So too, though the official view of the 1989 Tiananmen demonstrations was that they were "counterrevolutionary turmoil," Jiang declared that "this kind of civic action of daring to exercise rights and refusing to lie is not only not a crime, but also should be widely promoted and encouraged. The future of China lies in great part in nurturing and uplifting this kind of civic quality." To ask people to light candles at home on the evenings of June 3 and 4, to mourn "those heroic souls," Jiang maintained, "is not incitement to subvert state power." Rather, he said, "those who . . . insist on punishing ideas and prosecuting people with dissenting opinions are the real criminals among the Chinese people." He urged that the government "not imprison people merely for words." In his conclusion, Jiang pointed out that "For thousands of years, the Chinese people have been too accustomed to two approaches to the political domain—one is to be as docile as sheep, and the other is to rise up to overthrow the ruling group." He suggested that "the Chinese people do not want to continue this vicious cycle of either being docile or rising up and using force." He asked: "Simply by writing and talking, do I commit such a crime against heaven that I must be put to death?" as he declared himself innocent of the charges against him.[21]

Jiang was defended by Mo Shaoping, another lawyer in the post-Mao era, like Zhang Sizhi, who had defended Wang Juntao, who was willing to take on politically sensitive cases. Though repeatedly harassed by the authorities, he was one of a small number who defended political activists. Mo had studied law after stints in the army and as a clerk in the Beijing procurator's office. He opened his practice in the early 1990s in time to defend several of the Tiananmen political activists arrested after June 4.[22] He was one of the first lawyers to join a private practice when partnerships were permitted in 1992, and in 1995 he opened his own firm in Beijing.

Mo defended Jiang by reiterating that Jiang's action "does not in itself amount to incitement to subvert state power." Rather, he argued, it was "to revive people's memory, urge people to commemorate June Fourth, and to 'remind city residents not to forget these events.'" Mo stated, "to turn out the lights at home for one hour and light a candle [is] to show our respect and solidarity. This will constitute a silent . . . condemnation of the abrogation of justice in the name of 'stability.' It did not encourage people to rise up and overthrow state power . . . such silent, moderate, and non-violent forms of condemnation are only a critique or criticism of certain government actions."[23]

Mo also responded to the second charge against Jiang—that from 1996 through the spring of 1999 he had distributed to a few friends and others in his building in Haidian district, the university area in Beijing, and other locations an essay written by one Li Xiaoping, who was never identified, though the state asserted it was a pseudonym for Jiang. The essay was entitled "Thoughts on How to Peacefully Implement Fundamental Change in China's Social System." Mo declared that the act of giving an essay to others to read did not amount to incitement to subvert state power. Finally, Mo criticized the trial procedures, accusing the public security organs of abusing the defendant's legal rights by not notifying his family or work unit within twenty-four hours of detention or arrest. As Mo explained, "Abiding by the laws of the state is not only the obligation of ordinary citizens; it is also the obligation of the country's law implementation agencies."[24]

Jiang's arrest did not intimidate Ding Zilin and her network of June 4 families. Until then, their major methods for calling for a reassessment of the verdict on June 4 and seeking compensation for the families of the victims had been to send petitions to the NPC and other government offices and to commemorate the event annually by lighting candles. On June 4, 1999, the tenth anniversary, the group also took unprecedented legal action to attempt to bring to justice those responsible for the June 4 killings. They presented a petition to the Supreme People's Procuratorate, China's prosecutor general, signed by 108 relatives of people killed or injured on June 4. The petition contained evidence they had collected—the testimonies from twenty-four victims' families and three people who were injured, and the names of the dead and the injured. They asked that a criminal investigation be initiated to determine legal responsibility for the loss of life and the excessive use of force on June 4.[25] On May 24, 2000, Ding Zilin presented a supplemental statement that explained, "We are . . . a moral group demanding fair and impartial treatment.[26] In addition, the Tiananmen Mothers demanded the right to mourn peacefully in public; the right to accept humanitarian aid; an end of persecution of June 4 participants; the release from prison of those involved in the Tiananmen movement; and a full, public accounting of the June 4 events. They asserted that they were only exercising their political rights, to which they were entitled and they were not engaged in any illegal activities.

Despite continual rebuffs, warnings, surveillance, intimidation, and a brief detention in late March 2004 of two of the Mothers—Ding Zilin and the wife of a man killed on June 4—the Tiananmen Mothers continued their demands for a full accounting of what happened and compensation for the victims into the twenty-first century. At the same time, the Chinese government continued to warn against commemorations and increased surveillance of their homes each year around June 3–4.[27] In 2002 the Tiananmen mothers turned Ding's apartment into a mourning hall and lit candles in memory of their loved ones. In speaking about her son, Ding explained, "We have never held a public ceremony for him or any of the other victims of June 4 because the Chinese authorities won't let us."[28] On the fifteenth anniversary in 2004, the Tiananmen Mothers planned to start their memorial activities during the Qingming festival on April 4, but three of the Mothers, including Ding Zilin, were detained on trumped-up charges and were unable to do so. Nevertheless, despite the intimidation, the Mothers continued to commemorate the event among themselves. Despite the fact that the memory of June 4 was fading and the government's explanation that it had been necessary to use force against the demonstrators in order to prevent chaos had seeped into popular consciousness, Ding and the other Mothers continued to speak out publicly and petition the authorities to redress the wrongs done to their loved ones and reassess the Tiananmen events of the spring of 1989.

In addition to Jiang Qisheng, who was released from prison on May 19, 2003, after serving four years for organizing the tenth anniversary commemoration of June 4, a few other prominent dissidents joined their cause, such as cyber-dissident Huang Qi, who was arrested in 2002 for creating a Web site dedicated to helping friends and relatives of students missing since June 4, and He Depu, formerly of CASS, who was one of the few participants in the 1998 effort to establish an opposition party, the CDP, still at large until his arrest in fall 2002 in the lead-up to the Sixteenth Party Congress. The Tiananmen Mothers movement continued to attract former establishment intellectuals, whose political activities had led them to be expelled from the establishment, and ordinary men and women whose loved ones had also been killed or wounded on June 4. In addition to trying to change the official designation of the movement from "counterrevolutionary" to "patriotic" and demanding an official accounting of what happened on June 4, both groups sought to keep alive the 1989 Tiananmen movement's goal of political reform.

The Peace Charter Movement

Like the Tiananmen Mothers, the Peace Charter movement was another unofficial, grassroots movement that emerged in the 1990s without party permission. Its participants were disestablished intellectuals who attempted to express their grievances and to influence policy by organizing group petitions to the government. The use of petitions resonated with the Confucian practice of intellectuals' sending memorials to officials, and even to the emperor, on matters of conscience and principle. To remonstrate or to petition the government has been an accepted political practice throughout Chinese history. John Schrecker has pointed out that, beginning in the waning days of the Han dynasty, usually in times of trouble there were *qingyi*—"pure discussion" or "critical elite opinion"—movements composed of intellectuals and students working outside the centers of political power and without official approval to call attention to, or propose ways to improve or revise, the leadership's policies.[29] Even during the Mao era, individuals sent letters to Mao and party officials in an effort to make the leaders aware of problems and to urge them to live up to the highest ideals. Although they were acting without official sanction, their actions did not imply a direct confrontation with the state, but rather were efforts within the existing system to make the system work more effectively. In addition to their traditional moral authority, the remonstrators usually presented plausible arguments to show that their concerns also served the state's interests.[30]

While the petitions to the authorities in the 1990s resonated with past practices, they were qualitatively different. In Confucian times most of the petitioners or remonstrators were literati or members of the elite who sought to make their views on public affairs known or who were speaking on behalf of the people *(wei min shang shu)*. In contrast, in the 1990s ordinary people, as well as intellectuals, used petitions to protest policies and to recommend alternatives. Moreover, whereas in Mao's time petitioners remonstrated as individuals in the 1990s some petitioned as groups made up of both establishment and disestablished intellectuals as well as ordinary citizens. In the past such petitions, particularly those on specific political issues, could be disregarded by the leadership and their existence remained unknown to the population at large. But in the 1990s a number of the collectively organized petitions were also addressed to the international media and put on the Internet, and then reported back into China through VOA, the BBC, or the foreign and Hong Kong media—giving the petitioners' demands and concerns wider circulation and making them more difficult for the party leadership to ignore.

Even though petitioning the leadership to reform had been practiced throughout Chinese history, members of the Peace Charter group, as indicated by the group's name, were inspired not so much by China's own historical legacy, of which they knew little, but by the Charter 77 movement, begun in 1977 by Vaclav Havel in Czechoslovakia, which helped bring about the eventual collapse of Communist rule in Eastern Europe and the Soviet Union. These events in the former Leninist party-states had a dramatic impact on those seeking political reforms in China. Like a small number of the establishment intellectuals, the Peace Charter group sought to convince the party to introduce political reforms to accompany the economic reforms, but like the Charter 77 movement they also organized a multiclass grassroots alliance of disestablished intellectuals and workers to achieve their goal. Several of the leaders of the Peace Charter movement had participated in the Democracy Wall movement and the 1989 demonstrations. And like their Eastern European colleagues they sought to organize and give voice to demands for political reform coming from below.

The Peace Charter movement began with a petition issued on October 11, 1993, in Beijing signed by a number of individuals who called themselves "a group of Chinese citizens." Part of their message foreshadowed views that liberal establishment intellectuals would express in the late 1990s. They pointed out that "[as] historical facts of the contemporary world have fully shown, the rapid development of the market economy inevitably requires the adoption of political pluralization and democracy."

They similarly warned that "to prevent the intensification of the contradiction, which will inevitably bring the inevitable process of political change out of control . . . the authorities should now begin by adopting every possible means." Also like the establishment intellectuals, they expected that these political reforms would be carried out under party auspices: "The Peace Charter attaches great importance to . . . the fact that the CCP and its government are the only social force which can lead the mainland to peacefully effect the transition from centralism to plural democratic politics."[31] Yet the Peace Charter also called for measures that the establishment intellectuals had not publicly demanded, such as a reassessment of the events of June 4 and the establishment of political parties. Like their Eastern European counterparts, the group also called for human rights. They urged the party to "open up restrictions on political parties, respect resolutions of the United Nations regarding human rights questions, redress the wrongs of the '4 June' incident, release all political prisoners and establish a strategy for attaining a pluralistic democracy."[32]

Yet once again it was not so much what the Peace Charter group advocated as what they did in trying to achieve political reform that differed from the efforts of the establishment intellectuals. Rather than just remind those in power of their political and moral responsibilities and ideals, as their Confucian ancestors and dissidents in the Mao era had done, they joined with social groups besides intellectuals, and with followers in other major cities in addition to Beijing and Shanghai, to bring pressure from below for political change without the permission of the party authorities. A number of different people worked on and revised the Peace Charter. Among its drafters and organizers were individuals who had been participants in other political movements.[33] One such participant was Yang Zhou, who had attempted to set up a human rights organization in 1979 as part of the Democracy Wall movement, for which he was arrested and imprisoned for three years.[34] In late 1992 Yang co-founded a Shanghai-based China Study Group on Human Rights and held democratic salons in Shanghai's Fuxing Park. In March 1993 he founded another kind of human rights organization, the China Human Rights Association, to monitor China's human rights abuses, and he later officially submitted an application to register the association with the civil affairs authorities in Shanghai. Although the application was rejected, it was one of the first times a Chinese NGO on human rights that had no official links sought legal recognition.[35]

Another drafter of the Peace Charter was Qin Yongmin, a man in his forties from Wuhan who had been in and out of jail since 1970. His first run-in with the authorities occurred because he had criticized the Cultural Revolution in a diary. After the Cultural Revolution, he became a steelworker and participated in the Democracy Wall movement as an editor and writer of the unofficial journal *Sound of the Bell (Zhong sheng)*. He was also an organizer of the April 5 Study Society established during the Democracy Wall movement, for which he was again imprisoned in 1981. In addition to leaders from the Democracy Wall generation, members of the 1989 generation were also active in the Peace Charter movement. One of them, Ma Shaohua, an economics student at People's University in Beijing who had been a student leader in the 1989 Tiananmen demonstrations, was the author of *Eastern Europe, 1989–1993*.[36] As is reflected in the title, Ma and his colleagues modeled themselves after Eastern European activists in their efforts to reform China's Leninist party-state. The book was banned soon after it appeared.

Shortly after the issuance of the Peace Charter in Beijing, the leaders of the Peace Charter movement were arrested and were sent back to their home areas. Qin Yongmin was returned to Wuhan, where he was sentenced without trial to two years of labor reform; Yang Zhou was sent back to Shanghai, where he was sentenced to three years in a reeducation camp; and Ma Shaohua was imprisoned in Xi'an for eighteen months. In response to their arrests, the other eleven signatories to the Peace Charter issued a statement denouncing the authorities for violating the participants' civil rights as specified in China's constitution, and for trampling on the citizens' freedom of speech and assembly. They also demanded the release of their colleagues. Like their Eastern European counterparts who had asserted that their actions were based on constitutional and legal guarantees, members of the Peace Charter group asserted that they were acting within the limits of China's laws and constitution.

A similar petition signed by more than fifty people—among them intellectuals, workers, and owners of small businesses, as well as some of the people who had signed the Peace Charter, such as Yang Zhou—was organized in Shanghai and sent to the NPC in 1994. It demanded a multiparty system, freedom of the press, independent unions, and an inquiry into the events of June 4.[37] One of the people involved in the Shanghai group petitions was Bao Ge, a researcher at Shanghai Medical School who was also a member of Yang Zhou's China Human Rights Association. He added some new elements to the petition, calling for an effort to seek compensation from Japan for Japanese atrocities during World War II. Significantly, though he regarded the Shanghai petition as a continuation of the Peace Charter, he criticized the Peace Charter because it had called for democratization under CCP leadership. He urged development of democracy without party leadership.[38] Bao Ge was taken from his home on October 11, 1994, and sentenced without trial to three years of labor reform.[39]

Several members of the Peace Charter group also helped found the League to Guarantee Labor Rights (LGLR) in 1994 in Beijing. The LGLR was another multiclass effort of intellectuals working with other social groups, specifically workers. In addition to Yang Zhou, its leaders included the lawyer Zhou Guoqiang, the worker Liu Nianchun, Peking University legal scholar Yuan Hongbing, and Christian activist Xiao Biguang. This was the first evidence in the post-Mao period of Christian activists joining in the leadership of grassroots political movements. Although the LGLR had only a dozen or so founding members, they had connections with other unofficial labor groups in the country. Their aim, they stressed, was to protect the rights of workers through legitimate and legal channels. They, too, cited the Chinese constitution to support their actions—specifically article 35, which stipulates that citizens enjoy freedom of speech, publication, assembly, association, and demonstration.[40]

The lawyer Zhou Guoqiang exemplified the small group of intellectuals who could have been in the establishment but had chosen to make common cause with the workers. He had a degree in law and he was also a published poet. He had participated in the Democracy Wall movement and during the 1989 Tiananmen demonstrations, he had helped labor activist Han Dongfang set up the Beijing Workers Autonomous Federation. Like Li Jinjin of the SERI group, he was one of the few intellectuals who became involved with the workers' movement in 1989. He also joined Yuan Hongbing, lecturer in law at Peking University, and Wang Jiaqi, a legal scholar, in submitting a petition to the NPC in March 1994 that included proposals similar to those in the Peace Charter, such as asking the legislature to consider constitutional and legal revisions to allow workers the right to strike and organize nonofficial unions.[41] On March 9, 1994, the three men applied to the Ministry of Civil Affairs to officially register the LGLR, which they described as an interest group that supports the legitimate rights of working people and the political principles of the party.[42] The date was significant because it was the opening day of the NPC and a day before U.S. secretary of state Warren Christopher's arrival for a state visit. Despite their sensitive timing, however, all three men were detained soon thereafter.

The worker Liu Nianchun who was a leader of the Peace Charter movement also would have been an intellectual but for his political activities.
Along with his brother Liu Qing, he had participated in the Democracy
Wall movement, where he had been one of six editors of the influential literary journal *Today*. Though not ostensibly political, the journal made
a political statement in the aftermath of the Cultural Revolution by rejecting literature with a political message. Because of his role in Democracy
Wall, Liu was expelled from Beijing Normal College shortly before graduation and in 1981 was sentenced to jail for three years for "counterrevolutionary" propaganda because he had sent Liu Qing's prison diary out
of the country for publication. After release from prison in 1984, Liu
Nianchun faced police harassment and great difficulty in finding work, but
he continued to be politically active and later joined the 1989 protests. He
was detained on May 21, 1995, and sentenced to three years of reeducation
through labor.

Because the party had been on the alert against any alliance of intellectuals and workers since the establishment of Poland's Solidarity movement
of workers and intellectuals in 1980, its moves against the founders of the
Peace Charter and the LGLR were particularly swift and harsh. Legislation
to crack down on people who organized public petitions quickly followed
the detention of the Peace Charter organizers. Local party committees were
instructed to outlaw public petitions made by five or more people and to
restrict public assembly.[43] Whereas there was some leeway for freedom of
expression in the 1990s, there was little leeway for freedom of political association. Several of the views expressed by the Peace Charter group and
the LGLR were also voiced by intellectuals in the establishment, but the latter stated such views as individuals and therefore were allowed more leeway than those who organized with others, particularly other classes, to express similar political views.

Resistance of Former Political Prisoners

Another unofficial group that attempted to organize politically in the mid-
1990s was composed of recently released political prisoners of the Democracy Wall and 1989 Tiananmen movements. Most of them had been released in 1993, earlier than the conclusion of their sentences, in order to
boost China's chances of hosting the 2000 Olympics. Despite their early release, they refused to do the party's bidding. Xu Wenli of the Democracy
Wall movement, was freed after more than twelve years in prison, much of

it in solitary confinement. Wang Dan, who sponsored the democracy salons at Peking University in the late 1980s and co-led the 1989 Tiananmen
demonstrations, was released in February 1993, four months shy of completion of his four-year sentence. Unlike those accused of political trans-
gressions in the Mao period who admitted to all the crimes with which
they had been charged, these political prisoners emerged unrepentant.
Wang continued to assert that the 1989 student demonstrations were patriotic and their leaders did not deserve the punishment they received.[44] In
addition, in an open letter published in a Hong Kong journal, addressed to
"My friends at home and abroad who showed their concern for me," Wang
stated, "My past nearly four years in jail have reinforced my determination
to dedicate my life to the cause of the democratization of China. . . . I will
persist in my role as an open opponent acting within the limits of the
law."[45] Wang also called upon Chinese citizens and foreign observers to
monitor China's human rights record.

Using legal and nonviolent means to assert his rights, like Ding Zilin
of the Tiananmen Mothers, Wang Dan took legal action.[46] He filed suit
against the Beijing Public Security Bureau for violating his citizen's rights
by following and threatening him after his release.[47] A number of prominent intellectuals, established as well as disestablished, supported his suit
and collectively urged the government to stop harassing him.[48] This organized effort of support was led by Xu Liangying, an historian of science
who had been sent away for twenty years of labor reform during the anti-
rightist campaign for protesting against the designation of his students as
"rightists." Trained as a physicist, Xu had translated the works of Einstein
into Chinese during his term as a rightist. After his rehabilitation soon after Mao's death, he was made a member of the Chinese Academy of Sciences. Others who signed the appeal included Ding Zilin, Bao Zunxin (an
historian who had participated in the 1989 Tiananmen demonstrations),
and Liu Nianchun and Ma Shaohua of the Peace Charter movement. Despite their efforts, Wang Dan was detained again in May 1995.

Wei Jingsheng of the Democracy Wall movement, who had been sentenced in 1979 to fifteen years, was also released on parole in September
1993. He had served his time largely in solitary confinement from 1979 to
1985 because he had protested his innocence with hunger strikes. From
1985 to 1990, he was sent to do manual labor at a farm for criminals in remote northwest Qinghai Province. But soon after his release, he began
speaking to the foreign press, publishing articles in Hong Kong and

abroad, meeting with foreigners and diplomats, and expressing views similar to those he had expressed before he was imprisoned. Even though Wei was repeatedly warned that he would be rearrested, he continued to write articles and give interviews to foreign and Hong Kong publications, criticizing China's human rights abuses. Wei also published his prison letters in a Hong Kong journal. He was rearrested on April 1, 1994, supposedly because, among other things, he had met in Beijing with John Shattuck, the U.S. State Department official in charge of human rights.[49] Once again he was put on trial. But whereas during his first trial he had to defend himself, at least this time he was able to get his own defense lawyer, Zhang Sizhi.[50] Wei was sentenced once again to fourteen years, but owing to negotiations between the United States and China on human rights issues, he was released on medical parole and exiled to the United States in November 1997, as was Wang Dan in April 1998.

Chen Ziming, who headed SERI, was released on parole in May 1994, but his parole was revoked on June 25, 1995, after he took part in a petition drive calling on the Chinese government to tolerate peaceful political dissent. Suffering from cancer, Chen was released again on medical parole in 1997 on the condition that he not talk with journalists. Police were stationed around his apartment building, which he could not leave without police permission. This form of house arrest continued until his term was completed in 2004. His colleague Wang Juntao, who had initiated twenty-one hunger strikes during his five years in prison to protest ill treatment, was also released from prison early and was exiled to the United States in April 1994 in exchange for President Clinton's support for separating human rights issues from the annual U.S. Congress review of China's most-favored-nation (MFN) status. Wang's wife at that time, Hou Xiaotian, had been campaigning in the United States and other Western capitals for his release. Chen Ziming, who also was offered the option of exile, refused to leave China.

Min Qi, also a member of the SERI group and a former editor of the journal *Chinese Social Sciences*, was not arrested, but his identity papers and resident card were confiscated by the Public Security Bureau. In a March 15, 1993, letter to Qiao Shi, the head of the NPC, Min complained that without his official papers he was unable to get a job, marry, or study. "Officially, I no longer exist," he declared. Citing China's claim that it provided basic economic rights, Min asserted that he was being denied his basic means to subsistence. He said in an interview with a Japanese paper, "It is a fundamental right of a citizen not to be exploited or have his human rights violated by either individuals or administrative officials." He also declared that he would continue to work for the release of all political prisoners, including his colleagues.[51] These examples reflect another new phenomenon in the post-Mao period—political prisoners who not only were unwilling to admit to the charges against them, but who, when they were released, also were unwilling to accept the conditions of their parole or be intimidated into silence and inaction. Despite persistent official harassment, they continued to work for political reform and respect for human rights, the very issues for which they had been imprisoned.

Joint Petitions of Establishment and Disestablished Intellectuals

Until the 1989 demonstrations, with only a few exceptions, establishment intellectuals generally stayed away from nonestablishment efforts to bring about political change. Even during the 1989 demonstrations, few establishment intellectuals made direct contact with the student organizers. Initially there was little overlap in the names on the petitions of the establishment intellectuals and the petitions of the disestablished intellectuals, but their political activities often emulated and reinforced each other in the 1980s.

In the post–June 4 period, a small number of establishment intellectuals for the first time made common cause on political issues with people outside the establishment. The historian of science Xu Liangying was an example of an establishment intellectual who joined with disestablished intellectuals and others in the 1990s in organized petitions to the NPC and party leadership and maintained contacts with several of the recently released 1989 student leaders, such as Wang Dan. Despite his membership in the prestigious Chinese Academy of Sciences in the post-Mao era, Xu persisted in defending those whom he felt were treated unfairly. His actions, he declared, were inspired by his study of Einstein, who spoke out when he learned of political persecution and openly stated his views on major political events. If he remained silent, Xu claimed, he would feel that, to quote Einstein, he had "committed the crime of an accomplice."[52]

Xu's political views also changed radically in the 1990s as he reexamined his long commitment to Marxism, which he admitted had clouded his thinking. He wrote: "I am ashamed of the fact that although I dedicated myself to democratic revolution as a youth and demanded democracy and human rights from the Kuomintang, I erroneously believed Marxist dogma and understood little about the true meaning of democracy and human rights." At the same time, he also questioned the Western belief that the growth of a middle class would lead to democracy. He described the middle class that was emerging during China's economic transition as "some members who have gotten rich over night . . . others have become parasites within the bureaucracy. Even those who have made it in the market through hard work are only interested in economic issues which affect their own lives. Very few care about politics."[53]

Therefore Xu believed that it would be members of the intellectual class who would lead China to democracy. Yet his view of the intellectuals' role was at odds with China's intellectual establishment traditions. In order to establish democracy in China, Xu insisted, "there should be a group of intellectuals who are independent, with integrity and freedom to think and criticize. They should not be affiliated with any power group. . . . [and should] influence attitudes towards democracy in society through their ideas, their expression and their action." Moreover, he argued that democracy was not simply a matter of "majority decisions," "free elections," or "accountable government," though they were part of it, and he emphasized that "democracy should . . . advocate . . . all manifestations of the natural and inalienable rights of citizens."[54]

Xu Liangying was one of a small number of establishment intellectuals in the aftermath of June 4 to call publicly and directly for democratic political reforms. His most controversial article, "Reform Cannot Possibly Succeed without Political Democracy," appeared in the bimonthly *Future and Development (Weilai yu fazhan)*, published under the auspices of the Institute for Research on China's Future. In this article Xu criticized the fact that since June 4, public discourse was "only about economic reform and the development of productive forces, evading political reform and saying nothing at all about democracy." He argued that it was inappropriate for China's leaders to use the example of Asia's "four little dragons," the post-Confucian countries—Japan, South Korea, Taiwan, and Singapore—as models for China, because their economic development had begun with private ownership and a market economy already in place. By contrast, Xu wrote, in the process of the "transformation" of China's economic structure, "official speculation will surely thrive, corruption will run rampant and social contradictions will increasingly intensify to a point of no return, if politically there is no democracy and political power and bureaucrats are not under the supervision of the broad mass of the people and independent media."[55]

Xu also countered the party's criticism in the early 1990s of the concept of "peaceful evolution," which supposedly dominated intellectual circles: "Naturally the reform China needs should be a peaceful rather than a violent one. It should not repeat the old path of 'violent revolution.' Therefore reform is a kind of 'peaceful evolution.' In fact, 'peaceful evolution' is a synonym of 'reform.' It is by no means a tiger swallowing people. Why should we be afraid of it?" He concluded that "political democratization is a reliable guarantee for economic reform and the situation of stability and unity." He urged that political reform begin with guarantees of human rights, explaining, "It is first necessary to take effective measures to ensure the basic rights of citizens, which are granted by the Constitution of the PRC and the 'Universal Declaration of Human Rights' . . . especially to ensure citizens' freedom of thought, freedom of speech, freedom of publication, freedom of the press and freedom of assembly and association." Because China was a permanent member of the U.N. Security Council, he asserted, China had to abide by these stipulations. As radical as Xu's arguments were in the aftermath of June 4, what drew the government's ire was his assertion that "if human beings were only economic animals and growth of productive forces the sole indicator of social progress, then it would not be the four small Asian dragons, but Hitler's Germany that should be commended." Like the outcome of China's nineteenth-century self-strengthening movement, Xu declared, such an approach "is doomed to end in failure."[56]

Another senior Marxist humanist, Yu Haocheng, made a similar plea for democracy in the same issue of *Future and Development,* in an article entitled "Some Views and Expectations of China's Reforms."[57] Active in Hu Yaobang's intellectual network in the 1980s, Yu likewise pointed out the need to carry out political structural reform along with the reform of the economic structure in order to avoid chaos. He cited Deng Xiaoping's 1980 speech in which Deng stressed "the need to effectively restructure and improve the systems of the party and state in such a way as to ensure institutionally the practice of democracy in political life, in economic management and in all other aspects of social activity." Yu lamented, however, that these reforms had not been carried out because of the fear that a movement like Poland's Solidarity would develop in China. He specifically criticized those who equated democracy with anarchy: "In fact, anarchy is a form of punishment to bureaucraticism and a reaction to totalitarianism, and has nothing in common with genuine democracy. All turmoil and excesses are precisely the result of a lack of democracy, and not a case of 'excessive democracy.'" Like Xu, Yu insisted that it was necessary to democratize in order "to achieve genuine political stability and unity and not the other way around."[58]

Yu criticized "some people" who "underestimate the political consciousness of the masses, maintaining always that the conditions for the implementation of democracy in China are still not ripe, and that the establishment of democratic politics remains a remote thing of the future." He concluded his article with a quotation from the political report of the Thirteenth Party Congress, presided over by Zhao Ziyang: "It is not possible to achieve final success in economic structural reform unless political structural reform is also carried out."[59] Following the publication of these articles, the party committee of the Chinese Association of Science and Technology, which oversaw the journal *Future and Development*, ordered the journal banned, and in December 1992 it was closed down.[60] Still, about twenty thousand copies of the October issue were circulated before the ban.

Despite the party's rebuffs, Xu Liangying continued to organize and join with others to bring about political reform. In March 1994, reviving the Democracy Wall demand for human rights, he and six other intellectuals sent a petition to Jiang Zemin and Qiao Shi, head of the NPC, entitled "An Appeal for Improvement of the Human Rights Situation in Our Country." The signers were all well-known intellectuals whose activities had pushed them to the margins of the establishment. In addition to Xu's wife, the historian Wang Laili, the other signers were Ding Zilin and her husband Jiang Peikun, poet Shao Yanxiang, writer Zhang Kangkang, and Beijing Normal University physicist Liu Liao, who had also been purged as a rightist in 1957. The petition demanded that the government reassess the situation for "all citizens detained because of their thought and expressions of opinions." It asserted that "the right of freedom of thought and the expression of opinion is an inalienable right of modern man which brooks no interference."[61] Like the disestablished intellectuals, they timed their petition for the opening of the NPC session and the arrival of the U.S. secretary of state, Warren Christopher, in China. Xu provided a copy of the petition to the *New York Times* to be given to Christopher and expressed the desire to meet with him.[62] Clearly, Chinese advocates of political reform believed that international pressure could help improve the atmosphere for such reform in China as well as provide them with some protection from government reprisals.

Xu and his colleagues differed from most establishment intellectuals in the aftermath of June 4 in that their focus was on political rights, which the establishment intellectuals as well as the Chinese government downplayed in favor of economic rights. Ironically, in the aftermath of June 4, it was not the younger establishment intellectuals but a few of the older former Marxist humanists, such as Xu and Yu, who persisted in the 1989 demands of the student demonstrators for political reform. Moreover, in contrast to the party's view that human rights are to be granted by the state, they argued that human rights are inherent. As Xu's group petition stated, "humans should have independent personalities and dignity and enjoy inalienable and inviolable basic rights, the first of which is freedom of ideas and speech."[63]

Xu asserted that economic reforms needed not only political reforms, but also human rights, to be successful citing an old Chinese phrase: "To talk about modernization without mentioning human rights is like climbing a tree to catch a fish." The petition explained that the 1948 Universal Declaration of Human Rights asserted, among other things, that "everybody has the right to freedom of ideas, conscience and religion; everybody has the right to enjoy the freedom of advocacy and expression of views." Consequently, the petition asserted, "[as a] founder of the United Nations and . . . a member of the Security Council . . . [China] should be a pioneer in abiding by all United Nations conventions instead of a target of international blame because of the issue of domestic human rights." The petition further declared: "For this reason, we appeal to the authorities to bravely end our country's history of punishing people for their ideas, speeches and writings and release all those imprisoned because of their ideas and speeches." The petition pointed out that advocacy of human rights would not cause chaos but instead is based on the desire for stability: "We believe that only after human rights are respected and all rights of citizens are secured will society achieve true stability." Otherwise, it warned, "contradictions will intensify, causing unmanageable turmoil."[64]

Xu's petition was just one of several hundred collective petitions on a broad variety of topics that suddenly inundated Chinese government offices in the mid-1990s. The China News Agency reported that in the first half of 1994 there were 262 collective petitions, involving 5,674 people, calling these collective petitions unprecedented.[65]

Despite that fact that on January 1, 1995, Beijing attempted to prohibit collective petitions, petitions on political issues continued to pour into government offices. Several of them were organized by former political prisoners in coalition with former members of the intellectual establishment, such as a February 25, 1995, petition that was signed by twelve prominent political activists and sent to the NPC and the CPPCC.[66] It repeated complaints about the pervasiveness of official corruption, which was a public concern even of party officials, and the need for political reforms to deal with it. Again it was not so much what the petition said about rampant corruption, but the makeup of the petitioners, who were both establishment and disestablished intellectuals, that made it unusual. Among its signatories were former leaders of the Democracy Wall movement (Chen Ziming and Xu Wenli), some June 4 participants (historian Bao Zunxin, literary critic Liu Xiaobo, former editor of the journal *Chinese Social Sciences* Min Qi, and sociologist Zhou Duo), plus establishment intellectuals, such as Wang Ruoshui, a former editor of the *People's Daily,* and several famous writers, among them again the playwright Wu Zuguang. Although most of the twelve intellectuals had been arrested or detained at one time or another in the past, this was one of the first efforts in the People's Republic that brought together establishment intellectuals and political activists in an organized political effort.

Their petition pointed out that although anticorruption campaigns, launched in 1982, 1986, 1989, and 1993, had become more frequent and harsher, they had proven ineffective because "the malpractice of trading power for money by 'entering by the back door' has become a social practice and has been almost legalized." The ineffectiveness of the anticorruption campaigns, the petition explained, was due to the fact that there were no institutionalized checks on or supervision over the actions of the ruling party. The petition, therefore, called for the introduction of new institutions, such as an independent judiciary and an independent media, so as to reduce corruption. Only in this way, it explained, would it be possible "to reverse the present situation in which the ruling party is immune to restraint and supervision." Furthermore, it urged that people "be allowed to effectively restrain the ruling party's power through free elections" and that "the NPC and CPPCC should be transformed into legislative organs independent of the ruling party and establish an independent constitutional court to monitor and punish activities in breach of the Constitution carried out by the ruling party."[67] In other words, they were calling for a system of checks and balances that Deng Xiaoping and his successors had denounced as inappropriate for China.

At the same time, a number of scholarly journals circulating among like-minded establishment intellectuals made similar arguments for checks and balances, though less directly. One article in *Society (Shehui)*, entitled "Exercise Modern Social Control to Curtail Corruption," explained that "the root source of corruption . . . lies in the organizational structure of the CCP and the state, and launching of economic reforms has strengthened some of the prominent characteristics among them, including corruption in which work units play a central role." The article pointed out that "corruption is mainly the result of the absence of systems, laws and regulations and supervision."[68] But whereas the collective petitions had directly stated that political reforms were necessary to limit the corruption, this article merely implied it. Consequently, the editors of the journal *Society* were still able to continue publication, while the leaders of the collective petitions, such as Xu Liangying, were placed under surveillance.

Nevertheless, Xu continued to organize several additional petitions in 1995. Using the opportunity of the U.N. designation of 1995 as the Year of Tolerance, Xu drafted a petition issued on May 15, 1995, entitled "Greeting the U.N. Year of Tolerance and Calling for Tolerance in Our Own Country." The petition, commemorating the fiftieth anniversary of the founding of the U.N. and signed by forty-five people, was addressed to Jiang Zemin and Qiao Shi of the NPC and released to the foreign press. It repeated one of the demands of the Peace Charter group: political prisoners of conscience, including those imprisoned because of June 4, should be released as a way of demonstrating the government's political tolerance. The petition recounted persecutions of intellectuals from ancient times through the campaigns of the Mao era, specifically against the writer Hu Feng and his associates in 1955, in the anti-rightist campaign in 1957, and in the Cultural Revolution. It asserted that throughout its history, China had "recognized only one authority" and that "intolerance of a second voice still prevails today."[69]

Although the petition acknowledged that China's political situation began to improve in 1978 and that the above cases had been redressed, it pointed out that with the June 4 crackdown, the government again "began infringing on the basic rights of the citizens." Consequently, the petition urged the government to: (1) treat all views in such areas as ideology, political thought, and religious belief with a spirit of tolerance and "never again" regard individuals of independent thought and views as "hostile elements" or engage in attacks, surveillance, house arrest, or detention against them; (2) reevaluate the June 4 events and release those who remain in prison because of June 4; and (3) release all those who have been imprisoned because of their thoughts, religious beliefs, or speech. The petition quotes from classical Western political theory, including British historian Lord Acton's famous observation that "power corrupts and absolute power corrupts absolutely" and the 1789 French "Declaration of Human Rights": "The ignorance, neglect, or disdain of human rights is the sole reason for public misfortune and dishonest government."[70]

Once again, it was not the content of this petition that was unusual in the mid-1990s. Most of the ideas in the petition were being discussed in intellectual circles and academic journals, and appearing in other petitions as well. What made this particular petition different from the others was that the forty-five signatories included many well-known establishment intellectuals who for the first time were willing to place their signatures alongside those of political activists. Most of the signatories were prominent senior intellectuals, including scientists in the Academy of Sciences. Moreover, although the signatories of this collective petition were primarily establishment intellectuals, they also included people who were not only outside the establishment but under a political cloud, among them several former leaders of the 1989 Tiananmen demonstrations, such Wang Dan and Jiang Qisheng, famous Democracy Wall poet Huang Xiang, and Liu Nianchun, who was a member of the Peace Charter group and an organizer of disgruntled workers. Several more petitions on similar themes, with some of the same signatories, followed Xu's petitions.

Yet whereas the establishment intellectual signers of these petitions were able to continue their intellectual activities, most of the political activist signers were arrested or exiled abroad. A few of the petition organizers were detained as they sought to give their petitions to Western news organizations. Literary critic Liu Xiaobo, for example, was detained while delivering a petition signed by fifty-six writers, scholars, and former student leaders. Entitled "Draw Lessons from Blood," the petition declared that to ensure that June 4 "may never again occur, . . . citizens' acts of political participation" should be protected by major revisions in laws governing freedom of press and association, guarantees of basic human rights, and the establishment of an independent court.[71]

Just as the Soviet dissidents had urged their Communist government to live up to its constitution, China's established and disestablished intellectuals and political activists in the post-Mao era—sometimes separately, sometimes together—repeatedly urged China's leaders to abide by its constitution. As the "Draw Lessons from Blood" petition stated, "When a country draws up a Constitution stipulating rights and freedoms of its citizens, this is not merely an adornment to decorate the face of those who are in power; it is a sacred text holding that the government must guarantee the rights of its citizens."[72]

— 4 —

Ideological Diversity Challenges the Party

While disestablished intellectuals and political activists, in addition to a small number of establishment intellectuals, exerted pressure from below to bring about political reforms, diverse groups of establishment intellectuals used official journals, books, public forums, and petitions to argue for a variety of economic and political reforms. In the 1980s the establishment intellectuals who called for political as well as economic reforms had been predominantly Marxist humanists associated with the intellectual networks of the party leaders, but in the 1990s they were more diverse and without attachments to the current party leadership. Wide-ranging debates, without official direction or ideological constraints, erupted spontaneously on a broad range of topics—from the relevance of the traditional beliefs of Confucianism, Daoism, and legalism to May 4 liberalism, Maoism, and postmodernism.

In fact, there was more ideological diversity among the establishment intellectuals than among the disestablished intellectuals and political activists, whose major demands were for democratic institutions, human rights, a reevaluation of the 1989 student demonstrations, and the release of political prisoners. Even more unprecedented in the People's Republic was the emergence of diverse ideological groups within the establishment—neo-Maoists, neonationalists, neoconservatives, the new left, and liberals—that not only debated relatively freely among themselves, but also challenged the party's policies.[1] A few even challenged its political system. Although they did not specifically say that they were asserting their right to speak out on political issues, that was, in fact, what the various ideological groups did when they challenged the party's policies.

The debates among the politically oriented establishment intellectuals

95

primarily focused on how to deal with the serious social dislocations, increasing inequalities, and rampant corruption unleashed by China's economic reforms. These issues had become increasingly more urgent as the economic reforms accelerated in the 1990s. In the course of the debates, the various ideological groups offered differing diagnoses and remedies that diverged from one another and, more significantly, from the party's general policies. Consequently the 1990s witnessed vigorous political debates on fundamental political and economic issues. What was new in the People's Republic was that these ideological debates were conducted without the party's permission or the instigation of a political patron. Although the party leadership ultimately inserted itself into these debates when it believed the ideas being discussed threatened its authority, the debates themselves were generated independently and followed their own trajectories—until the party suppressed them and some of their exponents toward the end of the decade.

Ostensibly the 1990s could be considered the most stable, most prosperous decade in China's modern history. The economic reforms that took off in the mid-1990s brought remarkable economic growth, an expanding market economy, and increasing international economic integration. Yet there was a potential for great social instability from the by-products of these reforms—the accelerating social and economic polarization between the faster-growing coastal areas and the interior regions, the newly rich entrepreneurs and the workers in bankrupt state-owned industries, the villagers along the coast involved in nonstate enterprises and foreign trade and those in the poorer central and western areas, and the prospering urban dwellers and disgruntled farmers, whose economic growth in the aftermath of the land reform of the early 1980s had leveled off in the 1990s and whose farmland had been confiscated for infrastructure development, sparking the migration of millions of rural inhabitants into the cities in search of jobs. A three-year study by the Chinese Academy of Social Sciences (CASS), *Blue Book on Chinese Society, 2002,* found that at the start of the economic reforms, the richest 20 percent of Chinese households were four and a half times better off than the poorest; by 2002 the richest households had incomes nearly thirteen times greater than the poorest, a ratio close to that in the United States and far greater than that of the West European countries. Other statistics described an even more polarized society. In 2001 the average income in urban Shanghai was $1,330; in rural inland Guizhou Province, it was $165.[2]

Consequently, despite the economic growth and seeming stability, potentially destabilizing social, economic, and environmental forces unleashed by the economic reforms and rapid development provoked increasing public anger. This anger was expressed in accelerating demonstrations by workers, farmers, pensioners, and ordinary people against widespread corruption, official abuses of power, burdensome local taxes, demolition of housing for modern development, layoffs at failing state-owned enterprises, and unpaid health care, pensions, and wages. The continuing repression of believers in both old and new religions—such as worshippers in Christian home churches, the Falungong who sought to meditate without official approval, and ethnic minorities seeking more autonomy, particularly in China's northwest—also evoked more frequent, confrontational demonstrations in the 1990s and into the twenty-first century. A pervasive sense of insecurity about the future was widespread, as ordinary people as well as the leadership feared chaos *(luan)*, a specter that has haunted the Chinese people since time immemorial.

Most of the politically engaged intellectuals, whether on the left or the right of the political spectrum, and whether inside or outside the establishment, called for a variety of political and economic changes to alleviate the grievances induced by the economic reforms, or at least to channel the growing protests into less disruptive responses. Whereas the political discourse of the 1980s was dominated by the efforts of the Marxist humanists and technocrats, associated with the reformist party leadership, to bring about relatively liberal political and economic reforms, the intellectual discourse in the 1990s was the most pluralistic it had been since 1949, less directed by the top political leadership and more diverse in challenging the party's policies.

Because the various groups were divided even among themselves, it is only possible here to outline the broad spectrum of their views and point out their main divergence from the views and policies of the party leadership. The neo-Maoists sought to turn back the clock to the policies of the Maoist era before the Great Leap Forward (GLF); the neonationalists and neoconservatives sought recentralization of political power and less interaction with the international community; the new left looked to a revival of some aspects of Maoist social collectivism, the economic populism of the GLF, and the direct democracy of the Cultural Revolution; and the liberals called for individual and political rights, representative government, and an institutionalized system of checks and balances.

When these groups debated among themselves, they were generally left alone. As Perry Link has observed, "Nearly anything can be said in private, which is a big advance over the Mao years. And because academic journals have such small circulations, they are given somewhat more latitude than other publishing media. As long as scholars don't confront the top leadership head-on, they can write in scholarly journals pretty much as they choose."[3] However, when these debates spilled over into the public media and became organized, the party leadership regarded them as a direct challenge to the regime and suppressed them, along with their advocates. For brief periods of time, though, one group or the other was able to get its ideas debated and its views discussed in the public arena.

The Neo-Maoists

Ironically, the first group within the establishment to challenge the party leadership's policies in the 1990s was a coalition of retired party elders and economic central planners. Although they were called neo-Maoists, they opposed Mao's utopian policies of the GLF and the Cultural Revolution and sought to return to the strong state and state-run, planned economy established in 1949–1957. Ideological pluralism conflicted with their desire to return to the pre-GLF Maoist past, which was also characterized by one dominant ideology, but the impact of their efforts to assert their views nurtured an ideological climate in which a "hundred flowers" truly bloomed. The aftermath of the 1989 student demonstrations, the end of Communist rule in Eastern Europe, and the disintegration of the Soviet Union in 1991 initially evoked proposals to restore pre-GLF policies in order to avoid a Soviet-type collapse. China's party general secretary, Jiang Zemin, appointed in the aftermath of June 4 and the purge of Zhao Ziyang, was a former mayor and party secretary of Shanghai who had little experience in Beijing. He initially allowed a number of neo-Maoists to assume positions of authority, particularly in the propaganda apparatus, CASS, and the media. From these bases in the early 1990s they launched Mao-like campaigns against bourgeois liberalization and what they called "peaceful evolution." They also purged the remaining followers of former party general secretaries Hu Yaobang and Zhao Ziyang from these institutions and carried out witch hunts against political activists and student leaders of the 1989 demonstrations.

At the same time, the neo-Maoists opposed Deng's economic reforms and sought to reestablish the Stalinist central planning policies that China

had implemented before the Great Leap Forward. One of the most impor-
tant individuals calling for diversification of views was party elder Chen
Yun. A member of the Central Advisory Commission of retired party leaders, Chen had been one of the few people who had criticized Mao's Great
Leap policy at its inception for its deviation from Marxism-Leninism. In a
letter from the Central Advisory Commission submitted to the Central
Committee on April 14, 1992, entitled "Our Views and Points on Certain
Questions," Chen. asserted: "We should not evade discord or different
opinions. I do not think different opinions are necessarily bad in party
life. . . . Allowing debates and the expression of different opinions in the
party constitute the party's democracy." Chen advocated these liberal
methods, however, in order to express nonliberal ideas. The letter also
called for rebuilding Marxist-Leninist theories, and stated, "[we] should
understand that the biggest danger is the 'rightist' tendency and bourgeois
liberalization in the last 10 years." His purpose was not to achieve ideological diversity, but to return China to the pre-GLF economic policies that
Deng and his fellow economic reformers opposed.

The neo-Maoists used three state-sponsored journals that were under their direct control—*Pursuit of Truth (Zhenli de zhuiqiu), Contemporary Ideological Trends (Dangdai sichao),* and *Midstream (Zhongliu)*—and
sometimes even the editorial pages of the *People's Daily (Renmin ribao),* to
call for a return to an orthodox interpretation of Marxism-Leninism. As is
obvious in the title of an article in *Pursuit of Truth,* "The Division of Marxism into Factions Is Essentially a Repudiation of Marxism,"[5] they rejected
Western Marxism and Eastern European Marxism for "employ[ing] Western philosophy to 'transform' and 'reform' Marxism."[6] Specifically, the
neo-Maoists criticized the efforts of Hu Yaobang's intellectual network in
the 1980s to humanize Marxism. Articles in the *People's Daily,* under the
column "Only Socialism Can Develop China," criticized "erroneous views
that were widely spread in philosophical circles in the 1980s that put humanism into Marxist philosophy. These efforts, associated with the Frank-
furt School, Lukacs's philosophy, and existentialist Marxism, "tried to . . .
[set] up a 'dichotomy' . . . in which Engels and Lenin misinterpreted the essence of Marx's thinking." This particular article concluded that such ideas
were merely a reflection of Western humanistic thinking of a "small handful of 'elite.'"[7] Another *People's Daily* article urged, "We should criticize the
argument about the 'outdatedness' and 'pluralization' of Marxism and the
bourgeois viewpoint about 'human rights' and 'democracy.'"[8]

In addition, the neo-Maoists used their media outlets to challenge

Deng's economic reforms directly. They repeatedly asked whether the reforms should be called "Mr. Socialism or Mr. Capitalism," with the impli-
cation that the reforms were moving China in a capitalist direction: "[If we
do] not ask whether a reform is Mr. Socialism or Mr. Capitalism, it will
lead to privatization and marketization in economics, to a multi-party system in politics, and intellectual pluralization and will lead socialism to a
dead end." Another article asserted, "If one does not ask whether reform is
Mr. Capitalism or Mr. Socialism, it amounts to whether or not one upholds the four basic principles."[10] Even a *People's Daily* editorial on September 2, 1991, with the incongruous title "We Must Further Reform and
Open Up," said, "The reason we must ask whether it is Mr. Capitalism or
Mr. Socialism is because we have to maintain the socialist direction in order to maintain the dominant position of public ownership."[11] Although
this sentence was deleted from the editorial before it went to press, the
Hong Kong and international editions of the paper printed the original
version. Moreover, the *People's Daily* internal publication, *Internal Situation (Neibu qingkuang)*, on February 18, 1992, stated that "those who do
not want to ask the question whether it is Mr. Capitalism or Mr. Socialism
are either politically confused or followers of Gorbachev and Yeltsin."[12]
Thus, asking this question implicitly attacked Deng's economic reforms.

A revival of the Mao cult in the national media and popular culture in
the aftermath of June 4 accompanied the neo-Maoist challenge to the economic reforms.[13] Mao portraits, badges, and medallions were sold and
hung everywhere, most conspicuously on the rearview mirrors of Chinese
taxicabs. Such Maoist heroes as Lei Feng were revived, not only to fill the
ideological vacuum left by Deng's pragmatic policies, but also to return the
party to its original emphasis on ideology. As Wang Renzhi, the neo-
Maoist director of the Propaganda Department, wrote of Mao: "With the
passage of time, his mistakes appear to be minor when compared to his
contributions. . . . Negating Comrade Mao Zedong and Mao Zedong
Thought will certainly lead to negating the history and leadership of the
party."[14]

Initially, as Joseph Fewsmith points out, Deng attempted to respond to
the neo-Maoist challenge through four commentaries in the Shanghai
party paper *Liberation Daily (Jiefang ribao)*, written under the pen name
Huangfu Ping.[15] The neo-Maoists persisted in questioning the reforms until Deng embarked on his dramatic southern journey *(nanxun)* to the
showcases of the economic reforms, the special economic zones (SEZ) of
Shenzhen and Zhuhai in January and February 1992. The purpose of the

tour was to reenergize and reaffirm his determination to continue with his pragmatic economic policies. During the tour, Deng gave a series of lectures in which he explained that because neither socialism nor capitalism was solely characterized by plan or market, it did not matter whether the methods used were called capitalism or socialism, as long as they were economically productive. Deng's words paraphrased the aphorism Mao had attributed negatively to Deng during the Cultural Revolution: "It does not matter whether the cat is black or white, as long as it catches mice." Even though Deng, after the early 1980s, did not advocate political reform and in fact shared the neo-Maoists' commitment to a Leninist party-state, his persistent emphasis on pragmatic economic reforms as the country's number one priority represented a rebuff to the arguments of the neo-Maoists.

More directly, Deng attacked the neo-Maoists by arguing, as first attributed to Deng in the Hong Kong media, that vigilance was needed against the right but the main attention should be paid to guarding against the left.[16] The Chinese press did not report these remarks at the time. Furthermore, Beijing delegates to the Fourteenth Party Congress in October 1992 charged that in his report Jiang Zemin did not point out Deng's emphasis on the need to combat leftism as expressed during his southern trip.[17] Nevertheless, as the Hong Kong and foreign media continued to report on Deng's remarks, and knowledge about them gradually spread back into China, first reported in the Shenzhen *SEZ Daily* and then other newspapers, the incident revealed the role that foreign and Hong Kong media can have on events in China. Finally, in early March 1992, Deng's comments on his southern journey were issued as Central Committee Document No. 2 (1992) to party cadres at various levels and in October 1993 were published in his *Selected Works*. Deng declared: "China should maintain vigilance against the Right, but primarily against the 'left.'"[18] The contents of the Central Committee document soon became the main topic of news in China, broadcast on national radio, and splashed on the front pages of the party's major newspapers. This change in the media coverage signaled Deng's victory over the neo-Maoist-controlled Propaganda Department.

Yet, despite the official endorsement of Deng's 1992 warning about the left, the neo-Maoists continued to express their views in the journals under their control. Why were these journals funded by the state allowed to continue? In part, their major argument that Deng's economic reforms and the "opening up" to the outside world had undermined the basis of socialism and threatened the party's control had enough resonance within the party leadership, especially among the party elders, as seen from Chen Yun's letter, to win support. In addition, virtually all party leaders in the early 1990s feared that China might suffer a collapse similar to that of the former Soviet Union and Eastern European Communist states, neutralizing resistance to neo-Maoist ideas.

In addition, the neo-Maoists had the support of revolutionary elder Deng Liqun, who had carried out the campaign against spiritual pollution in 1983 as director of the Propaganda Department, until he was removed by Zhao Ziyang in late 1985. But in the aftermath of June 4 and the purge of Zhao, Deng Liqun returned to power as an adviser to the Central Committee's leading group on propaganda and was thus able to place his followers in high ideological positions. Maoist poet He Jingzhi replaced writer Wang Meng as minister of culture, Xu Weicheng became a deputy director of the Propaganda Department, Yan'an literary critic Lin Mohan became head of the All-China Federation of Literary and Art Circles, Gao Di became director of *People's Daily,* and Wang Renzhi became a vice president of the Chinese Academy of Social Sciences. Deng Liqun was also able to mobilize followers in the Central Advisory Commission, the Contemporary China Research Institute (which had ministerial status), and the Party History Research Office under the Central Committee in support of neo-Maoist views.

Although there was a lull after the publication of Deng Xiaoping's talks on his southern journey, by the mid-1990s the neo-Maoists resumed using their journals to warn that the party was losing its leading position in the economy to private interests and to denounce the admission of capitalists into the party. Bruce Dickson points out that the party began recruiting private entrepreneurs and other businesspeople into the party in the mid-1980s, with their numbers accelerating in the 1990s.[19] In reaction to these events, in late 1994 the neo-Maoist journals published articles opposing the admission of private entrepreneurs into the party and criticizing their influence on party decisions. One such article, "No Equivocation Possible about the Class Character of Private Enterprise Owners,"[20] charged that "people have noticed . . . that the owners of private enterprises in some places either overtly or covertly control and direct party and government cadres in grassroots organizations, provide services for them, and cover up both their ill-gotten gains and other illegal activities."[21] Responding to growing popular concerns about increasing official corruption, the neo-Maoist journals traced the origin of the corruption to the new business class) charging that "the corrosive influence of bourgeois ideology is what germinates corruption to begin with." When a party member becomes corrupt, "he first discards his communist ideals and pursues individual fame and gain, status and pleasure, and then slides further into economic crime and a degenerate lifestyle to become a corrupt element."[22] Therefore, the article explained, "bourgeois liberalization is both the expression of political corruption and the ideological and theoretical grounds producing corruption."[23]

The neo-Maoists also used their journals repeatedly to cite the collapse of the Soviet Union under the reformist rule of Mikhail Gorbachev as an example of what would happen to China if there were a dilution of Marxism-Leninism and a weakening of the Communist Party. The article "The Marxist Line of Party Building Must be Upheld," for example, noted that in the 1950s China's leaders and intellectuals hoped that "Russia's present was China's future," but the opposite was the case in the post-Mao era.[24] Although this article in *Pursuit of Truth* attributed part of the blame for the Soviet collapse to the strategy of peaceful evolution, "engineered by the Western hostile force," the article argued that in the final analysis in the Soviet Union and Eastern Europe "the ruling communist parties had gone wrong. They . . . no longer adhered to the Marxist guiding ideology, communist goals, . . . [and] democratic centralism." Specifically, the article blamed the Soviet Communist Party's last party secretary, Mikhail Gorbachev: "The leading group of the CPSU headed by Gorbachev reformed the party in accordance with the humane and democratic socialist ideology . . . which led to the ideological confusion and slack organization in the party. . . . Gorbachev opposed the Marxist principle that a political party is the concentrated expression of the classes and negated the proletarian character of the Communist Party. . . . He called for the transformation of the party into one that transcends classes and belongs to the entire people and nation." In addition, Gorbachev maintained that "the rights of the minority could be protected, party members' and citizens' free expression of views . . . could be guaranteed, and individual freedom and political rights could be ensured."[25] Similarly, an article in *Contemporary Ideological Trends* asserted that the collapse of the Soviet Union "was due not to a failure of Marxism, but rather the bankruptcy of Gorbachev's revisionist line."[26] It was such a scenario that the neo-Maoists sought to prevent in China.

Even though these articles, as well as many others in the neo-Maoist journals, attacked the intellectuals' emphasis in the 1980s on Marxist humanism and political reform, by the mid-1990s other articles resumed the attack on Deng's focus on economic reform. One article criticized thinking devoid of ideology that argues that "as long as the economy is going forward, it doesn't matter whether it is socialism or capitalism." The article claimed, "Class conflict still exists and will exist within a certain scope for a long time. Under certain conditions, it might even become acute."[27] Again, the Soviet experience was cited to denounce "[those who say] it doesn't matter whether it is socialism or capitalism as long as the lives of the Russian people are improved. But as soon as they switched to capitalism, the people's standard of living dropped dramatically."[28]

By 1997 the neo-Maoists even expressed nostalgia for some aspects of Mao's later years. An article in *Pursuit of Truth* asserted that "[although Mao] did not see the final outcome of the Soviet evolution in the 1990s, that outcome did prove his incisive and historic insight and vision in combating the problem of 'contemporary revisionism.'" The article admitted that the Cultural Revolution was a failure, but argued that it "does not prove that the motivations were wrong, . . . we need to treasure the rational parts of Mao's strategic thinking in his later years." While acknowledging that Mao may have overly stressed the role of class struggle, it claimed that "[this] does not mean abandoning all class struggle theory . . . not stressing class struggle is bound to blur the lines between socialism and capitalism, opening the door to 'peaceful evolution.'"[29] Finally, the article's authors asserted, they did not want "to see our spiritual civilization sacrificed in exchange for temporary economic development or superficial prosperity."[30]

In addition to the articles in their journals, the neo-Maoists in the mid-1990s also used an approach similar to that used by disestablishment political activists to disseminate their views. They issued a series of remonstrances, or petitions, called the "ten-thousand-character letters" *(wanyanshu)*, so named for their length, that were leaked to the foreign and Hong Kong media and then beamed back into China. Unlike the petitions of the disestablishment political activists, however, these letters were unsigned. Between 1995 and 1997, the neo-Maoists circulated four ten-thousand-character letters in Beijing. As in their journal articles, they attributed China's increasing unemployment, rampant corruption, and growing social and economic polarization to the acceleration of the privatization of the SOEs, the opening up to the outside world, and other economic reforms. Similarly, they argued that the reforms had betrayed the basic tenets of Marxism and socialism, resulting in the spread of unchecked bourgeois liberalization. Joseph Fewsmith points out in his analysis of these letters that they appeared directed against Deng's efforts since his 1992 southern journey to reenergize the economic reforms.[31]

Advisers to Jiang Zemin countered the neo-Maoists' arguments. Xing Bensi, vice president of the Central Party School, for example, in an article quoting Deng Xiaoping at length, argued that "a true Marxist-Leninist must comprehend, carry forward, and develop Marxism-Leninism in light of the situation of his time."[32] Again citing Deng, he maintained that "we need to develop the productive forces." In a direct attack on the neo-Maoists' tactics and in support of Deng's pragmatic approach, he wrote, "People should have the courage to try what they think is right, then sum up experiences they have gained, and abolish practices that are proved incorrect. Some people enjoy creating pointless arguments with others; as a result they waste a lot of time."[33] Finally, as the neo-Maoists continued criticizing the economic reforms in their journals, Jiang himself indicated that the party could not ignore the challenge from the remaining Maoists. In a speech on May 29, 1997, at the Central Party School, he charged that "the leftists are using contradictions in society to attack central authorities."[34]

In spite of the high-level counterattacks by Jiang and his spokespersons, the neo-Maoists, undaunted, persisted in using the journals under their control to criticize the economic reforms. During the months leading up to the Fifteenth Party Congress in September 1997, in an effort to prevent the accelerated privatization of state industry that was getting under way in the late 1990s, they revived the question of whether the reform was socialist or capitalist. An article in *Contemporary Trends* argued that "strenuous effort" must be made "to explain that upholding the public-ownership system as the mainstay is a must, and that in no way should we proceed with privatization."[35] They also continued to resist the continuing incursion of Western culture into China by trying to revive the Maoist emphasis on ideology, which had become increasingly irrelevant as China moved toward the market and opened up to the outside world. Another *Contemporary Ideological Trends* article stressed that "values, as a manifestation of ideology, are not passively subordinate to changes in the economic base, but aggressively and actively guide those changes. . . . The present rulers of the Western capitalist society are quite clear about the role of the value system in controlling society. . . . Infiltration, so-called by the foreign bourgeoisie, is to use its values to influence people." The article charged that "[in the past] Western colonialists used opium to poison the Chinese . . . [and] now the bourgeoisie tries to use its values to transform us."[36]

Rebuttal by the Marxist Humanists and the 1989 Generation to the Neo-Maoists

Deng's talks on his southern journey were primarily intended to relaunch the economic reforms that had lagged in the aftermath of June 4 and to regain the initiative against the neo-Maoists; they had little to say about political reform. Nevertheless, they sparked a flood of articles that simultaneously criticized leftism and called for political reforms. Most of the political activists involved in the 1980s grassroots efforts for political change, particularly the leaders of the Democracy Wall movement and the 1989 demonstrations, were imprisoned or exiled abroad after June 4. Still, voices calling for political reform were heard from the older generation of Marxist humanists, who had returned to high positions in the party hierarchy after the Cultural Revolution. Though some had been purged in the 1983 campaign against spiritual pollution and the 1987 campaign against bourgeois liberalization, they had not been imprisoned or completely silenced. They were joined by a small number of people who had participated in the 1989 demonstrations who, though criticized in the aftermath of June 4, also had not been completely silenced. In the early 1990s, members of these two groups joined together, without party permission or direction, to rebut the arguments of the neo-Maoists. More important, whereas by the mid-1990s the party's official spokespersons, as we have seen, also criticized the neo-Maoists' economic views, the Marxist humanists and members of the 1989 generation, in addition to criticizing the neo-Maoists' economic views, also called for political reforms, which Deng and the party leaders did not sanction.

After Deng's southern journey the neo-Maoists lost access to the *People's Daily* and the *Guangming Daily* and Maoist poet He Jingzhi was dismissed as acting minister of culture in June 1992, but the neo-Maoists still used their control over their three government-sponsored journals to propagate their views. By contrast, the Marxist humanists and 1989 participants had difficulty in the early 1990s gaining access to the mainstream party press. Therefore they resorted to a strategy—private book contracting—that had developed in the process of China's move to the market. As state book publishers lost their once-generous state subsidies, they became receptive to selling "book numbers" (ISBNs), which were required for every new publication, to independent book contractors and editors. The collaboration between state publishers and independent book contractors provided a way for the cash-strapped state publishers to raise money, while it gave independent intellectuals access to printing presses, providing them with the means to expand public space for their views. This collaboration also made it possible for independent book contractors and intellectuals to evade the stringent official publishing regulations and censorship. If one could not find a willing publisher in Beijing, one could find one in Guangzhou or Changsha. Or if a journal in Shanghai was closed down, one could find a publisher in Chongqing or elsewhere who was willing to resume publication for a fee. Therefore, (despite periodic bans, the growing market forces made possible the publication of a broad range of views, including political views)

The government was not unaware of this collaboration, as can be seen in a Xinhua News Agency report: "Today's illegal publications are not so easy to identify because they take legitimate book numbers that are borrowed or purchased, or because they are printed in the name of legitimate publishing houses." The State Council thus issued the document "Circular on Cracking Down on Illegal Publishing Activities," which charged that "the deluge of illegal publications has undermined the state's control of publications and interfered with the normal publishing order."[37] As in other aspects of post-Mao China, however, the growth of market forces overwhelmed the capacity of China's official censors and control mechanisms.

Several books published through this collaboration not only refuted the neo-Maoists' demand for a return to Mao's pre–Great Leap Forward policies, they went beyond Deng's message of economic pragmatism to demand far-reaching political reforms and ignored Deng's caution to be "wary of the right." The first book to rebut the neo-Maoists was *Historical Trends (Lishi de chaoliu)*, a collection of essays that appeared in April 1992, barely a month following the official release of Deng's southern-journey talks. Chinese People's University was listed as the publisher, but the university had merely sold a book number to allow publication. Although the book was subtitled *A Study of Deng Xiaoping's Southern Talks*, it said little about Deng's talks and focused on political reforms. The book was edited by Yuan Hongbing, a former law lecturer at Peking University. Born in 1953 in Inner Mongolia, Yuan had won a prize for teaching at the university. But he had been criticized for organizing Peking University professors in support of the students during the 1989 demonstrations, suspended from his position after June 4, and subjected to more than three years of investigation.

Most of the book's fourteen essays and three introductory articles were written by establishment intellectuals. Three of the authors had been associated with the Central Party School, one was from the Party History Research Office, two were from CASS, and one was from the Chinese Writers' Association. They were all well-known academics, intellectuals, and journalists who had been either purged or marginalized for criticizing party policies and for calling for political reforms. The book carried an inscription from party elder Bo Yibo, a vice-chairman of the Central Advisory Commission, whose calligraphy, "Reform and opening up make the people rich and the country strong," graced the front page.

Most of the essays primarily targeted the left. In opposition to the neo-Maoists' arguments for dealing with rampant corruption by returning to pre-GLF policies, several of the authors advocated political reforms. The editor Yuan Hongbing, in his introductory essay, after criticizing the neo-Maoists, charged that "Another characteristic of the leftist ideology is that it treats the individual as purely a political being. . . . In reality, [the leftists] regard all cultural phenomena in terms of class struggle."[38] Yuan then turned to the problems of the political system: "The monopoly over ideology inevitably leads to a monopoly over political power. Dictatorial power means that power cannot be limited by the people; when the people limit political power that is just the meaning of democracy. Facts have already proven that unrestrained power inevitably leads to the corruption of power. . . . Therefore, the leftist trend of thought tramples on democracy as well as breeds corruption." He continued, "In order to eliminate corrupt phenomena, it is necessary gradually to establish a complete system of laws and expression of public opinion. This can only be achieved by political system reform and it cannot be accomplished by limiting the economic reforms and opening up."[39] Deng Xiaoping had criticized leftism in the economy, but he had not criticized leftism in the political realm, nor had he called, as Yuan did, for transformative political reform.

Veteran editor Hu Jiwei also published an essay in *Historical Trends*, entitled "Mainly Guard against Leftism."[40] Hu was representative of a small number of party elders coming out of a Marxist tradition who called for political reforms; these included Li Rui, who once worked as Mao's secretary, and Yu Guangyuan, a political economist who in the post-Mao era spoke out repeatedly on political issues and sponsored efforts to initiate political reforms. Hu was also representative of the older generation of Marxist humanists in the 1980s who were associated with Hu Yaobang's intellectual network. After four decades of his fifty-year journalistic career working for the *People's Daily*, Hu was sent away for labor reform during the Cultural Revolution. When he returned to the paper in the late 1970s as editor in chief, he helped pave the way for Deng's economic reforms. However, he was dismissed in 1983 during the campaign against spiritual pollution. He then sought to draw up laws to protect journalistic freedom, which conflicted with Deng Xiaoping's insistence on political control over the media. When during the 1989 demonstrations Hu, as a member of the Standing Committee of the NPC, helped organize a petition drive to convene an emergency meeting of the Committee in the hope of finding a peaceful, negotiated resolution to the standoff between the students and government, he was suspended from his position on the Committee.

Despite the punishment, Hu continued to speak out, as he did in *Historical Trends,* where he criticized the left's resumption of control of the media after June 4. He argued that China had suffered enough from disasters resulting from leftist practices and should never again take class struggle as the key issue. He criticized those journals and newspapers still under the control of the neo-Maoists, specifically the editorial page of his former paper, the *People's Daily,* and warned that "their targets are not just confined to general experts, scholars in the ideology and theory, and famous activists in economic and political circles, because their ultimate goal is to overthrow leaders adhering to reform and opening up."[41]

Shortly after *Historical Trends* appeared, it was banned by the party committee of People's University and confiscated by the Beijing Municipal Public Security Bureau. Although about thirty thousand copies of the book had been printed and distributed, some twenty thousand unsold copies were confiscated.[42] Yuan Hongbing was suspended from Peking University in June 1992 for organizing publication of the volume. Yet, unlike in the Mao era, Yuan and his colleagues fought back against the party's repression. Yuan filed a lawsuit in the Intermediate People's Court in the name of the editorial committee of *Historical Trends* protesting the ban. When the suit was rejected, he then made an appeal to China's Supreme Court, but this was similarly rejected.[43] Despite the fact that such lawsuits almost invariably were rejected, filing suits against government harassment and persecution became another strategy the 1989 generation used to draw attention to specific political issues. Moreover, as William Alford has pointed out, "The mere act of filing a complaint enables litigants to juxtapose publicly the gap between the state's professed ideals and lived reality with a rare drama, clarity and moral force."[44] Yuan also demanded a public apology from the party committee of People's University and the Press and Publication Administration for the ban on *Historical Trends*.[45]

Furthermore, a number of former establishment intellectuals held an unofficial meeting at a hotel in Beijing, sponsored by the editorial committee of *Historical Trends*, among others, to condemn the banning of *Historical Trends*. In addition to the book's contributors, those in attendance included prominent intellectuals who had been criticized or expelled from the party for their dissident views and actions in the 1980s. Among the speakers were two former editors of the *People's Daily*, the Marxist humanists Qin Chuan and Wang Ruoshui, who had been purged along with Hu Jiwei in 1983, and the prominent playwright Wu Zuguang, who had been purged from the Chinese Writers' Association in the 1980s. Their speeches, resonating with Yuan's introduction, charged that it was leftism, not rightism or bourgeois liberalization, that had been the source of China's troubles since 1949. Their target, however, was not just the neo-Maoists. Like Yuan Hongbing, Wang Ruoshui pointed out that "the question of the absolute power of the ruling party gives rise to absolute corruption."[46] Several speakers also called for political liberalization to accompany China's economic liberalization.

Despite the banning of *Historical Trends*, several other books attacking leftism and calling for political reforms followed in its wake. One of them was *Memorandum against "Leftism" (Fang "zuo" beiwanglu)*.[47] Its editor, Zhao Shilin, worked in the Ministry of Culture's Bureau of Policies and Regulations. The "leftism" in the title referred to Marxist-Leninist ideologues as well as the neo-Maoists who opposed Deng's economic reforms of moving to the market.[48] Like the writers in *Historical Trends*, the authors of the essays in *Memorandum against "Leftism"* were establishment intellectuals who had been criticized for advocating greater freedoms during the 1989 Tiananmen demonstrations. The authors included famous writers, such as former minister of culture Wang Meng, Ba Jin, Xia Yan, and literary critic Li Zehou, and Marxist humanists, such as Yu Guangyuan, Zhang Xianyang, Sun Changjiang, and Wu Jiang. Although the thirty-six authors of the forty-seven essays in *Memorandum against "Leftism"* repeatedly quoted Deng on the need to fight leftism, they implicitly challenged Deng's view that economic reforms—the move to the market—could be carried out while maintaining the Leninist party-state. A major theme in many of the essays was that economic reforms had to be accompanied by political reforms in order for genuine reform to take place.

As in his essay in *Historical Trends,* Hu Jiwei again stressed the need to implement freedom of speech and press, as stipulated in China's constitution.[49] The title of his essay, "Freedom of Publication and Speech Is Not a Privilege of the Bourgeois Class," implied that these freedoms were beneficial to socialist societies as well.[50] He explained, "In capitalist society, freedom of speech and publication pushes society forward" because "[it] liberates the individual and activates social public opinion and encourages all kinds of ideas." Hu cited Marx, as well as other Communist revolutionaries who had expressed their appreciation for a free press, to prove the relevance of such freedom to socialist society. Several of the other essayists cited a number of Deng's pronouncements to make a similar argument. The writer Tang Dacheng, for example, approvingly quoted Deng's speech to writers in 1979 in which Deng stated, "What to write and how to write is something which only artists can resolve. On this issue, there must be no interference." Similarly, the Marxist humanist Sun Changjiang quoted from various speeches by Deng to demonstrate the failure of the Maoist policies. For example, he quoted Deng in "Establish Socialism with China's Special Characteristics": "The experience of the twenty years from 1958–78 has shown us that poverty is not socialism and socialism must eliminate poverty." Then, paraphrasing Deng, Sun asserted, "Practice is not only the criterion of truth, it is the only criterion of truth."[51]

Like *Historical Trends,* the book *Memorandum against "Leftism"* was banned by the party soon after its publication. The Propaganda Department and State Press and Publication Administration led an investigation. Nevertheless, by December 1992 fifty thousand copies of the book had already reached private bookstalls.[52] This development was indicative of another new phenomenon of China's market economy in the 1990s—though books were banned by the government, they continued to be disseminated by private booksellers. Moreover, as with the writers in *Historical Trends,* the authors of several of the essays in *Memorandum against "Leftism,"* such as Shao Yanxiang, Tang Dacheng, and Wang Meng, continued to criticize leftist attacks on writers at literary gatherings, as they did at a meeting of the Society of Contemporary Chinese Literature in fall 1992.[53]

Despite the banning of these two books specifically directed at "leftism," a third book, *China's "Leftist" Disaster (Zhongguo "zuo" huo)*, also attacking the neo-Maoists, was published in February 1993 by the Chaohua Publishing House, with a print run of fifty thousand. Printed opposite the title page of the book was a series of Deng Xiaoping quotes critical of the left, including the quote from his southern journey emphasizing the need to pay more attention to the left than to the right. This collection was authored by a group of writers working under the collective pseudonym Wen Yu. Among them were scholars in the Party History Research Center, the Party Literature Research Center, and CASS. In addition to its critique of leftism, the book continued the theme of the previous two books—that the principal factor affecting China's social stability was not the economic reforms, but the inappropriateness of China's political structure to the economic reforms. Several writers warned that if China were to undergo only administrative reform, without an accompanying political structural reform, then the economic reforms would be delayed, leading to rampant corruption and sparking tensions between party cadres and the masses. The two authors of the preface, Yue Jianyi, who had been deputy editor of *Pioneering Literature* before its closure in the aftermath of June 4, and Zhang Dening, noted that ultra-leftism was the chief source of all calamities in contemporary China.

The book, divided into fourteen chapters, presented a historical account of leftism in China from 1927 to 1991. Most of the essays recounted the harm caused by the leftism of China's party leaders—Qu Qiubai, Wang Ming, and Li Lisan in the 1930s; Mao's 1942 rectification in Yan'an; the 1950s campaigns against the writers Yu Pingbo, Hu Feng, and Ding Ling; the 1957 anti-rightist campaign; the dismissal of Peng Dehuai for his criticism of the Great Leap Forward at the 1959 Lushan meeting; and the criticism of Yang Xianzhen of the Central Party School for opposing the Great Leap Forward.[54] Two chapters cited examples of leftism during the Cultural Revolution, described as an "unprecedented disaster."[55]

The concluding chapter, entitled the "The Phantom Refuses to Leave," asked: "How can a nation vanquish 'leftism' . . . if even such misfortunes cannot awaken the unfortunate nation?"[56] The authors charged that the leftists were trapped in their dogmatic interpretation of Marxism and wanted to revive the "class struggle as the main principle."[57] They declared that it was time "to move out of this tragedy and toward a full, hopeful future."[58] This book, like its predecessors, was also banned soon after it appeared.

Despite these bans on unofficial critiques of the left, by mid-1992 several small scholarly establishment journals began to criticize the left while calling for political reforms. For example, an essay in the journal *Social Sciences (Shehui kexue)* by two members of the Heilongjiang Party Committee Propaganda Department charged that because of the long period of time during which people had been under the influence of "leftist" thinking, "we absolutized, and solidified the Soviet socialist model, and had an ossified understanding of the principles of socialism . . . it makes the life of the society subject to the will of senior officials, divorced from the masses, divorced from reality."[59] In November 1993, on the occasion of the publication of volume 3 of Deng Xiaoping's *Selected Works*, the newspaper *Law Daily (Fazhi ribao)* printed an article by a special commentator that interpreted Deng's talks on his southern journey as also emphasizing political reform, though they had not. The article explained that "political and economic structural reform should rely on each other and be coordinated. The pursuit of economic structural reform not accompanied by a corresponding effort in political structural reform is self-defeating, because it will immediately run into problems with human beings."[60]

In addition to the books and journals, a few high officials also began to speak out publicly in unprecedented ways against the neo-Maoists. Perhaps one of the most amusing rebuttals came from Tian Jiyun, vice-chairman of the NPC, in late April 1992 at the Central Party School, where he sarcastically called for the establishment of "Special Leftist Zones" (in contrast to the special economic zones that the neo-Maoists opposed) where the neo-Maoists could live. With tongue in cheek, unusual among Chinese officials, he advised, "Couldn't you establish a special economic zone for leftists? . . . Salaries would be low, prices of goods would be low, you would rely on coupons, you would have to stand on line to buy everything and suffer everything that goes along with leftism. . . . If we actually set up a place to do this, would anybody want to go?"[61]

Even Jiang Zemin, who hitherto had appeared hesitant to do so, criticized the neo-Maoists publicly. In a speech at the Central Party School on June 9, 1992, he repeated Deng's theme that "it is especially necessary to alert leading cadres to pay special attention to guarding against interference from 'left' tendencies."[62] Soon after, in the elections to the Central

Committee of the Fourteenth Party Congress in fall 1992, neo-Maoist officials Deng Liqun, Wang Renzhi and Xu Weicheng of the Propaganda Department, and Gao Di, the director of *People's Daily*, who had resisted publicizing Deng's talks on his southern journey, failed to be elected. Still, other neo-Maoists, such as Yuan Mu and He Dongchang who had been removed earlier from their positions, did manage to get elected, while reformist officials associated with Zhao Ziyang, such as Hu Qili and Yan Mingfu, were not elected to the Central Committee.

As seen with the appointments and dismissals of various officials, in the early 1990s there was a genuine struggle under way between those seeking to return to pre-GLF policies and those seeking to move China in new directions. This struggle was reflected in the decisions of the Fourteenth Party Congress in 1992. On the one hand, it established the concept of a "socialist market economy" that Deng had called for, but on the other hand, it dropped the demand for the separation of the party from the government. This reform to eliminate party committees from government organs was a potentially significant political reform that Zhao Ziyang had presented in his report to the Thirteenth Party Congress in 1987 and had begun to implement to a limited degree during his tenure. Also, in the run-up to the Fourteenth Party Congress there were articles in the party media countering Deng's admonition to pay more attention to the left by criticizing rightism and leftism equally. An article in *Liberation Daily*, for example, noted that "resistance to reform comes mainly from the 'left,'" but it asserted, "We must fight on two fronts at the same time . . . we must oppose rightism, as well as 'leftism.' . . . We have all learned from painful experience that wide-spreading liberalization can ruin socialism."[63]

Another round in the struggle between the neo-Maoists and a number of the older liberal establishment intellectuals occurred in the effort to limit the revival of the Mao cult and moderate the festivities to celebrate the centennial anniversary of Mao's birth planned for December 26, 1993, as orchestrated by Deng Liqun.[64] Thirty-two writers, historians, and scientists, among them the writers Ba Jin and Bing Xin and historian Zhou Gucheng, in mid-July 1993 signed a petition to the Central Committee criticizing the Mao cult and pointing out that its revival not only was a severe blow to the millions of innocent victims of the Cultural Revolution but also helped reinforce leftist ideology.[65] Ba Jin also called for the establishment of a museum dedicated to the Cultural Revolution. In August 1993 another fifty intellectuals, some associated with the small "democratic parties," submitted a collectively signed petition to Jiang Zemin that also expressed concern about the revival of the Mao cult. Despite the protests of both well-known and marginalized intellectuals, the CCP Central Committee General Office announced a five-day national symposium on Mao, which was attended by about five hundred scholars and officials.[66]

Ironically, the neo-Maoists' persistent opposition to the economic reforms and their demands for a return to pre-GLF party policies had a liberalizing impact, in that it provoked rebuttals from a variety of sources, using a variety of strategies, without being orchestrated by the party. Although the neo-Maoists' arguments and actions provoked the diversity of ideas that Chen Yun had sought, instead of giving the neo-Maoists dominance in the ideological realm, as Chen had also sought, their overall impact was to widen the parameters of political discourse and spark nonofficial as well as officially approved political debates on a number of controversial issues without the party's input, some of which directly challenged the party's policies.

Neoconservatives and Neonationalists

In the 1980s, students and intellectuals had focused on Marxist humanism and democratic institutions as the answers to China's problems. In contrast, in the mid-1990s the worldwide criticism of China's crackdown on June 4, along with U.S. opposition in 1993 to China's hosting of the Olympics in 2000 and persistent U.S. criticism of China's human rights abuses, evoked an upsurge of neoconservatism and neonationalism.

Those who expounded neoconservative and neonationalist views were mostly educated youth, including several sons and daughters of the party elite. They shared with the neo-Maoists a concern about preventing a Sovietlike breakdown in China due to the devolution of political and economic authority accompanying the move to the market, and they criticized Western capitalism, materialism, and individualism. Yet, unlike the neo-Maoists, who tried to revive Marxism-Leninism to deal with these issues, the neoconservatives and neonationalists advocated a recentralization of political authority and a revival of nationalism. Some of their ideas were derived from the neo-authoritarian views of a number of Zhao Ziyang's supporters in the late 1980s who had urged China to follow the examples of Singapore, Taiwan, and South Korea, where strong leaders first carried out economic development and maintained political stability for several decades before moving on to political reforms. But whereas the neo-authoritarians ultimately sought to develop a middle-class society from which gradually a democratic system could be built, the neonationalists and neoconservatives were primarily interested in ensuring a strong, centralized state and criticizing China's opening to the outside world, particularly to the United States and Japan. These views were accompanied by a revival of traditional values, particularly Confucian values, to fill the vacuum produced by the bankruptcy of Marxism-Leninism and disillusionment with the West.

Because Joseph Fewsmith discusses these streams of thought in great detail, only a few of the major neoconservative, neonationalist works of the mid-1990s will be mentioned here.[67] One of the most controversial was the book *Looking at China through a Third Eye (Di sanzhi yanjing kan Zhongguo)*, published in 1994. The author, Wang Shan, a deputy director of the College of Beijing Opera, writing under a pseudonym, was a member of the younger generation of writers who had experienced the Cultural Revolution. Whereas some members of the Red Guard generation, such as the participants in the Democracy Wall movement, sought a democratic solution to China's problems, others, such as Wang Shan, like the neo-Maoists, regarded the post-Mao economic reforms with dismay and looked back with nostalgia to Mao's more egalitarian society. Though Wang Shan had initially sympathized with the 1989 student protests, he subsequently believed that the June 4 crackdown was necessary to maintain stability. Yet despite its defense of the party's authority, Wang Shan's book presented an implicit critique of the party's economic reforms. As Fewsmith points out, the book reflects the neoconservative view that the economic reforms not only undermined the party's authority but also unleashed a host of destabilizing forces—corruption, crime, economic polarization, demoralization, and disruption caused by the migration of peasants from the countryside into the cities.[68] Fearing a social explosion, the book calls for restoration of a strong centralized government and unified ideology to hold the country together. It also defends Mao's rural policies of keeping the peasants down on the farm in order to prevent the millions who were searching for jobs from besieging the towns and cities, where, Wang Shan charges, they turned to crime and threatened China's social order.

The Shanxi People's Publishing House printed a hundred thousand copies of *Looking at China through a Third Eye* in March and May 1994.[69] Although the book initially encountered little official criticism, by mid-July

1994 it was restricted as reference material for those engaged in theoretical study, and in August 1994 it was banned. It was also criticized by prominent intellectuals, including the writer Wang Meng, who in the September issue of the important intellectual journal *Reading* described it as contemptuous of peasants, hostile to intellectuals, and negative toward the reforms.[70] In response to Wang Shan's fear that the reforms would provoke instability, Wang Meng asked whether China could be truly stable without reforms. As we have seen with the books rebutting the neo-Marxists, a work's being banned did not prevent pirated versions from quickly appearing in private bookstalls all over the country. The book was widely circulated and discussed.

Whereas *Looking at China through a Third Eye* represented a neoconservative critique of the post-Mao economic reforms, *China Can Say No (Zhongguo keyi shuo bu)*, a book jointly written by a group of young journalists and writers and published in May 1996 by Zhonghua Gongshang Lianhe Publishing House, exemplified the neonationalist critique of China's post-Mao foreign policy, specifically China's relations with the United States and Japan. The book attacked what it called the U.S. "containment policy" toward China in the aftermath of the cold war. As one of its authors explained, the book was modeled on Japanese writers' books bashing the United States, such as *Japan Can Say No.*[71]

Like the discourse of the neo-Maoists, the discourse of the neoconservatives and neonationalists expanded the ideological pluralism of the 1990s while it challenged the government's policies. Although their demands for stronger government controls and for a more anti-American, anti-Japanese foreign policy in some respects may have pleased the leadership, their criticisms implied that the leadership had responded ineffectively to both internal and foreign challenges. Demands for a recentralization of authority and reinvigorated patriotism reflected government policy in the mid-1990s, but explicit opposition to the open-door policy and anti-Americanism ran counter to Jiang Zemin's efforts to build good relations with the United States and to integrate China into the international community. One of Jiang's intellectual advisers, Xiao Gongqin, an associate professor of history at Shanghai Normal University, implicitly criticized these views when he asked, "Will nationalist ideas—an important asset for stimulating national cohesion in many countries after the Cold War—acquire a martial, belligerent and expansionist tendency in China?"[72]

In December 1996, the Propaganda Department and Press and Publica-

tion Administration banned *China Can Say No* and criticized it for being
"irresponsible" and causing "ideological confusion among readers . . . resulting in negative effects such as interference and impact on the implementation of the foreign policy of the state."[73] But again, as with the bans
on the books attacking neo-Maoism, this book, as well as variations of it,
such as *China Can Still Say No (Zhongguo hai keyi shuo bu)*, continued to
circulate widely at private bookstalls throughout the country.

The New Left

Another group of intellectuals of the younger generation, the new left,
took a different approach to dealing with the increasing economic inequalities, social polarization, rampant corruption, and what the new left called
"loss of humanistic spirit" that accompanied China's economic reforms
and opening up. Unlike the neoconservatives and neonationalists, most of
the new left (this label was given to them by others to distinguish them
from the old left—the neo-Maoists) had been educated or had spent time
in the West. And unlike the neo-Maoists, who used orthodox Marxism-
Leninism to criticize the reforms, the new left used the latest Western
critiques of capitalism and imperialism—neo-Marxism, postmodernism, poststructuralism, postcolonialism, and cultural studies—to criticize
China's economic reforms and foreign policy. Nonetheless, the new left
was a disparate group: some emphasized economic equality, others social
justice, and still others Maoist experiments. Like the neo-Maoists, the new
left expressed concern about the hardships that the workers and peasants had suffered because of the economic reforms. But whereas the neo-
Maoists sought to deal with these hardships by resorting to pre-GLF socialist practices, some members of the new left sought to resurrect the col-
lectivist landholding and village-based enterprises that had begun during
the commune movement of the Great Leap Forward. They even saw some
benefit in Mao's idea of "extensive democracy," which Mao tried to implement in the Cultural Revolution when he unleashed the youth to rebel
against the party and authority.

New-left discourse began in the mid-1990s and was published primarily
in the journals *Reading*, the intellectual journal that earlier in the decade
had been an outlet for liberal thinking, and *Frontiers (Tianya)*. In the second half of the 1990s, under the guidance of the literary scholar Wang Hui,
who became a co-editor in 1996, *Reading* began to publish new-left views

and academic discourse. Wang Hui had received his Ph.D. from the Institute of Chinese Literature of CASS, but like other members of the new left, he had also spent much time abroad. Other new-left exponents were Cui Zhiyuan, a political scientist who was educated at the University of Chicago and had formerly been a professor at MIT, who emphasized "economic democratization" rather than political democratization;[74] Wang Shaoguang, a Yale-educated Ph.D. who worked in Hong Kong and stressed the need for a strong government; Zhang Xudong, who taught at New York University and edited and wrote a number of books in English on the intellectual milieu in China in the 1990s; Gan Yang, the editor of the influential book series "China and the World" who resided in Hong Kong; and Hu Angang, who headed a research center at Tsinghua University and whose statistical studies detailed the increasing economic and social disparities in Chinese society.

Like the neo-Maoists, the new left called attention to the fact that the privatization of state industries and China's integration into the global economy had deprived vast numbers of workers and pensioners of their social status, social security safety net, and economic rights, producing an underclass of laid-off workers, poorly paid pensioners, and migrant rural workers flooding to China's cities in search of jobs. Specifically, they focused their criticism on the widespread corruption that accompanied the process of privatization of the SOEs and the establishment of new enterprises, which they attributed to the collusion between local officials and new entrepreneurs. Like the neo-Maoists and the neoconservatives, the new left wanted the state to play a more assertive role in dealing with these problems. However, unlike the neo-Maoists who sought to address China's problems by appealing to Marxism-Leninism and calling for a return to the pre-GLF Mao era, some members of the new left urged a return of other elements of the Maoist legacy, such as the egalitarianism, rural collectivism, and economic decentralization introduced during the Great Leap Forward and Cultural Revolution periods. The new left also extolled workers' management of factories, though they did not talk about workers' unions.

Cui Zhiyuan described the new left as searching for new concepts to describe China's current problems and new ways to deal with them.[75] He looked for inspiration from a variety of Western sources—from the analytical Marxist School, the new evolutionary theory of Stephen Jay Gould, Western critical legal studies, and the American New Deal. Noticeably absent were references to Chinese thinkers. Although Cui praised Sun Yatsen's land policy, he was primarily influenced by Henry George's program of publicly owned land, which Cui supported in opposition to the principle of private property that was advocated by liberal intellectuals and the post–Jiang Zemin leadership. Cui defined economic democracy as "co-operative landholding"—that is, land not owned by the state or by an individual, but collectively owned by the people of a village. He distinguished between the capitalism he opposed, which he defined as economic monopolies, and the market, which he supported. Although Cui approved of village elections, he had little to say about political democracy in general. He called for a strong central government to ensure that laws against corruption were implemented. Like others in the new left, his views were more abstract and general than practical and specific. He was more concerned with developing new conceptual visions and language to describe China's current economic and political developments than with implementing concrete programs to bring about change. Like several other new-left adherents who saw some benefit in the Maoist idea of "extensive democracy," Cui recommended carrying out the Cultural Revolution every seven or eight years in order to sustain a "democratic dictatorship."[76]

One of the models that Cui and several of his colleagues cited to demonstrate the success of economic democracy was Nanjie, a village in Henan Province that was graced by a huge white marble statue of Mao Zedong. Nanjie exemplified the collective ownership they sought to reinvigorate. Although in 1981, at the beginning of China's land reform in the post-Mao period, Nanjie had introduced individual farming and two dozen village enterprises and joint ventures, it had reverted back to collective ownership in the late 1980s. By the beginning of the twenty-first century, it had grown from a village of more than three thousand people into an industrial area with more than ten thousand inhabitants, with contracted-out factories and five Sino-foreign joint ventures. Nanjie residents had no private businesses or property; all of their earnings belonged to the collective, which, Xinhua News Agency reported, provided about 70 percent of the daily necessities and welfare benefits needed by its inhabitants. Each family had free housing, and everyone was guaranteed lifelong employment, free education, and medical care.[77] The new-left advocates of economic democracy, however, did not mention that Nanjie's success could be attributed to China's involvement in a market and international economy that bore little relation to the commune economies introduced by Mao in the GLF.

Whereas Cui was searching for new concepts, Wang Hui, the editor of *Reading*, focused on differentiating the views of the new left from those of the Marxist humanists of the 1980s, and particularly their successors, the liberals of the 1990s, whom he called neoliberals or "conservative liberals." In an important article, "Contemporary Chinese Thought and the Question of Modernity," published in late 1997 in the journal *Frontiers*, Wang charged that the intellectuals influenced by Western liberal ideas of freedom, individual rights, and modernization theory were incapable of understanding the economic and social upheavals caused by China's economic reforms.[78] Their idea of the "good society," Wang asserted, "not only failed to accompany the market economy in coming into existence, but the market society has given rise to new and in some ways even more intractable contradictions."[79] He also criticized their demand for "the gradual establishment of human rights and a parliamentary system to limit the power of the rulers through the expansion of freedom of press and speech" (this was understood as political freedom)." He charged, "In thus completely excluding the significance of direct democracy to democratic practice, these scholars even came to regard the widespread participation of the populace as the hotbed of authoritarianism." This sort of "idea of democracy," he insisted, "runs in complete opposition to any actual understanding of the spirit of democracy."[80]

Calling this concept of democracy "the New Enlightenment thinking of the 1980s," Wang acknowledged that it had "provided an enormous source of liberation for the reform of Chinese society and it dominated and still dominates intellectual discourse in China." But, he added, "it has gradually lost not only its ability to critique but also its ability to diagnose problems in contemporary Chinese society." As Wang explained, this kind of thinking was "unable to come to an understanding of the fact that China's problems are also the problems of the world capitalist market and that any diagnosis of those problems must come to terms with the steadily increasing problems produced by the globalization of capitalism. Finally, it was unable to recognize the futility of using the West as a yardstick in the critique of China."[81]

While, as Wang charged, the liberal intellectuals may not have offered a relevant diagnosis and remedy for China's current problems, it is not clear that Wang did either. His diagnosis of China's situation was bleak. He pointed out that "China's increasingly deep involvement in globalized production and trade has led to increased complexity in the domestic economy and to inevitable systemic corruption. . . . This corruption has seeped into every aspect of the political, economic and moral spheres, giving rise to serious social inequities at every level." But like Cui, Wang's analysis of these problems did not provide specific measures with which to deal with them. Instead he called for a search for new intellectual concepts and institutions. As Wang explained, "The reconsideration of China's problems by placing them in the context of globalization is an urgent theoretical problem." Such thinking, he wrote, "may prove for Chinese intellectuals to be a historic opportunity for theoretical and institutional innovation."[82]

Unlike the neo-Maoists and even the neonationalists, whose anti-market and anti-American rhetoric was at a much higher decibel than the party leaders could tolerate, and the liberals, whose demands for political reforms led in the late 1990s to the purge of their major exponents from the intellectual establishment, the views of the new left generally encountered little interference or opposition from the party. Although they challenged the government's market-oriented and economic internationalist approach, new-left intellectuals continued to publish articles in *Reading*, which was published by a government-owned publishing house administered by the Bureau of Journalism and Publications, and in other government-sponsored journals.[83] By contrast, early in the twenty-first century most of the journals of the neo-Maoists and liberals were closed down.

One intellectual, the economist He Qinglian, figured prominently in the discourse of the mid-1990s, but she did not fit into any one group. She shared the new left's moral outrage at the growing inequalities and rampant corruption, but did not share their anti-Western, anti-globalization stance. Although she frequently quoted Karl Marx to substantiate her arguments, she did not share neo-Marxist views. Moreover, rather than debating and criticizing the liberals' approach to China's problems, as the new left did, she directly criticized the party leaders for their unresponsiveness to the plight of laid-off state workers and the millions of rural poor who were left behind by the economic transformation. She also substantiated her criticisms with copious economic data. Although in her critique of the economic reforms she was as indignant about the growing inequities as the neo-Maoists and the new left, and her criticisms often overlapped with theirs, she did not call for the egalitarianism and collectivism of the Mao era nor did she seek neo-Marxist solutions. Instead, she recommended a few democratic institutions—free press, civil society, and rule of law—to deal with the increasing class divisions and social injustices that she denounced so vehemently.

He Qinglian was a member of the Cultural Revolution generation and in a number of interviews with Western journals she attributed her moral outrage at China's increasing economic polarization to her experience in the Cultural Revolution.[84] Born in 1956, she was only ten at the start of the Cultural Revolution. But her father, a doctor of Chinese medicine in their hometown in Hunan, was brutally persecuted, became half mad and half paralyzed, and died when she was sixteen. She then survived by earning a pittance carrying bricks and pushing carts. Like Chen Ziming and other Democracy Wall activists, in the later part of the Cultural Revolution she found a circle of friends who had become similarly disillusioned with Mao and had begun to question everything they had been taught.[85] She likewise took advantage of the limited freedom at that time to read widely, particularly nineteenth-century Russian literature. He Qinglian's Cultural Revolution experience instilled in her "a sense of moral responsibility that stayed with her ever since."[86]

Following Mao's death, He Qinglian studied history at Hunan Normal University in Changsha and then did graduate work in economics at Fudan University in Shanghai in 1985. In 1988 she went to Shenzhen to become a newspaper reporter and to write for small scholarly journals. In 1993 she joined the *Shenzhen Legal Daily*. The extremes of wealth she encountered in the Shenzhen SEZ exemplified the inequalities that she railed against in her articles and books: new entrepreneurs, bankers, prostitutes, and gangsters coexisting with destitute migrants from the countryside and inland cities in search of jobs. He Qinglian characterized China as moving toward joint rule by the government and the mafia, which she condemned as "systemic corruption."[87]

He Qinglian described these developments in *China's Pitfalls (Zhongguo de xianjing)*, which she sent to nine publishers in 1996, all of which rejected it. The book was published in Hong Kong in 1997 and attracted the attention of intellectuals; it was then published in Beijing in the spring of 1998 as *The Pitfalls of Modernization (Xiandaihua de xianjing)*. Its publication in China was facilitated by Liu Ji, who had been an adviser to Jiang Zemin in Shanghai and had been transferred by Jiang to Beijing in 1993 to become a vice president of CASS. Liu placed He Qinglian's book in his book series, Contemporary Chinese Problems, published by Today's China Publishing House (Jinri Zhongguo chubanshe).[88] Jiang's intellectual advisers from Shanghai ranged from conservatives, such as Wang Huning, to those of a more liberal persuasion, such a Liu Ji. Like He Qinglian, Liu Ji had also suffered during the Cultural Revolution when, as a graduate of

Tsinghua University, he was charged with being a counterrevolutionary and was criticized at mass meetings.

With Liu Ji's assistance, He Qinglian's *Pitfalls of Modernization* became an immediate success in China and was sold nationwide in bookstalls and subway stations.[89] It was estimated that about three million copies (including pirated editions) were in circulation. Like her other writings, *The Pitfalls of Modernization* described China's economic reforms as the plunder of state property, carried out through the use of political connections, a process that she called "the marketization of power."[90] This process transferred wealth, but, she complained, it "does not produce wealth." During the first decade of reforms in the 1980s, she pointed out, party officials and their friends and children enriched themselves mainly by manipulating the public funds and supplies under their control. Officials would procure raw materials or commodities at fixed prices and then resell them on the private market at market prices. It was this kind of official corruption, He Qinglian asserted, that helped spark the 1989 demonstrations.

Equally as dangerous, she argued, were the inequalities that accelerated dramatically after Deng relaunched the reforms in 1992, when the economy grew at unprecedented rates and the disparities between the rich and poor and between the coastal and the inland regions increased rapidly. At the same time it became the norm for state workers and pensioners to be paid late, only partially, or not at all. He Qinglian acknowledged that any transition from a planned to a market economy entailed corruption and inequalities, but because the existing system bred corruption, those engaging in corruption, she declared, were not punished.[91]

He Qinglian added a "moral" dimension to the ideological debates of the 1990s. Along with her abundant use of statistics and economic data, she castigated the economic reformers for lacking a sense of moral responsibility. She accused them of emphasizing production and their own gain, without any concern for an equal redistribution of state assets. In chapter 6 of *Pitfalls*, "A Market Devoid of Any Moral or Ethical Constraints," she lamented that the "loss of moral values and the spread of material desires . . . threaten the very vitality of our nation's spirit." She argued, however, that the main reason for this moral decline "is not that economic transactions of the market have somehow destroyed our attention to nonmaterial 'ultimate' concerns, but rather that the totalitarian practices employed during the process of primitive accumulation undermined any sense of social regulation and fairness."[92] She specifically blamed the power holders, friends or relatives of influential power holders, or in some cases self-employed businesspeople, whom she charged had "the ability . . . to abuse . . . reform by converting state-owned property into personal assets."[93] As she explained, officials converted "reform into an opportunity for shifting huge amounts of state property and assets into their own hands," an activity she called "rent-seeking activity" *(xunzu huodong)*.[94]

Furthermore, He Qinglian charged, despite the transition from a planned to a market economy, the government still played a central role by interfering in and managing the economy, "thereby giving power holders at all levels a golden opportunity to participate in the distribution of wealth for their own personal benefit." These rent-seeking activities, she complained, "have been subject to few or no constraints. . . . Whether it is the dual track price system, shareholding reform, real-estate development, or the transfer of property rights of state-owned enterprises, each and every one of these activities is characterized by pervasive rent-seeking." What upset He Qinglian was that "people with insider information and special-access channels, who controlled huge amounts of capital began to manipulate the market for their own interest."[95]

He Qinglian is sometimes categorized with the new left, primarily because of her moral outrage at the increasing inequalities and the corruption inherent in the collusion between officials and new entrepreneurs. But unlike the new left, she suggests some types of political reform to deal with the issues rather than searching for new theoretical concepts or denouncing the liberals or globalization as being responsible for China's problems. In her view, "Political power should have been separated from the economy in such a way that government would serve as a rule maker and arbiter." She insisted that "administrative power . . . [be] restrained and insulated from economic activities." But, she declared, "no such reform has yet hit China."[96] She also called for a more open media to focus attention on corruption, for NGOs to act as watchdogs, and for the establishment of a legal framework to regulate the market economy.

He Qingling was the one person associated with the new left who was punished for her writings. Although her writings were scholarly and filled with statistics, in her frequent public appearances on television she made her more academic descriptions of the wholesale theft of state property, and the increasing tensions between the ordinary people and the ruling elite, readily accessible to the general public; therefore the party regarded her as a greater threat than the more theoretical new-left intellectuals. For example, in an appearance in late April 2001 on a Hunan television program, *Speak Up*, she described a housing dispute between twenty-five laid-off workers and their company in Guangzhou.[97] Although the workers had signed housing contracts with the company in 1994 and had paid money to purchase the rights to use the houses built by the company, when they were laid off they lost these rights and were asked to move out. They brought their case to court, but it was rejected and they had no avenue of appeal.

On the television program, He Qinglian insisted that "the issue was not one of preserving the sanctity of the law, but of answering the question of how to ensure the basic legal rights and interests of the workers. The enterprise must guarantee the legal rights and interests of the workers, including in relation to housing. It cannot renege on its historic liabilities." She then described the standoff between the workers and the company in Marxist terms: "When the gap between the comfortable lifestyles of a minority of the rich and the poor lifestyles of the vast populace becomes too large, then extremely vicious class struggle results. This is exactly as described in Marx's *Communist Manifesto* and why the movements of socialism and communism swept the world. . . . Marx was holding up a mirror for the world to see its own evil ugliness."[98]

Despite her repeated quotations from Marx, or more likely because of them, He Qinglian encountered serious trouble from the authorities. Even before her appearance on *Speak Up*, in the summer of 2000 she was removed from her position as an editor of the *Shenzhen Legal Daily* and assigned to a lowly position in its research department.[99] In 2001 she published *We Are Still Watching the Stars Above* (*Women rengran zai yangwang xingkong*), in which, in addition to continuing to address the issues of corruption, inequalities, and the breakdown of the social fabric, she ridiculed the idea of the "three represents," Jiang Zemin's justification for bringing China's new business class into the party. He Qinglian called the "three represents" another pretext for enriching the already privileged. The book was immediately banned and editors at newspapers were told not to publish her articles. While her unremitting critique of the social dislocations caused by the economic reforms echoed that of the new left, it could be that her demands for more media transparency and for NGOs to act as a check on government, which overlapped with the demands of the liberals, in addition to her appearance on television, were regarded by party leaders as the most direct intellectual challenge to their authority.

Of the various ideological groups presenting views that diverged from the party's in the second half of the 1990s, the liberals were the only group to challenge the prevailing political structure of the Leninist party-state directly. Unlike the other ideological groups, the liberals agreed with the government's move to the market and integration into the world community, but they differed from the government and the other ideological groups in that their major focus was on reforming the existing Leninist party-state and moving China in the direction of democracy. Their views would dominate the final years of the twentieth century.

— 5 —

The Flowering of Liberalism, 1997–1998

Whereas neo-Maoism, neoconservatism, and neonationalism dominated the political discourse in the aftermath of June 4 and the collapse of the Soviet Union in 1991, and the new left dominated in the mid-1990s, liberal discourse, which in the 1980s had climaxed with the 1989 demonstrations, slowly revived by the late 1990s. Those engaged in this discourse were primarily the older generation of Marxist humanists of the 1980s and intellectuals of the 1989 generation.

A more open official environment that began in the spring of 1997, leading up to the Fifteenth CCP National Congress in fall 1997, facilitated their efforts to promote political reforms. However, liberals' specific demands for freedom of speech and association and a system of checks and balances were regarded by party leaders as a threat to their authority. The most outspoken liberals were repressed and deprived of access to the media, but unlike in earlier periods of repression in the post-Mao era, they found a variety of ways to continue to assert what they considered their right to speak out on important political issues.

A Liberalizing Environment

Soon after Deng Xiaoping's death in February 1997, Jiang Zemin began to present his own views on political issues. In his speech of May 29, 1997, at the graduation ceremony for the Central Party School, for the first time he publicly criticized the neo-Maoist arguments and renewed Deng's warning that "the main danger comes from the left."[1] Most of Jiang's report at the Fifteenth National Congress on September 12, 1997, was devoted to a discussion of the economic reforms and a reiteration of Zhao Ziyang's view, expressed at the Thirteenth Party Congress, though not attributed to Zhao, that China was in the "primary stage of socialism," which allowed for the existence of a variety of economic institutions—state, cooperative, private, and foreign.[2] His report also contained a relatively short discussion of political reform, but its content was sufficient to provide some vague support for those advocating liberalism. Emphasizing the need to rule the country by law, the report declared that "all work by the state proceeds in keeping with law, and . . . socialist democracy is gradually institutionalized and codified so that such institutions and laws will not change with changes in the leadership or changes in the views or focus of attention of any leader." Furthermore, it stated that the party supports "holding democratic elections, making policy decisions in a democratic manner, instituting democratic management and supervision, ensuring that the people enjoy extensive rights and freedom endowed by law, and respecting and guaranteeing human rights. In developing socialist democracy, institutions are of fundamental, overall, stabilizing and lasting importance."[3]

Jiang Zemin's report was most supportive of grassroots democracy: "The grassroots organs of power and self-governing mass organizations in both urban and rural areas should establish a sound system of democratic elections, and keep the public informed of their political activities and financial affairs so as to enable the people to take a direct part in the discussion and decision-making concerning local public affairs and welfare undertakings, and exercise supervision over the cadres." Yet even though the report endorsed some democratic practices, it reaffirmed the Leninist party-state: "The party plays the role of the core of leadership at all times, commanding the whole situation and coordinating the efforts of all quarters."[4] Nevertheless, there was enough in the report's discussion of democratic methods, and its unprecedented mention of human rights, to provide an impetus for liberals to call for the establishment of democratic procedures.

As at the Thirteenth and Fourteenth Party Congresses, competitive multicandidate electoral methods were used at the Fifteenth Party Congress to select the members of the Central Committee.[5] At the two previous party congresses the margin of elimination was never higher than several percentage points, but at the Fifteenth Party Congress there were 10 percent more candidates than positions.[6] Furthermore, Jiang Zemin's adviser Wang Huning, in an article in *People's Daily*, stressed the need to move ahead with political reform. Wang pointed out that the Fifteenth

Party Congress report explicitly stated that "the in-depth economic reform . . . require[s] us to, . . . continue to push forward the country's political structural [reform]." He explained that "On our way ahead, there still exist new contradictions and new problems that can only be resolved through deepening reform." Wang, however, did not see political structural reform as an effort to change the political system. Rather, he saw it as a way to "ensure that the party can always give play to its role as a leading nucleus in making overall plans and coordinating the work of all fields." He explained: "Political structural reform . . . is aimed not at changing the fundamental system of socialism but at improving those . . . mechanisms that are not suited to . . . [its] development." And he concluded: "Upholding the Four Cardinal Principles is an impassable political threshold."[7] Thus, the four basic principles enunciated by Deng Xiaoping on March 30, 1979, at the Theory Conference, principles that essentially demanded adherence to the Leninist party-state, continued to be given precedence in the Jiang era.

Similarly, although Jiang at times seemed supportive of political reform, his main emphasis continued Deng Xiaoping's stress on economic and administrative reform and the rule of law to curb corruption. Like Deng, Jiang directed his criticism of the neo-Maoists primarily at their opposition to economic reforms, such as their opposition to separating government from business and advancing the privatization of state industry, not to their adherence to the Leninist party-state. Also, although Jiang, like Deng, called for "socialist democracy," he defined it primarily as improving government efficiency and establishing the rule of law in business and as a mechanism for limiting corruption rather than reforming the political system.

Nevertheless, a number of the party's official mouthpieces, when calling attention to the few official statements promoting political reforms in the Fifteenth Party Congress political report, emphasized its political system reform. The party's theoretical journal, *Search for Truth (Qiushi)*, for example, pointed out:

"We need to politically safeguard the people's rights. . . . Practice has proved that we cannot count on ideological education alone for solving the existing, prominent problems regarding party and government style at the current stage and for eliminating the serious, bad, and corrupt phenomena among a small number of cadres within the party. Instead, to achieve this, we need to perfect the democratic system, reinforce the legal system, and improve the democratic supervision mechanism. Only by perfecting the regulatory mechanism under which power is exercised according to law, by practicing democratic election, democratic decision-making, democratic government, and democratic supervision . . . will we . . . ensure that people will enjoy all democratic rights according to law, that corrupt phenomena will be eliminated."[8]

The article also admitted that "[A]fter liberation we did not conscientiously and systematically establish various systems for the protection of the people's democratic rights," and that "our country's legal system is very much unsound."[9] Another *Search for Truth* article, while emphasizing party leadership, sought to dispel the connection made by a number of party leaders between democracy and the anarchy of the Cultural Revolution. (Democracy does not mean rejecting centralization, discipline, or party leadership) Democracy is not the same as anarchism."[10] This article pointed out that "under the constitution and other laws, not only are the people entitled to a range of civil rights, but they are also empowered to manage state affairs."[11]

China's increasing interaction with the rest of the world, particularly with the West, in the late twentieth century was another factor promoting a more liberalizing environment. In 1998 China was visited by a series of important foreign dignitaries, including U.S. president Bill Clinton in June, Mary Robinson, the U.N. high commissioner for human rights, in September, and French prime minister Lionel Jospin in November. In addition, China signed the U.N. Covenant on Civil and Political Rights in October 1998 and had already signed the U.N. Covenant on Economic, Social, and Cultural Rights in 1997. The easing of controls at home was part of China's effort to create goodwill abroad, particularly with the United States and other Western countries. The flowering of Chinese liberalism in 1998 correlated with China's deepening engagement with the international community, particularly on human rights issues.

Intellectuals of a Liberal Persuasion

Exactly one hundred years after China's Hundred Days of Reform in 1898, which were ultimately to lead to the beginnings of political change during the last years of the Qing dynasty, the year 1998 ushered in public political discourse on fundamental political reforms in the People's Republic. And like the Hundred Days reformers, the major exponents of liberalism and political reforms in the late twentieth century were establishment intellectuals, primarily scholars. They worked at think tanks, universities, newspapers, and governmental commissions, or they were in retirement; they presented their ideas on political reform in books, intellectual journals, public forums, and other channels.

Those proposing a wide variety of political reforms represented a broad ideological spectrum, from the older generation of Marxist humanists, who still couched their calls for political reform in Marxist language, to younger intellectuals from CASS and the universities, who supported their arguments by citing a range of Western liberal thinkers from Adam Smith to Karl Popper. Although none of the establishment intellectuals proposed a multiparty system or direct elections of the political leadership by universal suffrage, they did advocate other institutions associated with liberal democracy: some stressed freedom of expression and association; others called for more competitive elections. A number were concerned with iner-party democracy; others with grassroots democracy. A few promoted an elected parliament. Virtually all, however, called for a political system based on some form of checks and balances and rule of law. What they had in common was their shared emphasis on the need for political system reform in order to deal with the rampant corruption and accelerating economic and social inequalities accompanying the economic reforms.

Establishment intellectuals expressing liberal political views in the late 1990s differed from members of the intellectual networks of the 1980s that had formed around party secretary Hu Yaobang and his successor, Zhao Ziyang, in that they were relatively more independent of political patronage. Not only did China's accelerating market economy and openness to the outside world make this independence possible, but they themselves desired more intellectual and economic autonomy. Furthermore, with the fall of the Berlin Wall in 1989 and the collapse of the Soviet Union and the Communist states of Eastern Europe in 1991, the liberals in the 1990s, unlike their predecessors in the 1980s, did not seek to base their views on Marxist humanism, nor did they call for reform within a Marxist-Leninist framework.

Virtually all of them, though, cloaked their demands for political reforms with the Marxist argument that when the economic substructure changes, there must also be changes in the political superstructure. Without such political changes, they warned, contradictions would arise that would undermine the substructure. Nevertheless, even though Marxist-

Leninist-Maoist ideas still influenced some older officials, as seen with the neo-Maoists and a small number of younger intellectuals of the new left, Marxism-Leninism waned as an inspirational force for most intellectuals in the late 1990s, particularly as the liberals drew increasingly from a variety of Western sources to buttress their views. Another change was that the views and activities of the liberal establishment intellectuals and the disestablishment political activists at times echoed one another, though only rarely did these groups join together in political action.

Liberal Discourse

The liberals in the 1990s addressed the same question that concerned the other intellectual groups—how to deal with the growing corruption, economic and social polarization, and increasing alienation spawned by China's economic reforms. The answers they offered to these problems, however, not only differed from those of the other intellectual groups, but were regarded by the party as the most threatening to its authority. The other groups challenged the party's move to the market—the neo-Maoists sought to return to the pre-GLF Mao era, the neoconservatives and neo-nationalists called for recentralization of political and economic authority, and the new left proposed populist forms of economic and political democracy based on the Maoist experiments in the Great Leap Forward and the Cultural Revolution. In contrast, the liberals' call for the establishment of democratic institutions of checks and balances and representative government directly challenged the party's monopoly on political power and the very nature of the unlimited Leninist party-state on which party power was based.

Strangely enough, economists, who hitherto had generally stayed clear of political issues, were among the first to speak out publicly in the late 1990s on the need for fundamental political reforms. One of the most prominent was Peking University economics professor Shang Dewen, 65, who in August 1997 prepared a proposal for political reform and sent a copy to Jiang Zemin.[12] Shang also offered his proposal to Chinese newspapers, but they refused to publish it. Like the political activists, he then contacted the Voice of America (VOA) and the BBC, which broadcast his views back into China. Shang's views attracted attention because this was the first time this well-known economist had publicly deviated from the party in the forty-two years he had been a party member.[13]

Born into a poor peasant family in Shandong Province, Shang had joined the Communist Party as a youth. During the civil war he was in charge of a platoon in Mao's army when it marched into Shanghai. After 1949, apart from a period working in the countryside in 1960 during the Great Leap Forward and another year in Jiangxi Province during the Cultural Revolution, Shang had taught at Peking University since his graduation in 1958. By 1997 he was only one year away from retirement.[14] He admitted that he had never before openly questioned or challenged the party's authority. In fact, in 1960 he was chosen to guard the rightists who had been expelled from Peking University. Students put up posters attacking him during the Cultural Revolution, but his party record, class background, and revolutionary credentials had protected him. Although he stood on the sidelines during the 1989 demonstrations, his views hardened after the tanks were sent in to crush the demonstrators; Shang believed that the party should have engaged in dialogue with the students instead of using military force to end the standoff. Although several of his children tried to dissuade him from speaking out publicly, by 1997 he believed that it was time to open up debate on previously taboo subjects.

Even though Shang's methods for publicizing his views were new for an establishment intellectual, like his older establishment colleagues he couched his proposals in Marxist rhetoric. He warned of turmoil and chaos if the leadership continued its economic reforms, such as privatization of the SOEs, without also restructuring the political and legal systems. What was new was that an establishment intellectual was saying that China needed political restructuring that involved not merely administrative or legal reforms, which were also promoted by party leaders, but a fundamental change in the political system. In opposition to Deng Xiaoping's warning after June 4 against any system of checks and balances, Shang specifically recommended the establishment of just such a system.[15] He acknowledged that when "anyone brings up separation of powers, people become frightened." But he asserted that this was because of "political ignorance." He insisted that "whether from a Marxist or Western economic view, political system reform is necessary and urgent."[16]

Shang described the dangerous tension between the modern market economy and the Leninist party-state. The collapse of the Soviet Union, he explained, was caused not "by the evil deeds of the individual overconcentration of power by Stalin at the center, but by the fact that the system was no longer appropriate for international economic relations."[17] He pointed out that "Leonid Brezhnev missed the opportunity to make the changes that could have saved socialism, saved the system, and saved the Soviet Union."[18] Similarly, Shang noted, "The greatest problem facing China now is the contradiction between the market economic system and the current political system."[19] He recommended that members of China's parliament, the NPC, be elected.[20] Moreover, he insisted that "the head of the military must be a civilian" and that "journalists should have laws on which they can rely in order to expose and supervise government."[21] Establishing a balance of powers to limit political power, Shang believed, would benefit both the economy as well as society. In July 1998, Shang further proposed the establishment of special political zones to experiment with democracy, patterned after the SEZ experiments with economic reform.[22]

Though not offering political blueprints or expressing themselves so publicly, other economists also spoke out in 1997 on the need for political reform, likewise emphasizing the need to make the superstructure reflect the substructure. One such economist was Zhang Yuanyuan of Ji'nan University in Guangzhou, who asserted that in the move toward private ownership, "political reform is indispensable to matching the market economy."[23] He explained that "deepening reform would inevitably lead to a clash with the existing rigid political mechanisms. It would be paradoxical to continue encouraging state firm managers to embrace the market without modifying the political structure."[24]

Even official economic advisers of the government became public advocates of political reform. One of the most outspoken was the prominent economist Dong Fureng, who in an interview in *China Economic Times* (*Zhongguo jingji shibao*) called for speedier development of democracy and the legal system as the way to solve the social and economic problems arising from China's transition from a planned to a market economy. Similarly basing his arguments on the Marxist requirement of consistency between the substructure and the superstructure, Dong pointed out that "although the superstructure has seen some reform, it has failed to adapt itself to the economic base. . . . The primary thing in reforming the political system is to suit . . . the needs of the economic system."[25] Political reform was necessary, he believed, in order to prevent vested interests from thwarting economic reforms. As he explained, "When social resources are allocated by the government, the will of officials plays a decisive role. . . . [It] replaces and supersedes the law. . . . The market economy . . . needs the law to maintain market order and the rights and interests of all quarters." Moreover, he noted, "only when information is transparent can the market operate successfully."[26] Dong also urged that the people's congresses, at both the central and local levels, strengthen their monitoring of government; he cited local congresses in several provinces that had voted down candidates or proposals put forward by the authorities as a form of monitoring. Specifically, he cited the people's congress in Wuhan that had rejected a proposal by the municipal government dealing with unemployment, which Dong applauded as "part of a very important democratic progress."[27]

In 1998 two journals—*Reform (Gaige)* and *The Way (Fangfa)*—became major forums for liberal views. *Reform* had been established in 1988 in Sichuan Province under the auspices of the Chongqing Academy of Social Sciences. Its founder, Jiang Yiwei, had been a party leader in Sichuan before the revolution and at that time had distributed an underground paper called *Forward Reform*. After 1949 he was trained as an economist and worked at CASS from 1978 to 1985. About ten thousand copies of *Reform* were published every two months, and it appears that the journal was accountable only to Jiang Yiwei, its founder.

On the occasion of its tenth anniversary issue in January 1998, *Reform* published a speech given by Li Shenzhi, a former policy adviser to Zhou Enlai, which advocated political reform, as is clear from the speech's title, "Also Push Forward Political Reform" (Ye yao tuidong zhengzhi gaige).[28] Born in 1923 to a wealthy merchant family in Wuxi city, Jiangsu Province, Li received a Western-style education and graduated in economics from Yenching University, the precursor of Peking University, before joining the party in the early 1940s. He was labeled a rightist in 1957 for questioning one-party rule and as a result was ostracized for almost two decades. However, after Mao's death in 1976 he was rehabilitated to advise on foreign policy. He accompanied Deng Xiaoping on his visit to the United States in 1979 and served as a special assistant to Zhao Ziyang during his visit to the United States in 1984. Li then became a vice president of CASS and established the Institute of American Studies there in 1981. But after June 4 he was dismissed because of his criticism of the crackdown. Unlike during the Mao period, though, when he was silenced, in the late 1990s he became one of the most public and eloquent advocates of liberalism and political reform.[29] His essays, which appeared in both *Reform* and *The Way*, unreservedly proclaimed his liberal political agenda.

In his speech on *Reform*'s tenth anniversary, Li observed, "What intellectuals care most about is not improvement in their lives, but tolerance of freedom of expression." But, he lamented, "political reform" has not advanced." One of the reasons for this, he insisted, was that China had "rule by law" but not "rule of law." He explained, "The difference between rule by law and rule of law is that no one is above the law in a country with rule of law." But Li noted that since ancient times China has been accustomed only to rule by law, in which the emperor imposes the law. The greatest shortcoming of China's cultural tradition, he believed, was the lack of human rights. Whereas new left advocate Wang Hui had disparaged the trend of globalization, Li welcomed it because China could not "persist in its unique concept that the foremost right of human rights is the right of survival. We should adopt the worldview that human rights are the rights of citizens." To establish a country with the rule of law, Li said, "A necessary condition was that people fully have the consciousness of citizens."[30]

In another talk at *Reform* on July 11, 1998, this time on the twentieth anniversary of the post-Mao economic reforms and opening up, Li resumed the theme of his earlier speech. Even though it had been only eight months since his last talk, he described the need for political reform as being more urgent than ever because of the current East Asian economic crisis. Though the crisis was economic in nature, Li depicted it as a political crisis due to the crony capitalism and the connections between bureaucrats and business. Suggesting that the same phenomena existed in China, he decried the fact that in addition to China's lack of rule of law, China's "economic activities do not have transparency." In the belief that the impetus for political reform "comes from looking back into one's history," Li declared, "Our present reform originated from rethinking and criticizing the Cultural Revolution. Deng Xiaoping theory received near unanimous support because the majority of people suffered the bitterness of the Cultural Revolution and wanted to eliminate it." At the same time, Li discounted the view of some establishment intellectuals and the party leaders that "if the economy continues to develop, then democracy naturally will follow." He asserted that "this kind of thinking is not supported by world history. First, the economy is not always able to develop continuously." Moreover, "the starting point of a genuine democratic system must be appropriate and there must be strong public opinion in order to lead and awaken the people. Because democracy is an enterprise of the whole people, whatever system is carried out, it is necessary to have as many people as possible with a deep understanding of democracy."[31]

Another article in the tenth anniversary issue of *Reform* was written by the well-known economist Mao Yushi, who in 1998 also became an outspoken advocate of the need for political reforms to accompany China's economic reforms. Like Li Shenzhi, Mao Yushi, born in 1928, was branded a rightist in 1957, his works were banned from publication, his salary cut, his job taken away, and his privileges revoked. He was from a revolutionary family, but when he was invited to join the CCP during the 1980s he refused. Though he held a position in the Institute of American Studies at CASS, Mao and some of his colleagues established an independent economic think tank, called Unirule, in 1993 in the wake of Deng's efforts to revitalize the economic reforms.

The chief activity of Unirule was to explore and develop new academic areas of inquiry.[32] Mao organized a forum to discuss a new Chinese translation of *The Constitution of Liberty* by Friedrich Hayek, the philosopher and economist who was one of socialism's harshest critics and a proponent of individualism and property rights. Unirule organized a biweekly forum, where scholars freely talked about their research on theoretical and policy issues; it also published research reports and created its own Web site, China Review, to disseminate its reports.[33] In 1998 Mao Yushi wrote a long essay, "Liberalism, Equal Status, and Human Rights," in which he praised Western liberalism and called for human rights.[34] He stressed respect for individual rights, including the right for individuals to pursue their self-interest, and argued that market economies also needed a loosening of political controls in order to develop fully.[35]

The reformist revolutionary elder Li Rui, Mao Zedong's onetime secretary, also published in *Reform*'s January 1998 issue. His article was an abridged version of a letter he had written to an unidentified comrade in the central government on September 10, 1997, in which he complained of continuing leftist influence in the party. Li Rui charged that "for more than 20 years between 1957 and 1978, our Party took a long 'leftist' erroneous path from the Anti-Hu Feng and rightist campaigns . . . to the decade-long disastrous 'Cultural Revolution.'" After the party began the post-Mao reforms, he said, "the 'leftist' pernicious influences are still here even at present." Although these views overlapped with Deng's talks on his southern journey, Li Rui then quoted from Deng Xiaoping's August 18, 1980, speech warning about the overconcentration of political power in the hands of individual leaders. He pointed out, "After 17 years, problems criticized by Deng's [1980] speech, such as . . . overconcentration of power . . . , the inability to separate the functions of the Party from government administration, the substitution of the Party for the Government, the abnormal inner-party democratic life, and the imperfection of the legal system have not been solved well." Whereas the overconcentration of political power was a concern of Deng, it was not a concern of Jiang Zemin, who had undone much of the separation of the party and government begun under Zhao Ziyang in the late 1980s. Li Rui was also a strong opponent of the Three Gorges Dam, which was promoted by prime minister Li Peng. He continued to denounce the project's disregard of environmental issues. "We should take into account the issue of natural and ecological environment. One-third of land in China has been hit by soil erosion." And he asked rhetorically: "What kind of foolish and bad things have we done in flood control?"[36]

The other major journal expounding liberal views in 1998, *The Way*, was established under the auspices of reformist party elder Yu Guangyuan, who had sponsored several liberal journals and study groups since the 1980s. Yu registered *The Way* under the Natural Dialectical Association in Shanghai, whose unit *(danwei)* was the Association of Science and Technology with which Yu was affiliated. In 1998, at Yu's suggestion, *The Way* was moved to Beijing so that it could be more actively involved in political affairs. In addition to publishing articles on political issues, it also organized lectures by its authors around the country.

In March 1998 *The Way* published a special issue on political reform. The articles called for limited government, establishment of private property rights, separation of party and government, a system of checks and balances, and freedom of the press. In one of the articles, entitled "Promote the Legalization of Socio-political Life," the author, Wang Yan of the Institute of Political Science at CASS, differentiated between political system reform and the administrative reform advocated by Jiang Zemin and Prime Minister Zhu Rongji.[37] In fact, Xinhua News Agency reported a reduction in the number of ministry-level departments, from 40 to 29, under the State Council in early 1998 and a decrease in the number of organs under the ministries, which were cut by a quarter, with a 50 percent cut in staff.[38] Wang declared, "To limit political reform to administrative reform is to simplify political questions into technical questions."[39] He pointed out, "Since ancient times, China has emphasized administrative reform, but ignored reform of the political system. Consequently, this has led in recent times to China's impoverishment." By contrast, Wang described political reform as "the establishment of a parliamentary system." He also called for the government to abide by the constitution, which he defined as "regulating public rights and establishing legality on a rational basis."[40]

Wang Yan's article, as well as several others in this issue of *The Way*, re-

vived discussion of separating the party from the government, which had
been promoted by Zhao Ziyang and his advisers. Wang stressed that the
party and the state should not have the same horizontal organs because
this leads to redundancies; responsibilities should not be mixed together,
and government and party should have different responsibilities. This argument not only challenged the Leninist party-state, the central tenet of
the People's Republic, but also challenged Jiang Zemin's reversal in the
1990s of Zhao Ziyang's earlier efforts to separate the party from the government. Wang provided one of the clearest arguments for the separation:
"When the party is substituted for the government, it only regulates the
government power, but not the party's power." Furthermore, "When the
party is substituted for the government, the political power of the state
cannot be supervised by the constitution. On the other hand, since the
practice of the power of the state lacks a rational basis for a two-way feedback channel, it is easy for the leaders to make mistakes." Wang therefore
urged that in addition to separating political power from the economy and
allowing market forces to direct the economy, in the political realm "legal
methods and regulations should be used to govern and carry out policies."[41]

Another article in the March issue of *The Way*, entitled "Freedom of
Ideas and Democratic Politics," by Hu Weixi, a professor of intellectual history at Tsinghua University, pointed out the discrepancies between what is
written in China's constitution and the existing situation. Even though
freedom of expression is stipulated in China's constitution, Hu asserted,
"there is a very big difference between what is in the constitution and the
actual reality." He explained that freedom of expression is a prerequisite for
good government because "popular participation in government without
the citizens' concern for politics and society is difficult to imagine; and
freedom of ideas is a prerequisite for this." Hu added, however, that freedom of ideas and popular participation are not just questions of individual
consciousness. He outlined four conditions necessary for these freedoms to
become a reality: (1) The society must have tolerance—politicians must
encourage people to speak truthfully and must not suppress or attack
those who express differing and opposing views. (2) There must be independent public opinion; the people themselves must have the right to publish newspapers and publications freely and the right to report news and
express ideas freely. (3) Citizens must have the right to obtain ideas and
news and interpret events freely, which means more transparency in gov-

ernment affairs. And (4) Government repression of the "ideological freedom" of citizens must be revealed and investigated. Hu acknowledged that
"some people's greatest concern is that freedom of expression will lead to
ideological confusion and opposing ideas." But he argued that because "at
present, China is undergoing a period of structural transformation as economic reform deepens, political reform unavoidably must be put on the
agenda." Moreover, in order to complete several difficult tasks of economic
reform, "reliance on a small number of officials and experts will not do; it
is necessary to mobilize the whole of society to participate and that requires 'freedom of ideas.'"[42]

Many of the articles calling for political reform that were published in
Reform and *The Way,* as well as in several other journals and newspapers in
1997 and 1998, including even a few in *People's Daily,* were collected together in two major volumes that appeared in July and September 1998, respectively: *Political China: Facing the Era of Choosing a New Structure,* and
Liberation Literature 1978–1998.[43] The concentration of the arguments for
political reform in these two volumes gave the liberals' proposals a greater
impact than their publication in a variety of disparate journals and newspapers had done.

Just as significant as these books' content was the fact that their economic sponsors were members of the new business class, who were beginning to use their profits to try to influence political change, thus revealing
the beginnings of a burgeoning bourgeoisie. Up to this point there had
been only a few entrepreneurs who supported political reforms, such as
Wan Runnan, the head of the Stone Group, a private computer company,
who set up a think tank in the 1980s to study political reform and supported the 1989 demonstrators in Tiananmen Square with telecommunications equipment and money. But most of the rising entrepreneurs, as the
new left and others repeatedly pointed out, had colluded with local officials to improve their own economic positions. Because they desired to
join the party as a way to improve their economic status, most stayed away
from efforts to engender political change.[44] Nevertheless, both of these volumes were funded by private businesspeople, some of whom had gone into
business because they had been excluded from the intellectual establishment, owing to their participation in political activities in the 1980s. By the
late 1990s they were able and willing to fund such political endeavors.

Political China was edited by Dong Yuyu, an editor at *Guangming Daily,*
and Shi Binhai, a thirty-six-year-old journalist from Shanghai. Shi was ed-

ucated in law and was both a member of the editorial board and a commentator for *China Economic Times*. He had also been active in the 1989
demonstrations. His contacts with several businesspeople helped finance
the publication of *Political China* by Today's China Publishing House, the
same publishing house that had published the books sponsored by Liu Ji,
though in this case the publication did not appear to have any relationship
with Liu Ji. Because the thirty-two authors of the volume's essays were
well-known scholars, journalists, and ex-officials, ranging from Jiang adviser Wang Huning, who called for political reform under party leadership,
to Liu Junning, a political theorist at the Institute of Political Science of
CASS who discussed the formation of a bourgeoisie, the publication of the
book quickly became a cause célèbre.[45] The first edition ran to thirty thousand copies, most of which sold out quickly.[46]

The purpose of *Political China* was immediately clear from the quotation by Deng Xiaoping that faced the title page: "If we only carry out economic system reform and do not carry out political system reform, then
the economic system reform will not work because it will encounter obstacles from the people. . . . Whether all of our reforms will succeed ultimately
will be determined by political system reform." The foreword was written
by the reformist party elder Jiang Ping, a former dean of the Chinese University of Politics and Law who had supported the students in 1989 and
was removed after June 4. Entitled "Political Reform Cannot Be Delayed,"
the foreword conveyed in simple but powerful language China's pressing
need for political reform. Jiang explained that the delay was due to the fact
that political reform "is a sensitive issue because it might affect real interests." But, Jiang asked, "how can practical problems in the political system
be resolved by doing nothing?" He cautioned that "the more one waits,
the more difficult it becomes." To create a more open atmosphere for discussion of political reform, Jiang Ping urged that "the right of people to
express themselves freely be implemented so as to form a citizens' consciousness which will be the basis for a legal society and provide a social
foundation for the rule of law."[47]

One of the contributors to the volume from the younger generation
was Yu Keping, director of the Institute of Contemporary Marxism under
the Central Bureau of Translation. Although his article "Overcome the Di-
lemma between 'Political System Reform and Social Stability'"[48] endorsed
China's emphasis on economic reform before political reform as a more
stable approach than the Soviet Union's carrying out political reform be-

fore economic reform, he expressed concern that "political defects threaten the nation's social and political stability and eventually will undermine its economic growth." Yu presented two contrasting current views on political reform, one that "economic growth needs a stable social environment and slow political structural reform . . . [and] we must carry out well-planned political system reform that cannot be done quickly" and the opposing view that "political reform must be done more quickly, otherwise economic reform will be undermined." Yu, however, suggested that China "must find a third road." Although "traditional stability is static and order is maintained by suppression, modern stability which is required by a market economy is characterized by a kind of balance in a process by means of continual adjustments to achieve a new equilibrium." Therefore, Yu recommended that "one way for citizens to express dissatisfaction is through appropriate channels and then the relationship between the citizens and the government will be adjusted." Warning that the old methods can no longer maintain stability, Yu concluded that "social stability and political reform go together and do not contradict one another."[49] In another article in the same volume, Yu urged political engagement, explaining that when people withdraw from public debate and activity, "the conditions for dictatorship are created; without expanding the political participation of citizens, we cannot talk about democratic government."[50]

An essay by one of the editors, Dong Yuyu, entitled "The Road to the Rule of Law Is through Political System Reform," directly contested Jiang Zemin's approach in his report to the Fifteenth Party Congress, which stressed the rule of law without reference to political system reform. Dong asserted that "in a dictatorial system, one must follow orders of the ruler and conform to his wishes. This kind of order makes people feel insecure and society is without justice." Dong warned that "as soon as there is any freedom, this way of maintaining order through force can lead to a social crisis and the beginning of a loss of order." Therefore, he explained, the establishment of "neutral impersonal laws is the basic condition to maintain authority and to promote social justice. In a country with the rule of law, rulers are bound by the law; without law, rulers rule through directives." Therefore Dong insisted that China must undergo political system reform in order to establish the rule of law. Furthermore, it must ensure the basic rights of the citizens as determined by the constitution. Although "citizen participation in politics," Dong granted, "is not governing, it is systematized actions according to a legal process that influences the political situation." Like his colleagues, Dong urged that "we must take the constitutional rights in the legal books and put them into action." He warned that "if we delay the process of political system reform in order to avoid disorder, then that can only delay the time of the disorder. This kind of delay might lead to an even bigger social disorder." Once a citizen obtains and uses freedom of information and expression, then there is a basis for citizens to carry out other democratic rights. Dong concluded, "Rule of law limits the state's power by means of establishing regulations and procedures for using power."[51]

As seen in Dong's and others' essays, most of the authors in this volume, like their May 4 predecessors, emphasized the freedom of expression stipulated in China's constitution as a prerequisite for citizenship participation in political affairs. Several authors focused specifically on the need for laws to guarantee freedom of the press. Zhang Ximing of the Institute of Journalism of CASS, in his article "The Rule of Law for the News and Social Development," called for laws to protect the rights of those who report, criticize, and comment on the news.[52] He stressed that "legal protection is one of the required preconditions for the news media to carry out public opinion supervision and social responsibility." Moreover, he emphasized, media freedom is important for maintaining stability because conflicts discussed in the news are outlets through which they can be resolved. In addition, media freedom "reflects all kinds of social points of view and allows people to see whether policy makers are resolving or avoiding contradictions in society." But Zhang complained that "in the 1990s, the effort to reform the media had stopped."[53]

Ma Licheng, a political commentator for *People's Daily,* in an essay entitled "Supervision by the News Is Not Mr. Capitalism," insisted that freedom of the press is not an institution that exists only in capitalist societies.[54] He described it as "one of the most powerful tools guaranteeing civil rights, rule of law, and restrictions on corruption." Like others, Ma quoted from Jiang Zemin's Fifteenth Party Congress report to support his argument, stating that "develop[ing] the function of public opinion supervision" and "increased supervision of all levels of cadres, especially of the leading cadres, prevents the abuse of power." Ma cited *Southern Weekend (Nanfang zhoumo)* in Guangdong as China's best newspaper because it exposed wrongdoings as well as carried out supervision. He acknowledged that "some people believe that to increase supervision by the news gives society a bad face." But Ma countered "to reveal darkness will increase the light." Likewise, he recognized that some people believe that supervision by the news will negatively influence social stability, but "the situation is just the opposite." He concluded that "supervision by the news is a product of man's enlightenment; it is neither capitalism nor socialism."[55]

Another journalist at *People's Daily*, Zhu Huaxin, published an article in *Political China* entitled "Grassroots Democracy," in which he defined democracy as the establishment of a complete set of political procedures starting at the grass roots. Zhu specifically cited the competitive elections in China's villages as one democratic procedure and argued that the party's view that "only when the people's livelihood improves will they be able to carry out democracy" is a "misunderstanding of democracy." He asserted that "a democratic society does not need to be organized by people with higher degrees." Furthermore, it "is not sufficient for a citizen just to develop a democratic consciousness; he must also master the methods of participating in politics." As Zhu explained, "Democracy is not only a noble, humane value and political belief, it also includes practical operational procedures and techniques." Therefore, Zhu looked not to the elites, but to the villages, where peasants had been participating in self-government since the late 1980s, as the source of China's democracy. In conclusion, Zhu urged that direct elections be extended to the township and then the county levels. Zhu's essay expressed the growing realization of both the established and disestablished intellectuals in the 1990s that the development of democracy in China was not merely the mission of the educated elite. In fact, it was the peasants who were leading the way.

The liberal nature of *Political China* was reflected not only in the views of most of the writers, but also in the fact that it included a few political thinkers of a more conservative persuasion and even opposing views. An article by Jiang's adviser Wang Huning had a title similar to those of the other essays—"Continue to Push Forward Political System Reform."[57] And like the other authors, Wang repeated the Marxist theory on "the need to make the political superstructure more appropriate to the economic base." He explained that "as the market economy develops . . . it encounters contradictions and new problems that must be resolved by deeper political reform." But Wang's definition of political system reform was primarily administrative reform, which differed from the systemic reforms recommended by most of the other contributors to the volume. Wang described this reform as "self-perfection of the socialist system; it does not aim to reform the basic system of socialism, but to reform some specific administrative parts that are inappropriate to the development of social production and the people's demands." Moreover, he asserted that "the four basic principles are the political limits beyond which the political system reform cannot go. . . . To abandon these basic principles will deviate from the correct direction and political system reform also will not be accomplished."[58]

As if in response to Wang Huning's stress on perfecting the prevailing system, Wang Guixiu of the Central Party School, in an interview, called for immediate political change.[59] Unlike most of the contributors to *Political China,* who stressed gradual political reform, Wang called for revolutionary change of the political system. He explained, "Reform, which is one kind of revolution, contains two meanings: one is that reform is the self-perfection of the socialist system; the second is that reform is a revolution against the existing shortcomings in the original system." Wang endorsed the second approach because "the older institutions which limit social development must be basically eliminated." He acknowledged that one of the reasons for avoiding political structural reform was fear of ending up like the Soviet Union and that "the common view is to have reform of the economic system first and then to have political reform. This is the perfect way to defer political reform to the future." But he insisted that this means that reform of the political system will not take place.[60]

The views expressed in the interview were followed by an article in the same volume in which Wang Guixiu further explained his demand for immediate political reform. Like others in the volume, Wang stressed that "political system reform and economic system reform should take place in coordination with one another." He pointed out that China "has a high degree of concentration of political power that is inappropriate for a market economy." Consequently, he warned, "the sequential approach will bring about conflict between the reform of the political and economic systems," which will result in a "new authoritarianism and concentration of political power, even dictatorship and reliance on a political elite."

Wang noted that in Europe, political development came before economic development, and he specifically criticized the argument of the neo-authoritarians of the late 1980s, who believed that limitations on democracy and freedom help economic development. Although the neo-authoritarians had "faded away" as a group, Wang asserted, their ideas still persisted. Like others in this volume, Wang not only cited Deng's speech of August 18, 1980, denouncing the concentration of political power, he also cited another Deng speech, of June 28, 1986, in which Deng pointed out that economic reform without political reform will lead people to seize power and warned that unless political reform was carried out "on the same scale as economic reform," economic reform would be thwarted.[61]

In another article written around this time and published in the *Workers' Daily (Gongren ribao)*, Wang Guixiu again equated political system reform with a new revolution, because it will have to deal with the problem of "excessive concentration of power." He pointed out that because "the power of the Party committees is frequently concentrated in a few secretaries, in particular the first secretary," the party secretaries "have the final say. The Party's centralized leadership for this reason often is changed into leadership by one person." Hence there is "no separation of Party and government, the Party takes the place of the government . . . the Party takes the place of the masses etc." Finally, "The power of the organization is concentrated in the hands of the primary leaders, and becomes 'a high degree of concentrated power in the hands of an individual leader.'" Wang calls for a revolution to reform this system, but except for calling for the separation of party and government, he does not spell out what institutions will replace the party-state.[62]

The other important collection of articles calling for political reform in 1998 was *Liberation Literature 1978–1998*, in two volumes. This collection was compiled by a former political scientist at Peking University, Chen Bo, who had been imprisoned for his participation in the demonstrations in 1989 and was released two years later. After his release, unable to get a position in the intellectual establishment because of his political activities, Chen went into business, and like the economic sponsor of *Political China*, he used some of his earnings to sponsor political activities with which he sympathized. Chen also participated in a small group of liberal thinkers, among them Li Shenzhi, who met together once a month to discuss political issues. Using the penname Li Yu, he engaged in contract publishing— buying book numbers from an official publisher and then contracting out the production and marketing of the books.[63] In this case, the publisher was the well-known Economic Daily (Jingji ribao) Publishing House.

Like the authors in *Political China*, the writers in this compilation ranged from Marxist humanists and members of Hu Yaobang's and Zhao Ziyang's networks in the 1980s (published in volume 1) to a miscellaneous group of well-known intellectuals of the 1990s (published in volume 2). The essays written in 1998 were collected in the last section of volume 2, which was prefaced with a brief introduction in bold type, paraphrasing the major theme of most of the essays in that section: "Among all the things which people value, freedom is the most valuable." Consequently, "For everyone to enjoy freedom, a system of checks and balances must be established that will allow society to develop in an orderly manner and prevent an opening for a reckless dictator."[64]

The original title of the volumes, *From Marxism to Liberalism,* reflected the shift in the intellectual thinking of the writers from Marxist humanism in volume one to liberalism in volume two. But because the original title was considered too controversial, the two volumes were published under the supposedly more neutral title *Liberation Literature.* Initially the volumes were sold in official bookstores, but they were soon banned. Nevertheless, like other banned books, they circulated underground and at private bookstalls and were widely read and discussed. Several of the writers in volume 2 also had articles in *Political China.*

One such writer was political theorist Liu Junning, an outspoken advocate of liberal democracy in the late 1990s who also published in both *The Way* and *Reform.* Although Liu's education and positions made him a member of the establishment, his liberal political views had pushed him to the margins of the establishment by the late 1990s. Liu defined liberalism as "individual freedom based on a government strong enough to protect individual rights but limited by an independent judiciary and the press." He also believed that property rights were necessary for the establishment of human rights because "they provided the independent material conditions necessary for the exercise of political and civil rights."[65]

Liu's intellectual journey to these views had evolved gradually from his personal and intellectual experiences and in some ways exemplified the intellectual journeys of other Chinese liberals of the 1989 generation. Born in Anhui in 1961, Liu was too young to be a member of the Cultural Revolution generation, though it had a profound impact on him through his family's experience. He and his parents lived together with his grandparents in a small town where his grandfather, a party member and the manager of small store, was criticized harshly during the Cultural Revolution as "a capitalist roader." Despite the fact that his own father worked in an SOE and both his parents were lower-ranking cadres, they were poorly educated. Nevertheless, Liu passed the highly competitive exams in 1978 to attend Anhui University. Upon graduation in 1982 he went to work at the Institute of Political Science at CASS in Beijing. As more open political discussions took place in the media and academia in the mid-1980s, Liu's political ideas began to develop and he started publishing articles in 1986, mostly in *Research on Political Science (Zhengzhixue yanjiu)*, on the relationship between economic and political development from a comparative perspective. He also participated in the debates between the neo-authoritarians and liberals in the late 1980s.

From April to August 1989, Liu worked for China's official news agency, Xinhua, in Hong Kong, where he had the opportunity to read many books that he could not find at home. Although he was not in Beijing during the spring 1989 student demonstrations, he was deeply affected by the events of June 4, which he watched on television in Hong Kong. That experience provoked disillusionment with Marxism-Leninism and an appreciation of Gorbachev's efforts to transform the Soviet Union. Liu's reading of de Tocqueville, *The Federalist Papers*, and John Locke also helped move him in a liberal democratic direction. In 1991 he received an M.A. and in 1993 a Ph.D. in political theory from Peking University, and then he returned to the Institute of Political Science of CASS. In 1995 Liu began publishing the journal *Res publica (Gonggong luncong)*, which contained translations of Western essays on political theory as well as articles by Chinese political scientists. The choice of articles in *Res publica* reflected Liu's abandonment of belief in reform within the existing Leninist political system and his desire to promote liberal democracy in China.

Liu Junning published an article representative of his views in *The Way*. Entitled "Protection of Property Rights and Limited Government," it was later reprinted in *Liberation Literature*. Like the other contributors to that collection, Liu repeated the Marxist view that "as soon as the economy changes, the political structure must change." For Liu, this meant that when an economy moves to the market, the government must protect private property rights. In contrast to the neo-Maoists and the new left, Liu saw private property rights as necessary for economic reform and ultimately for political reform, which he believed entailed "a restructuring of the political system." Liu explained that "as long as we acknowledge a market economy, then we must acknowledge that the goal of the government is to protect each person's private property." Such a system, he insisted, must protect the rights of all people to private property and not just the rights of a few. Otherwise it will lead to an "oligarchy or authoritarian system." Consequently, it was necessary that property rights be clearly defined by law. In addition, Liu called for a revision of China's constitution, which "still stipulates that private ownership be supplementary to public ownership." He urged that the constitution be changed "to acknowledge that property rights are the individual inalienable sacred rights of citizens." Liu also advocated the establishment of a limited government, which "cannot use its power to discriminate, harm, or confiscate a person's property; the purpose of government power is to protect a citizen's property and basic rights."[66]

In conclusion, Liu paraphrased the Western concept of "no taxation without representation": "The protection of property demands that each citizen participate, discuss, and supervise government in a systematic way because the maintenance of government is based on taking the citizens' wealth and the citizens have the right to ask how that wealth is spent."[67] In another article, entitled "Society Run by Appointments and Society Run by Elections," also reprinted in *Liberation Literature,* and originally published in *China Reform Paper (Zhongguo gaige bao)* on January 16, 1998, Liu added competitive elections at all levels as another check on political authority.[68] As he explained, "in a society based on appointed and unlimited government, power is unrestrained and people's rights are unprotected; the people or rule of law have no influence." By contrast, a society based on elections produces limited government in which "the highest level of power and every level of power is checked, restrained, and supervised and all levels are open to free competitive elections and are responsible to the electorate."[69]

Liu was also one of the few intellectuals in the late 1990s who articulated the need for the formation of a bourgeoisie, which was another reason he stressed the establishment of private property. In "Protection of Property and Limited Government," one of his four articles published in *Political China,* he described the newly formed middle class as being not merely an adjunct of officialdom, which is how it was viewed by the neo-Maoists and the new left, but an independent class, based on the establishment of private property rights.[70] He explained that individual property rights and a free market economy will not automatically lead to democracy, but without property rights and markets it is impossible to have democracy. Furthermore, "in the past, the demand for political system reform came mostly from a number of scholars and theorists," but "in the future it will come from people who own their own property." While observing that the political reform fever of the 1980s did not broach the topic of limited government, Liu asserted that China must move from market reform to limited government to democratic politics. As he explained, "people are searching for a system that will prevent the abuse of power" and because "a market economy can limit the power of the state," it "establishes the pre-conditions for government noninterference in people's economic activi-ties." When a society has property rights and economic freedom, then the people demand rule of law, supervision of government, and protection of individual property.

In addition to articles, journals, and books calling for liberal democratic institutions, another venue for liberal discourse in 1998 was public forums. In this more informal setting, views and criticisms were expressed even more directly and emphatically. One such forum was held at Beijing Hotel under the auspices of the World and China Research Institute, a relatively independent NGO headed by Li Fan, whose business consulting and mar-ket research activities provided him with funding for the institute. Li Fan was also active in promoting grassroots elections at the township level. Various speakers at the forum expressed the fear, hinted at in articles and books, that the slow pace of political reform not only would thwart the economic reforms but also could lead to a social explosion in China.[72] Qin Hui of Tsinghua University's History Research Center asserted that China was in "a stagnant situation, with neither an effective democracy nor an effective dictatorship," but with an "ineffective dictatorship." At another point in the discussion, Qin Hui explained that "the obstacles to political reform are real interests." Like Liu Junning, Qin Hui called for a change in ownership rights as a way "to make a breakthrough to political reform." He urged that "state-owned firms should be sold, otherwise they will be stolen."[73]

Similarly, Wang Yan of the Institute of Political Science of CASS pointed out: "At present . . . we don't have democracy based on law and we have a central government that has lost authority in local areas. . . . In this stag-nant situation, with no democracy and ineffective dictatorship *(lansui de quanzhi zhuyi)*, one can ask 'why are you qualified to rule?' . . . . Therefore, to carry out political reform and increase government power, we need to implement democratic politics." Wang even regarded the grassroots ap-proach of village elections as too slow. He lamented, "If we wait for direct elections by each level, then we will have to wait for a hundred years." *People's Daily* commentator Ma Licheng then chimed in that "it is a slow pro-cess that can go wrong." Ma also questioned whether political reform will resolve China's accumulated problems, explaining that "the longer one waits, the bigger the political revolution," which Ma described as having the potential for becoming "a political revolutionary explosion."[74]

Several of the speakers blamed their fellow intellectuals' inaction for the failure to implement political reforms. Li Fan observed, "If intellectuals only talk about political system reform, then it won't succeed." He also rejected a proposal, put forth by fellow panelist Ma Licheng at a previous discussion, that the CPPCC could supervise the party, explaining that because "the party gives the CPPCC money, the CPPCC cannot supervise the party." Li Fan favored competitive elections, arguing that "only if we have fair elections will we finally have change." Yet, not surprisingly, one of the intellectual participants interjected that democratization "from bottom to top [is] not as good as from top to bottom."[75] In fact, several speakers at the forum criticized the corruption and clan influence in the village elections. Li Fan at least practiced what he preached—he helped organize an unauthorized election for township head that took place in Buyun Township in Sichuan in 2000.

Liberals' Participation in Ideological Debates

Like the other intellectual groups, the liberals also engaged in vigorous debate among themselves and with others, further opening the parameters of discourse in the late 1990s. Whereas the new left directed their arguments primarily against the liberals and the economic reformers, the liberals in the late 1990s directed their arguments primarily against the neo-Maoists. An example is the book that Ma Licheng of *People's Daily* wrote together with Ling Zhijun, a senior reporter at the paper, to rebut the neo-Maoists.[76] The purpose of *Crossed Swords (Jiaofeng)*, as reflected in its subtitle, *A Faithful Record of the Three Rounds of Ideological Emancipation in Contemporary China*, was to describe the ideological struggles, or "crossed swords," since 1978 between the post-Mao reformist intellectuals and the neo-Maoists. *Crossed Swords* appeared in March 1998 in the series sponsored by Liu Ji and published by Today's China Publishing House. Although the book depicted Jiang Zemin as a crusader against the leftists and implied that Jiang favored political reform, the main intention of the book was to promote political reform in the process of criticizing the neo-Maoists.

Though slightly older than people in the Cultural Revolution generation, Ma Licheng, born in 1946, could be identified with that generation. Initially he had stayed away from the turmoil of the movement and taught at a middle school, but in 1971, like many others feeling betrayed by the purge of Lin Biao, Mao's supposed successor, he began to question the Cultural Revolution as well as the rise of the Gang of Four. He also became concerned that China's political system lacked nonviolent methods with which to bring about change. After the Cultural Revolution ended, Ma began to write for the *China Youth Daily (Zhongguo qingnian bao)* and then in the mid-1980s went to the *People's Daily,* where he became a political commentator.

In *Crossed Swords,* Ma and Ling chronicled the neo-Maoist articles, speeches, and statements, some public, others less so, and identified the authors behind the pen names. They argued that by insisting on public ownership as the backbone of the economy, the neo-Maoists challenged the reform agenda of China's present leaders. Specifically, they criticized the ten-thousand-character letters written under Deng Liqun's auspices, without directly mentioning Deng's name.[77] To counter what they called "leftism," the authors called for "three ideological liberations: liberation from individual worship, the planned economy, and state ownership."[78] Although they seemed supportive of Jiang Zemin's policies, in their conclusion they asked when the next liberation will take place.

Some 150,000 copies of *Crossed Swords* were published in one month. It quickly became a best seller with two million copies in print, some of them printed illegally.[79] With excerpts from the book reprinted in newspapers and journals, *Crossed Swords* attracted much publicity. In addition, two senior reformist party elders publicly supported it. Wan Li, former chair of the NPC, who had retired in 1993 and had helped introduce the contract responsibility system—that is, China's land reform—and Wang Daohan, former mayor of Shanghai and adviser to Jiang, recommended *Crossed Swords* to others. At the same time, the book provoked vigorous debate between market reformers and state planners. Ma Licheng estimated that in 1998 the three neo-Maoist journals had printed at least fifty-two articles savaging him and *Crossed Swords* and accusing him of seeking to bring down the party and to replace socialism with capitalism.[80]

While criticizing the party's economic reforms, several of the articles in the neo-Maoist journals denouncing *Crossed Swords* appeared to defend Jiang Zemin's political views. One of them, published in *Contemporary Trends* by a young instructor at the Dalian Naval Political Institute, praised Jiang's assumption of power in the aftermath of the turmoil of the late 1980s.[81] The article asserted, "This round of ideological emancipation restored those things turned upside down by bourgeois liberalization; it liberated the people's understanding of socialism from the bondage of bourgeois liberalization and put it back on the right track." But *Crossed Swords*, it charged, "smeared this round of emancipation of the mind, saying it put a 'shackle on China.'" It also charged that *Crossed Swords* "hates the third generation leading group . . . because this emancipation completely disrupted the timetable of 'peaceful evolution' of forces at home and abroad and completely changed the kind of domestic political climate that almost destroyed China's socialist future."[82]

In addition to such articles, the neo-Maoist journals also convened forums to condemn the book. At one such forum, in celebration of the publication of the one-hundredth issue of *Midstream* in late April 1998, one of the speakers, Wei Wei, warned, "The guiding ideology of this book is to negate the four cardinal principles . . . and incorporate China into the Western capitalist system."[83] The latter point also coincided with the new left's critique of the liberals.

Like the democratic activists and others, the neo-Maoists turned to the courts to defend their rights. In June the editor in chief of *Contemporary Trends*, Duan Ruofei, sued the writers of *Crossed Swords* and its publisher for violation of intellectual property rights.[84] He charged that they had quoted without permission from an article that first appeared in his publication, the third ten-thousand-character letter, for which Duan asserted that his magazine owned the copyright, and they had distorted its meaning. In his suit, Duan Ruofei claimed that in the fall of 1996 and early 1997, because of efforts in certain theoretical circles to break away from public ownership, he had written an article "Several Theoretical and Policy-Related Issues concerning the Need to Uphold the Dominant Position of the Public Ownership," in which he stressed the dominant position of the public economy.[85] Signed by an anonymous "special commentator," it was never openly published but was carried by *Contemporary Trends* as a restricted commentary. Duan charged that Ma and Ling had taken extracts of his article without permission and pieced them together, resulting in a total distortion of the original intent, seriously twisting its theoretical and political views and infringing on Duan's rights and interests in terms of copyright. Duan demanded that they be ordered to halt publication of their book, make a public apology, and pay two hundred thousand yuan in compensation.

In rebuttal, Ma and Ling argued that although Duan's article had not been formally published, it had been made public to many units in the form of a "comment-soliciting edition," and it had also been published in

Hong Kong, where it had not violated anyone's copyright. Moreover, the defendants asserted that they were simply enjoying their right to express their views under protection of the constitution and the law. The trial, held in November 1998, was one of the first to be open to the public, including journalists.[86] But Duan himself did not appear because he claimed his social status was much higher than that of the defendants.[87] The judge deferred a verdict and advised the parties to settle out of court. Despite its inconclusive verdict, this incident demonstrated that both sides of the political spectrum in the 1990s resorted to the courts to resolve conflicts.

Although the State Press and Publication Administration asked the officials in charge of Today's China Publishing House to explain why *Crossed Swords* had been published, and the Propaganda Department in October 1998 ordered its news organizations not to discuss the book any further, *Crossed Swords* was not banned and Ma and Ling continued in their jobs at *People's Daily*. Moreover, undeterred by the vociferous reaction of the neo-Maoists, Ma and Ling proceeded to write another book, *Shouting: Five Voices in Contemporary China (Huhan: Dangjin Zhongguo de 5 zhong shengyin)*, which was published by Guangzhou Publishing House after a number of publishing houses in Beijing had rejected it.[88] *Shouting* discussed the emergence of five voices after 1978—mainstream economic reformism, dogmatism of the neo-Maoists, nationalism as expressed in the book *China Can Say No*, feudalism as in the revival of Confucianism, and democracy as expressed at Democracy Wall. Whereas *Crossed Swords* reflected the expression of two voices, the purpose of *Shouting* was to show the coexistence of a number of different voices in post-Mao China that challenged the party's policies and values.

Other Venues for the Expression of Liberal Views

In addition to journals, books, public forums, and debates, the centenary anniversary of the establishment of Peking University in 1998 provided another occasion for liberal discourse and an opportunity to assert political views that differed from the party's. To counter the party's use of the occasion to extol the university's patriotic tradition, Liu Junning arranged for the publication of the book *Peking University's Tradition and Modern China: The Harbinger of Liberalism*,[89] a selection of essays written before 1949 by prominent Peking University faculty members, praising the uni-

versity's efforts to promote human rights, the rule of law, and democracy.
It included excerpts of essays by Cai Yuanpei and Yan Fu, the university's
first and second presidents, who introduced to the university a liberal arts
curriculum and toleration of a variety of viewpoints. In addition, there
were essays by one of the leaders of the Hundred Days of Reform, Liang
Qichao; the pragmatist philosopher Hu Shi; and a founder of the Chinese
Communist Party, Li Dazhao. The diverse views expressed in the essays
exemplified the kind of liberalism Liu advocated.

The book's preface, written by Li Shenzhi, pointed out that since Peking
University's inception in 1898, liberalism had been the dominant intellectual trend and had spread to other universities and the intellectual
community at large. Although elements of liberalism could be found in
Confucianism and Daoism, until the establishment of Peking University,
Li asserted, intellectual endeavors had not been "separate from political
power." But starting with its first president, according to Li, the university was open to all views, ideologies, and debates until 1957, when Mao
Zedong purged and condemned its president, Ma Yinchu, for criticizing
Mao's policy to increase births during the Great Leap Forward. Li wrote,
"Through comparisons and choices in the world over the last two or three
hundred years, especially mankind's largest experiments in China for over
a hundred years, we already have plenty of reasons to believe that liberalism is the best and most universal value." Furthermore, "The revival of the
liberal tradition, originating at Peking University, will bring a free China
into a globalizing world, and will be beneficial and glorious for the whole
world."[90]

Liu Junning's opening essay in the book specifically attributed the end of
Peking University's liberal tradition to the Communist revolution. Even
though Liu acknowledged that liberalism had never entered deeply into
Chinese society, except among a number of educated people, he sought to
revive that liberal tradition, which he described as "the only ideology that
is tolerant of other ideologies including those that are opposed to it. . . .
Liberalism is tolerant and open to other ideas." He used the conventional
Western description of a liberal as someone who "may oppose your views,
but will uphold your right to express them." He pointed out, however, that
"tolerance is not equal to agreement." Because Peking University embodied
this liberal approach until 1949, Liu asserted that "Peking University and
modern liberalism cannot be separated from each other."[91]

Even more challenging to the party's views than the book on Peking

University's liberal tradition was a speech on Karl Popper's philosophy, entitled "Open Society and Its Enemies," that Liu gave to law students at Peking University in October 1999. Liu described Popper's view of an open society as one based on individual freedom. Liu specifically criticized the demand to "unite around a political leader or leadership core"—a current Jiang Zemin dictum. He again called for free and competitive elections. Someone who was in the audience wrote to Jiang Zemin complaining about Liu's talk. Around the same time, Liu held interviews with foreign journalists and he wrote an article published in a Hong Kong journal calling attention to the need for constitutional reform to abolish the four basic principles. His major theme was that China cannot wait for the market to bring about democracy and that the Chinese must "learn democracy by making democracy" and "defend the rights of ordinary people by participating in politics."[92]

Liu was subsequently attacked in the neo-Maoist journals. One article in *Midstream*, by Peking University professor Zi Yu, written on December 12, 1999, was entitled "Who Is Influencing the Ideas of University Students?"[93] The article charged that "Liu Junning . . . criticizes collectivism, and then socialism, Lenin, Stalin's first socialist country, our leader Mao, and others during Mao's years and the idea of the party center with Jiang Zemin as the core leader as individual worship. He ridicules that America never united around Clinton, so then why in China do we have to unite around a core? He strongly advocates capitalist liberalism and criticizes collectivism to advocate individualism. Even more frightening is that among the people who worship Liu Junning the most are the freshmen." Zi Yu declared: "Our government and schools should stop this; otherwise our nation will change its color." He even impugned Liu's patriotism: "I wonder whether Liu Junning is Chinese."[94]

For these views, Jiang Zemin ordered Liu Junning dismissed from the Institute of Political Science at CASS along with others at CASS who advocated political reform. The Guangdong newspapers and journals, which were the most daring politically, were specifically ordered not to publish articles by these well-known scholars.[95] Thus, the liberal flowering of 1998 slowly faded away by the end of the century.

Yet unlike previous decades when censured writers were dismissed from their positions and could not find another place in the establishment, Liu Junning received an invitation almost immediately to join the Institute of Chinese Culture under the Ministry of Culture—though the position came with little in the way of remuneration or benefits. Nevertheless, with the move to the market and the outside world, Liu was able to support himself as a freelance writer by publishing in Hong Kong and abroad, and even occasionally in China under a pseudonym, and once and while under his own name.[96] The economist Mao Yushi, who was dismissed from the Institute of American Studies of CASS, continued to work in his own consulting firm, Unirule, which was economically successful. Thus, those purged from the establishment were able to find other outlets from which to express their views and, at times, challenge the party.

Li Shenzhi and the Fiftieth Anniversary of the People's Republic

Despite the dismissal of a number of liberal reformers from CASS and elsewhere in late 1998 and 1999, the retired Li Shenzhi continued to speak out forcibly against the Leninist party-state and in favor of political reform. An essay he wrote on the fiftieth anniversary of the Communist revolution, "Fifty Years of Storms and Disturbances: Soliloquy on National Day Evening," represented his most scathing critique of the party. The essay was written in reaction to what Li called the party's "triumphalism" and "lack of introspection" on the fiftieth anniversary of the People's Republic.[97] He began writing the essay on October 1, 1999, and completed it on October 9. It was posted on the Internet, without his approval, in December 1999.

Li's essay movingly revealed the transformation of a loyal party member, whose experiences during the Mao years had turned him away from Marxism-Leninism and toward liberal ideas, as he searched for a way to protest against party policies and save his country from future catastrophes. Li's transformation epitomized the transition from "comrade" to "citizen" among a number of his generation in the late twentieth century. He described himself as a young, idealistic, dedicated Communist Party member of twenty-six when China held its first National Day on October 1, 1949. Although he recalled that "it was quite impossible for me to express such emotions in words at the time," he discovered that the writer Hu Feng had succeeded in doing so in a long poem, "Time Has Now Begun," published in November 1949 in several successive issues of *People's Daily*. Hu Feng's poem extolled the virtues of the People's Republic. Wrote Li, "I am sure that in Tiananmen Square that day every single person felt it. China had said farewell forever to the past . . . to backwardness, to poverty and to ignorance, and had set out on a completely new road, to liberty, equality and fraternity." But Li added: "What I could never have imagined then, and what I am sure Hu Feng would never have been able to imagine either, was that less than six years later, a decree from Chairman Mao himself would identify him [Hu Feng] as the leader of a 'small counter-revolutionary Kuomintang clique,' and he would be thrown into prison and languish there for a quarter of a century."[98] It was not until three years after Mao's death that Hu Feng was finally rehabilitated.

Furthermore, Li continued, he never imagined that during the anti-rightist campaign, he himself, "who had an unblemished record," would find himself "labelled a 'capitalist rightist element.'" As Li explained, "the revolution had devoured its own children." He added, "This was only the beginning. . . . When the tenth anniversary and the twentieth, took place, I was undergoing reform through labour." Despite this treatment, Li admitted, "It was not until after . . . I was to hear Mao say, 'I am Marx and Qin Shihuang [the Qin dynasty's first emperor] rolled into one.' Only then did I wake up . . . to a common thread, . . . as Lord Acton put it, 'power corrupts and absolute power corrupts absolutely.'" Li asserted: "The nearly thirty years of the People's Republic up to 1976 could thus be said to have been a reign of terror."[99]

In spite of the reforms, Li's disillusionment extended into the post-Mao period. Although he acknowledged that the Deng era allowed a greater degree of freedom of personal expression, he wrote that "Anyone who knew anything about civil rights could not but feel that in essence nothing in the system or the ideology had changed, and we were still living in a Maoist system, with a Maoist ideology . . . continuing to exist in a state of moral servitude." Li's disillusionment turned to despair after the June 4 crackdown. Though again recognizing Deng's historic contribution, he declared that "his use of the army to suppress the student demonstrations in 1989 was an unforgivable crime." Moreover, although Li appreciated the fact that a large number of books were published after June 4 on the anti-rightist campaign and the Cultural Revolution, he asserted that there is "no evidence of self-examination or even glimmers of awareness of the whole of the Chinese people's sense of history and how they feel." He explained that "the reason for the dearth of truly accurate and honest studies of the Maoist period is that the leaders of the country want to stop people from knowing the truth . . . [they] refuse to open the files and will not permit such research." Li lamented the fact that "the youth of today are totally ignorant of these events."[100]

In addition to this ignorance, Li pointed out that "The covering up and falsification of history reached new heights with the grand celebration that marked this country's fiftieth anniversary. The national shame and all the disasters of the past fifty years were vanished away. The criminal who should bear the greatest part of the responsibility for that shame . . . is obviously Mao." By contrast, Li praised "leaders, such as Hu Yaobang and Zhao Ziyang, who worked so hard [to correct Mao's mistakes] . . . and made such great contributions to the country. . . . [They] are not even mentioned in the history of the past fifty years. . . . All that remains in this version of history is lies." Li warned that "to overstate the national strength of China . . . allow[ing] extreme nationalism to continue unchecked and to develop unhindered, is dangerous indeed."[101]

In conclusion, Li declares, "I still place my hopes in the idea of 'peaceful evolution' that the elderly economist Qian Jiaju proposed eight years ago, on the disintegration of the Soviet Union." Li warned, "If democracy is not implemented, the corruption that the people find so repugnant will only become worse as they try to fight against it." Perhaps Li's most daring challenge to Jiang Zemin's government was his singling out of Taiwan's Chiang Ching-kuo as a model of leadership, because "He [Chiang] lifted restrictions on the press and on the formation of political parties in Taiwan after the Kuomintang held a monopoly on power for sixty years." Li urged that "China lift the restrictions on the freedom of the press and on the formation of political parties . . . summed up in the traditional Chinese saying: 'A sage is the man who seizes the moment.'"[102] That was what Li was attempting to do in his denunciation of the party's celebration on its fiftieth anniversary. But the fiftieth anniversary also marked the end of the unprecedented liberal discourse in the late 1990s calling for political system reform.

— 6 —

The Establishment of an Alternative Political Party

The China Democracy Party

While establishment intellectuals were forming their own groups and engaging in relatively wide-ranging ideological debates in journals, books, and public forums in the late 1990s, intellectuals who had been pushed out of the establishment because of their past political activities tried to set up their own nonofficial think tanks to deal with political issues. Though these think tanks resembled the SERI group of the 1980s, the participants in some of the 1990s nonofficial think tanks proposed more radical political reforms than those suggested by SERI or the establishment intellectuals. In addition to calling for the rule of law, freedom of expression and association, representative legislatures, intraparty democracy, and grassroots elections, the participants in several of these nonofficial think tanks proposed a number of political reforms that were rarely mentioned by the establishment intellectuals, including the formation of a multiparty system, independent labor unions, and nationalization of the military.

Forerunners of the China Democracy Party

These nonofficial think tanks emerged among the thousands of NGOs that were established in China in the late 1990s. The 1999 U.S. State Department Human Rights Report estimated that in 1998 there were fifteen hundred national-level quasi-NGOs, two hundred thousand social organizations, and seven hundred thousand nonprofit organizations registered under the auspices of the Ministry of Civil Affairs.[1] Tony Saich has shown that some of these NGOs were planting the seeds for a civil society by generally setting their own agendas.[2] Nevertheless, as Saich also acknowledges,

161

most of the registered NGOs sought advocacy roles in nonpolitical areas, such as women's issues, the environment, health care, education, and consumer rights, though these issues had political implications.

Within this context, a small number of disestablished intellectuals, without official auspices or registration with the Ministry of Civil Affairs, set up their own groups and engaged in more direct political action. One such effort was launched by Fang Jue. A native of Beijing, born in 1955, Fang was a member of the Cultural Revolution generation who had spent four years working in the fields of Shaanxi Province. In 1978 he passed the national examinations and entered the economics department at Peking University, where he was active in the 1980 local election campaign in which Wang Juntao and Hu Ping had participated. After graduating in 1982, Fang worked at the Institute of Political Science of CASS, under Yan Jiaqi, who was later purged for his participation in the 1989 demonstrations and then sought exile in the United States. Subsequently, Fang worked in the Water Resources and Electricity Ministry under the State Council, and then became a vice-director in the Planning Commission in Fuzhou, Fujian Province. In 1995 Fang left government to start his own trading company, which provided him with a relatively independent source of income that he used to promote liberal political views. In November 1997, Fang presented a program for political reform, entitled "Put Political Reform Back on the Agenda: A Call from Inside the System," which he distributed to members of the Central Committee, high-level government officials, and the foreign media.

Although Fang was the sole signatory, he insisted that his program represented the collective efforts of several hundred middle- and upper-level government officials, including Central Committee members, who were disappointed by the lack of political reform following the Fifteenth Party Congress.[3] His program called for the establishment of democratic institutions. Specifically, it proposed universal suffrage and direct elections at all levels of the people's congresses, from the counties to the higher levels, so that "the traditional People's Congress, which has a half-century long history, will be transformed into a modern legislature that truly and independently exercises its power to legislate, to determine the composition of the government and to supervise the administration."[4] In contrast to the hesitation of establishment intellectuals who feared giving universal suffrage to the uneducated, Fang Jue's program asserted: "The current degree of economic development, education and citizens' political consciousness satisfies the necessary conditions for the election by universal suffrage of the People's Congress representatives above the county level." It further explained that "free, fair and direct elections . . . legal channels for participating in national affairs with equal opportunity and competition will be created."[5]

Fang's program also called for a multiparty political system, an idea that establishment intellectuals rarely mentioned in public discourse. In addition, it urged that individuals be allowed to establish independent newspapers, journals, publishing companies, broadcasting and television companies and be permitted freely to organize associations to protect the interests of special groups and the public interests of political as well as nonpolitical groups. On the issue of freedom of association, the program declared: "Political groups that aim to advance democratic reform should be a legal constituency in an open political system." In addition, it called for the establishment of independent labor unions, farmers unions, merchant guilds, professional associations, and religious groups.[6]

(In contrast to the CCP's emphasis on economic rights, Fang's program defined civil and political liberties as the core of human rights.)Though the NPC had ratified the U.N. Covenant on Economic, Social, and Cultural Rights in March 1998, Fang Jue's program asserted that it was "all the more important for China to sign, as soon as possible, the International Covenant on Civil and Political Rights." China did sign the latter in October 1998, but it still had not yet been ratified by the NPC at the end of the twentieth century and therefore was supposedly unenforceable in China. Fang Jue's program also urged that international human rights and religious organizations be allowed to establish organizational relations with China, and that the International Committee of the Red Cross be allowed to inspect the conditions in Chinese prisons. The program addressed some other sensitive issues by not only urging the reversal of the official verdict on June 4 but calling for full Tibetan autonomy within China, explaining that before 1950 China had had only limited suzerainty over Tibet. Disputing the Chinese government's assertion that the Dalai Lama wanted independence, the program pointed out that "the former Tibetan government has already publicly announced that it will no longer pursue the complete independence of Tibet." It endorsed a system of "full autonomy," which "may be a realistic arrangement that can bring long-term stability to Tibet."[7]

Although Fang Jue claimed that he was acting on behalf of others, he provided no evidence of an organized group behind his program. Still, he had been invited to participate in the China Development Union, an organized group that had been founded in Beijing by another former intellectual and official, Peng Ming, who had likewise turned to business. Peng Ming, who was forty-two in 1998, was a party member and a graduate of Wuhan Agricultural Sciences Institute, and had worked in the Shoudu Iron and Steel Policy Research Office and the Ministry of Aeronautic and Astronautic Industries, which was controlled by the military. Since 1986 Peng had conducted research on economic theories, structural reforms, and development strategies and had published scores of articles on these subjects.

With the profits from his investments in real estate and textile exports, Peng founded and funded his own think tank. Like the SERI group, the examples of Fang Jue and Peng Ming demonstrate that China's move to the market made it possible for a small number of individuals to use their own economic resources to attempt to assert their political independence.

Although the China Development Union claimed to have thousands of members nationwide, there was no evidence to support this claim. Nevertheless, a group of twenty to thirty scholars, journalists, students, and acquaintances met every Saturday in an office on the twelfth floor of the China Development Union building in Beijing, ostensibly to talk about environmental issues, while at the same time they also discussed political issues, grassroots elections, and human rights.[8]

At a December 1998 meeting of about twenty people, the topic under discussion was the fiftieth anniversary of the Universal Declaration of Human Rights, at which Jiang Zemin publicly had acknowledged that human rights encompassed civil and political rights as well as economic rights.[9] Peng hailed China's signing of the U.N. Covenant on Civil and Political Rights as "great progress" and expressed the hope that "once it is ratified, the pact will oblige China to observe the rules on matters of human rights."[10] Other meetings of the group discussed such sensitive topics as establishing a federal and multiparty political system as well as nationalizing the military.[11] Some of the views expressed at these meetings were also being discussed by intellectuals all over China—in research institutes, bookstores, universities, parks, hotels, and private homes. But it was not so much the topics discussed as the organized nature of the discussions on sensitive political issues that was unusual in the People's Republic.

Equally unprecedented until the late 1990s was the fact that the participants in the China Development Union's discussions included people from both inside and outside the establishment, including former political prisoners. One attendee, for example, was Democracy Wall participant Ren Wanding, who had spent altogether ten years in prison and who helped organize the discussion on the fiftieth anniversary of the Universal Declaration on Human Rights. The Democracy Wall leader Xu Wenli, who had spent twelve years in prison, also attended some of the meetings. Unlike the participants in the SERI discussions, who were mainly intellectuals and businesspeople, Ren and Xu were workers who had been deprived of establishment careers because of their political activities. On October 4, 1998, Peng Ming and Xu Wenli jointly urged the NPC to enact a law abolishing the requirement that NGOs had to have official approval, so as to guarantee true freedom of association and conform to international practices and U.N. conventions. On October 4–5, 1998, the China Development Union held its "First National Congress" in Beijing, where forty-five delegates, supposedly representing 3,058 members, passed a constitution.[12]

Whatever the intentions of the participants in the China Development Union, in late October the police closed down the union's offices and without a search warrant confiscated its fax machines, computers, and documents, including details on its membership. Though the union was registered in Hong Kong, it was declared illegal because it was not registered in Beijing. Peng Ming was detained. Upon his release, he escaped the country. At about the same time, Fang Jue was sentenced to four years in prison. Shortly after his release four years later, he was detained again; he was exiled to the United States in January 2003.

Another form of organized nonofficial political activity in the late 1990s was the establishment of independent watchdog groups. One such group was the China Corruption Observer, set up in early 1998 by An Jun, age forty-six, an official at the Xinyong City Supply and Marketing Cooperative Cotton and Hemp Company in Henan.[13] The group attracted some three hundred members from twelve provinces. After a little over a year, the China Corruption Observer sent information on about a hundred corruption cases to the domestic and international media and to the government's "letters and visits" departments that dealt with complaints from the public. In September and October 1998 the group tried to register with the local civil affairs bureaus, but its applications were repeatedly rejected as "illegal and unnecessary."[14]

On July 16, 1999, An Jun was detained by the police; he was subsequently arrested and charged with incitement to subvert state power and seeking to overthrow the socialist system by means of fabricating rumors and slander and distributing articles that harmed the party and state leadership. He was also charged with listening to VOA. At his trial in November 1999, An Jun argued in his own defense that in setting up the group he had been acting as "a responsible citizen."[15] On April 19, 2000, he was sentenced to four years in prison for subversion.[16] The suppression of this independent watchdog group, as well as other similar groups, was to make clear that only the government, not individual citizens or groups organized on their own initiative, was allowed to expose the rampant corruption that both the government and ordinary citizens regarded as so destructive to Chinese society.

Seemingly in response to these efforts to form nonofficial NGO advocacy groups, a national conference on NGOs and social stability was held on November 23, 1998. Politburo member Wei Jianxing asserted that in recent years NGOs "in general played a positive role in the society, but also created some problems that need to be urgently addressed."[17] Wei estimated that there were nearly a million NGOs in China, in all fields, including politics. But he cautioned, "we need to streamline our working system on the management of NGOs to better maintain the social stability, and to further strengthen their internal management mechanisms," insisting that "they must properly handle the relations between reform, development and social stability and always put social stability at the top of all priorities."[18] The message was clear: only governmental bodies, not nonofficial NGOs or autonomous groups, were to deal with China's critical problems.

The Background of China Democracy Party Members

Even more unprecedented in the People's Republic than the nonofficial political think tanks and groups discussing political reforms or seeking to deal with critical issues on their own initiative was the organized attempt to establish the China Democracy Party (CDP) in 1998. This was the first significant effort to establish a multiparty system in the People's Republic. Like the liberal establishment intellectuals and the nonofficial groups, participants in this effort sought to use legal, moderate, nonviolent methods to bring about political reform. Its members have been described as "a loosely linked group of political activists" who stressed their loyalty to the government and the preparatory nature of their actions.[19] They also referred to China's constitution as the basis for their actions. They differed from other nonofficial political groups in that they not only organized discussions and presented petitions demanding freedom of association and a multiparty system, but also sought through their actions to establish an alternative party. Although their efforts were eventually thwarted, the very fact that they organized publicly, published newsletters, and held meetings on and off for almost a year was in itself something formerly unheard of in the People's Republic.

A facilitating factor in the CDP's establishment was its use of the new telecommunications technologies, which by the late 1990s provided the potential to break down the separation between intellectuals and ordinary citizens and to coordinate and rapidly organize a movement on a national scale. Whereas previous nonofficial organized political activity rarely moved beyond Beijing and Shanghai, through the Internet and the other new technologies the CDP was able quickly to create a broad political organization on a nationwide basis.

Not only were members of the CDP able to communicate and coordinate through the Internet and cell phones, but, as in 1989, their views and actions were publicized by the international media and then broadcast back into China, particularly via VOA and Radio Free Asia, which had been set up in 1996. Political scientist Teresa Wright, in her important article on the background of the members of the CDP, singles out the role of computer technician Frank Lu Siqing,[20] who after a decade of political activism in China escaped to Hong Kong in 1993 and became an important source of information on various nonofficial and dissident activities in China. He conveyed information about the CDP that reached not only the international media but also political activists back in China.

Although the participants in the CDP ranged in age, education, and experience, Wright's study shows that many of the leaders were members of the Cultural Revolution generation and participants in the Democracy Wall movement or were leaders of the 1989 demonstrations. Wright was able to find information on 83 CDP leaders; 14.5 percent had participated in the Democracy Wall movement, and 25.3 percent in the 1989 demonstrations. Nearly 5 percent had experience with labor activism. Some participated in the Peace Charter movement and the underground labor movement of the mid-1990s. Despite repeated punishments for past political activities, or perhaps because of them, these individuals and their colleagues continued to try to bring about political change. Only a small percentage of CDP members came from China's current student generation. A few CDP leaders had participated in the China Development Union discussions. The leaders included both "educated" and "ordinary" citizens; nearly half of the most prominent CDP leaders were workers employed in factories or engaged in unskilled or semi-skilled labor. About 11 percent were professionals, and 14.5 percent were intellectuals. Although about 4.8 percent were self-employed, there is little evidence that China's emerging middle class played much of a role in the CDP leadership.[21]

Even though a number of the leaders had attended universities, because they had been barred from engaging in intellectual and professional pursuits owing to their past political activities, they were forced to do unskilled labor. The inclusion of intellectuals with workers or intellectuals who became workers in the same organization was also unprecedented in the People's Republic. Unlike the May 4 and May 13 movements in China during the early decades of the twentieth century, or Solidarity in Poland and Charter 77 in Czechoslovakia, there is little evidence of intellectuals and workers in the People's Republic joining together in common cause until the late 1990s. During the April 5, 1976, demonstration in Tiananmen Square and the spring 1989 demonstrations, both workers and students played major roles, but usually in separate endeavors. It was not until after the party's declaration of martial law on May 19 that members of the Wang Juntao–Chen Ziming group tried to form a broad coalition including workers in joint action with students, professionals, and intellectuals. And even then, the relationship was stormy and brief.

Whether or not its members originally came from the intellectual class, the CDP's inclusion of both intellectuals and workers as well as other social groups in its organization was the development that the CCP had feared most since the early 1980s establishment of Solidarity in Poland that ultimately overthrew the Polish Communist Party. The CDP reflected the breakdown of the division between intellectuals and workers in the late 1990s and demonstrated that individuals from a variety of backgrounds and classes were willing to work together to bring about political change.

Procedures Used in Organizing the CDP

Wang Youcai, who had participated in the 1989 Tiananmen Square demonstrations, initiated the first attempt to establish the CDP. He began this effort in Hangzhou, Zhejiang, where he was born on June 29, 1966, to peasant parents.[22] When he was a student at Zhejiang University, he participated in a demonstration in 1986 demanding more freedom of association and speech, but at that time he and his classmates were primarily concerned with achieving these freedoms on campus. After graduating from the university in 1987, Wang attended Peking University to pursue graduate studies in physics. During the 1989 student demonstrations in Tiananmen Square, he was in charge of coordinating the joint actions of students in Beijing's various universities. Before the June 4 crackdown, he was the secretary of the Beijing Student Autonomous Federation, the independent student organization established during the demonstrations. Following the June 4 crackdown, he was number 15 on the government's list of the 21 most wanted student leaders.[23]

Wang was sentenced to four years in prison, but owing to international pressure, in November 1991 he was sent back to Hangzhou, where he secured a job at a telecom equipment company.[24] He later did a variety of jobs, made possible by China's move to the market. During this time, he concluded that democracy would come to China not through holding demonstrations, but through efforts to carry out political change from the bottom up. He sought to learn about the village elections, which had been occurring under the party's auspices since the late 1980s. To find out about them, Wang contacted people in the countryside involved in the elections, villagers with some high school education, small private business owners, and peasants. Even though there were more candidates than positions in the elections for village head and village council, his informants criticized the nomination process because it was controlled by the village party committee. Believing that such village elections were not truly democratic, Wang concluded that democracy could not be achieved within a one-party system; it was necessary to have a multiparty system to ensure a fairer nomination process.[25] Thus, he launched the effort to establish an opposition party, the CDP, beginning at the local level.

A facilitating factor in starting the CDP was the introduction of NGOs in the 1980s and their exponential growth in the 1990s. In late 1997 Wang proposed to a number of colleagues the creation and legal registration of an opposition party by utilizing the same procedures used to legitimize NGOs—registering local preparatory committees of the CDP at the local offices of the Ministry of Civil Affairs, the office in charge of registering NGOs.[26] After local preparatory committees were set up and registered with the local civil affairs bureaus in a number of provinces and cities, Wang's plan was to form a national preparatory committee of the CDP registered with the Ministry of Civil Affairs in Beijing; this in time would develop into an alternative national party.[27] It was to be a long, gradual process, but Wang believed that "a ruling party and an opposition party are the prerequisites for a constitutional democracy and a system of checks and balances."[28]

Wang also planned strategically. He timed his effort to register the first local preparatory CDP to the visit to China of American president Bill Clinton in June 1998. Clinton's visit was followed through the fall of 1998 by visits of a number of foreign leaders, including the U.N. high commissioner on human rights, Mary Robinson. Wang believed that the government would be less likely to crack down in order to avoid embarrassment and censure from the international community.

Thus, just hours before the start of Clinton's visit, Wang, with another former 1989 activist, Wang Donghai, and a student, Lin Hui, applied to register the CDP Zhejiang Preparatory Committee with the local civil affairs bureau in his hometown of Hangzhou. They also posted the announcement "Open Declaration on the Establishment of the CDP Zhejiang Preparatory Committee of the China Democracy Party" on the Internet, which explained that the purpose of the CDP was to create a multiparty system. It stated, "The CDP firmly believes that a government must be established through the conscious approval of the public [and must be] established through free, impartial, and direct democratic elections. . . . [It] firmly oppose[s] a monopoly of news and publications, and oppose[s] any groups with vested interests carrying out a policy of obscurantism by force or through economic threats." In contrast to the CCP's view that human rights are given by the state, the declaration declared that human rights are inalienable: "The CDP firmly believes that the various articles on human rights in the 'Universal Declaration of Human Rights' are the equally sacred and inviolable rights of mankind that come with birth." Finally, the declaration stated that the CDP's purpose was "to establish a mechanism of separation of political powers; to allow the political powers to restrain each other and . . . to realize the nationalization of the army."[29] Following the launching of the Zhejiang branch of the CDP, another one of its founders, Wu Yilong, embarked on a nationwide tour to describe the registration procedures and to help set up other local preparatory committees.

The efforts to register local branches of the CDP elicited a variety of responses from the authorities. Because the applications by Wang and others to register preparatory local CDP branches were not rejected outright and local officials appeared uncertain how to respond, CDP leaders were initially encouraged to continue. For example, when Xie Wanjun, a Shandong student leader in 1989 who had encountered difficulty finding a job after graduating from Beijing Agricultural University, sought with a colleague to register the second preparatory CDP branch on September 10, 1998, with the Shandong civil affairs bureau, officials told them that in order for their application to be accepted they had to fulfill three conditions: they had to show assets of about fifty thousand yuan, provide details about their headquarters, and give the names of the main organizers and at least fifty CDP members.[30]

Among the other founders of the CDP was Qin Yongmin, who was the initiator and spokesperson for the third local preparatory committee, which was set up in Wuhan, Hubei. Qin received a response similar to that received in Shandong.[31] An active participant in the Democracy Wall movement, in which he had been an editor and writer of an unofficial journal and an author of the Peace Charter in 1993–94, Qin had been in and out of labor camps since the Cultural Revolution.[32] After his last release, he worked as a self-employed businessman, first selling fabric from a market stall and later opening a small bookstore in Wuhan. Qin was an example of an intellectual who had been forced to become a worker and small businessman because his Cultural Revolution experience and subsequent political activities had blocked him from holding a position in the intellectual establishment.

In mid-October 1998, Liu Xianbin and three colleagues attempted to register a CDP branch in Sichuan. Liu had been active in the 1989 Tiananmen demonstrations while he was a student at People's University in Beijing and had been sentenced to two and a half years in prison.[33] After his release, he was expelled from the university and was unable to find work. He then returned to his home province of Sichuan, where in 1994 he became concerned about the increasing plight of China's peasants. In addition to Charter 77 in Czechoslovakia and Solidarity in Poland, Liu was inspired by the nonviolent struggle of Mahatma Gandhi for Indian independence and Nelson Mandela's fight against apartheid in South Africa.[34] He explained his reasons for participation in the CDP: "The modern democracy movement should be an open and transparent endeavor . . . employing open and lawful methods." Moreover, "Protections for the basic human rights and civil rights of the people are created through open and lawful means." He emphasized that "the primary force of the movement comes from the general public, not an elite minority. . . . The movement itself operates on a system of democracy, not oligarchy. . . . [and] employs a strategy of gradual progress."[35]

A multiclass membership—of marginalized or disestablished intellectuals, owners of small businesses, and ordinary workers—was typical of most branches. The CDP's multiclass nature was exemplified in the Hunan branch. It was headed by Tong Shidong, age sixty-five, an assistant professor of physics at Hunan University, who established a Hunan University Preparatory Committee for the CDP in October 1998, and Liao Shihua, a factory worker and labor organizer in Hunan's capital city of Changsha, where he had organized protests outside government offices against corruption and against cuts in housing and medical benefits for workers at the Changsha Automobile Electrical Equipment Factory.[36]

Along with the efforts to establish provincial preparatory CDP branches at the local level, other CDP members used a new tactic in September 1998 when they applied by mail directly to the Ministry of Civil Affairs in Beijing to register a regional branch in Liaoning, Jilin, and Heilongjiang provinces as a Northeast Preparatory Committee of the CDP.[37] Around the same time, a Shanghai branch also submitted a registration by mail to Beijing.[38] However, when on September 16, 1998, five veteran political activists in Beijing, among them Ren Wanding of the Democracy Wall movement, attempted to register a CDP preparatory committee in Beijing, they were blocked from doing so.[39] Despite the rebuffs, the effort continued, in part emboldened by China's October 5, 1998, signing of the U.N. Covenant on Civil and Political Rights, which among other things sanctions the formation of political parties. Although China's signature on this covenant received relatively low-key coverage in China's official press—an article about China's U.N. ambassador signing the covenant in New York placed at the bottom of the front page of the *People's Daily*—within the next several weeks a number of CDP members took advantage of this propitious moment to speed up the process of registration. They brought together various provincial preparatory committees into one national organization and appeared to be headed toward creating a national party.[40]

Moving beyond Wang Youcai's local efforts, Xu Wenli attempted to expand the CDP to a regional and then national level. Along with Qin Yongmin, Xu had the longest record among CDP leaders of trying to assert political rights in the People's Republic. For having organized and edited the journal *April 5 Forum* during the Democracy Wall movement, he had been later sentenced to fifteen years. He spent three of those years in solitary confinement, during which time he had not been allowed visits by his family. Nor was he allowed to listen to radio broadcasts, read newspapers, or watch television, because he had secretly written a document, *My Defense Statement*, that was smuggled out of prison in 1984. But when China was trying to create a favorable international image in its efforts to be selected to host the 2000 Olympics and to receive permanent most-favored-nation (MFN) status from the U.S. Congress, Xu had been paroled in May 1993, three years before completion of his sentence. On November 6, 1998, with a group of Beijing-based veterans of the Democracy Wall movement, Xu announced the establishment of the "First CDP National Congress Preparatory Work Group."[41] On November 10, 1998, the CDP National Preparatory Committee issued an open letter appealing to the State Council to be allowed to exercise the "natural right to organize a party" in accordance with the freedoms of association, expression, and assembly stipulated in the Chinese constitution and the U.N. Covenant on Civil and Political Rights.[42]

Shortly before his rearrest on November 30, 1998, Xu Wenli issued a statement, explaining that the CDP had been inspired by the 1898 political reformers, Sun Yatsen, and participants in the Hundred Flowers movement, the April 5 demonstration, and Democracy Wall.[43] These events, Xu declared, were "all crucial stages for the course of democracy in China." The statement acknowledged that, since the launching of the economic reforms, "the living standard of most people has improved," but it cautioned that "the polarization within society is becoming increasingly evident" as manifested in "growing public resentment against the regime for instituting massive layoffs" and the "peasant protests against exorbitant taxes and levies." These resentments could be lessened, the statement asserted, through political reforms. It argued that economic problems "cannot be resolved by mere economic means, but must be solved within political areas." It warned that if these problems "cannot be solved well, it will have political consequences."[44]

Xu's statement also emphasized the CDP's peaceful, moderate approach. It urged that political reforms be a "gradual process, for in modern Chinese history there have been many radical, revolutionary storms inflicting much pain on people, but achieving little in terms of people's democratic rights." Therefore, a slow process must be adopted to end "the one party autocracy, . . . protecting human rights and freedom, [and] rebuilding a constitutional democracy." The hope was for "the emergence of a pluralistic, multi-party political environment." Accordingly, the statement urged political activists to shift gradually from "a 'street politics' approach to parliamentarianism . . . instituting an electoral process and to strive for the participation of democratic activists in that process."[45]

Sensitive to the role of the international community, the statement advised that at present the focus should be put on "human rights . . . through the help and pressure of the international community, the CCP has recognized that human rights is a very serious problem, which have at times caused China to 'lose face' and damaged its international image." It urged that the Chinese government ratify the U.N. Covenant on Civil and Political Rights and "follow the same standards in protecting the rights of its citizens," adding, "The international community and China's democratic activists should monitor the behaviors of the CCP in accordance with the Covenant and must criticize the CCP if it fails to implement the Covenant." Finally, the statement called for a reevaluation of the 1989 Tiananmen demonstrations and for the party to make a public apology to the relatives of those killed on June 4. It concluded by calling for a relaxation of "the controls on free speech and guarantee that nobody will be persecuted for expressing different views."[46]

While Xu and others were seeking to establish a national organization, they also continued to try to establish a regional CDP. On November 9 they joined with a former Democracy Wall participant from Tianjin, Lu Honglai, to form a CDP Beijing–Tianjin Regional Party Branch, with Xu Wenli as chair. Xu's decision to set up a party branch rather than a preparatory committee, which had been the approach until then, implied that the CDP already considered itself a functioning party rather than a party in the process of formation. By early March 1999 there were twenty-nine CDP organizations nationwide, including nine party branches, nineteen preparatory committees, and one national committee.[47]

The CDP's Other Political Activities

A number of CDP leaders were also actively involved in organizing workers.[48] It is not surprising that, as a resident of Wuhan, where many large bankrupt SOEs were rapidly dismissing workers in the late 1990s, Qin Yongmin was also active in the nonofficial labor movement. Qin was the principal author, with three co-authors, of a December 22, 1997, declaration calling on workers to organize independent unions through legal means. They cited as the basis for their declaration China's 1997 signing of the U.N. Covenant on Economic, Social, and Cultural Rights, which included the right to establish independent labor unions (although when it ratified this covenant in February 2001, the NPC omitted the clause allowing independent labor unions).[49] The December 22 declaration stated: "Only by depending on ourselves can we fight those who punish workers arbitrarily or fire workers without reason."[50] In Hunan, where independent workers groups, such as the Changsha Workers Autonomous Federation, had formed during the 1989 demonstrations, members of the Hunan CDP were active in demanding the release of labor leader Zhang Shanguang, who had been imprisoned for attempting to organize an association to protect the rights of laid-off workers.[51]

The CDP founders also established watchdog groups and published newsletters to monitor China's compliance with the human rights covenants. Xu Wenli applied on March 20, 1998, for permission to publish a newsletter, *China Human Rights Watch,* a nonofficial observer of human rights among the people, that was to be transmitted in China via email and to the outside world by fax.[52] His application, addressed to the Central Committee, State Council, NPC, and CPPCC, referred to Foreign Minister Qian Qichen's March 12, 1998, statement that announced China's intention to sign the Covenant on Civil and Political Rights. It explained that *China Human Rights Watch* would ensure that "the party will abide by the covenant and stop infringing on human rights."[53]

Similarly, on that same day, March 20, 1998, Qin Yongmin applied to establish a newsletter, *Citizens Rights Observer,* in Hubei. In justifying his application, Qin cited clause 19 of the U.N. Covenant on Civil and Political Rights, which provides for freedom of expression.[54] Although Qin's effort to register the newsletter in Wuhan was rebuffed, the newsletter was faxed to foreign journalists and then its contents were reported back into China through the foreign media. The newsletter described workers' demonstrations in Hubei and neighboring provinces against the party's policy of privatizing or closing state industries, which had led to the dismissal and unemployment of millions of workers in China's inner provinces. It later reported specifically on a demonstration by some two hundred workers in Wuhan, who were protesting against the halving of their salaries and carried posters reading "Fight to the End."[55]

In addition to setting up independent watchdog groups and newsletters, members of the CDP attempted to participate in local elections. CDP member Yu Tielong, for example, a practitioner of Chinese medicine, ran for village head in a village near Hangzhou in 1998.[56] One of five candidates, Yu formed a campaign team with two other members of the CDP. During the brief campaign, he promised to raise funds to buy chemical fertilizer, to address the teacher shortage, to open village accounts to inspection, and to get young people to support their elderly relatives—all major concerns of the local community. Although Yu won the election, the authorities refused to recognize the results and installed someone else.[57] Clearly the CCP saw participation by CDP members in grassroots politics as a threat to its authority.

Another CDP member, Zhao Changqing, a factory worker from Hanzhong, Shaanxi, also tried to run in a local election for delegate to the local people's congress in early 1998. Zhao, age twenty-eight, was a former student demonstrator who had served six months in prison for his involvement in the 1989 demonstrations in Tiananmen Square.[58] He distributed leaflets, entitled "The Will of the People and the Truth," protesting against a ruling by the factory management where he worked that he could not run in the election. The leaflet explained that a clause in the election law stipulated that any citizen can be a candidate, provided that he or she has the support of ten voters. Zhao had already collected sixty signatures from colleagues at the Nuclear Industry General Company Factory No. 813. But the factory management decided that only party members with a higher standing than deputy director could run in the local elections. Zhao was detained and, after a month in prison, was placed under house arrest.[59] When he attempted to return to work in February, he was laid off and the factory management confiscated money sent by friends to help him.[60] In early March 1998, Zhao and eight others wrote to the NPC demanding rehabilitation of Zhao Ziyang and recognition of the victims of June 4. On April 1, 1998, Zhao was formally arrested.[61]

Despite these setbacks for CDP members in various local elections, in fall 1998, when Beijing held local elections for delegates to the local people's congress at the district and county levels, in which organizations and groups of more than ten voters could recommend candidates, three CDP members put themselves forward.[62] Among the three was He Depu of CASS, who had participated in Democracy Wall when he founded a magazine called *Beijing Youth*, as well as in the 1989 demonstrations. The three issued a statement that asked: "What can you do as an ordinary person? You can try to become a representative or you can vote for people who stand for us . . . it is time to get rid of corruption."[63] They charged that the previous representatives had failed to stand up to the party and government to protect people's rights, and declared, "What we need are representatives who are not afraid of authority, who can insist on the truth and who can stand for the people." Their statement urged the voters: "even if we are not allowed to be formal candidates, please write our names on the election papers."[64] But the police seized the printed declaration when they tried to distribute it.[65] Although the election law stipulated that only ten signatures were needed to run in the election, He Depu had collected thirty-two signatures outside a factory in the Chaoyang district of Beijing.[66] Those who had signed were later summoned by the factory boss and told that He's candidacy was invalid. At the same time, He was physically attacked by state election workers.[67] Consequently, he declared that the local elections were "much worse" this time around than they had been in 1980, referring to the last time he ran for local office in Beijing and lost by a narrow margin. "Back then," he said, "I could at least hold open campaign activities, now they've been banned."[68]

CDP Resistance to Repression

At the same that members of the CDP were setting up preparatory committees in various provinces and carrying out a variety of local political activities, the authorities began to take action against the CDP leaders. On July 10, 1998, shortly after President Clinton left China, Wang Youcai, who had tried to register the first CDP branch in Hangzhou, was detained. On August 7 he was charged with "inciting to overthrow state political power."[69] Because the offense of "counterrevolution" had been eliminated from article 105 of the 1997 penal code, "subverting the state" became the charge used by the government against those seeking freedom of expression, association, and assembly. Nevertheless, though charged with "organizing, scheming or acting to subvert the political power of the state and overthrow the socialist system," Wang was released a few weeks later, on August 31, under a form of residential surveillance.[70] His release was seen as a result of international pressure, another indication that under certain circumstances and at certain times, such as when China desires better relations with the United States and other Western countries, outside pressure, as the CDP leaders suggested, can influence the government's actions. Other leaders of the effort to register the CDP, such as Liu Lianjun and Xie Wanjun of Shandong, were also detained, but they were released after thirteen days.[71] Dozens more were detained, but most were held only briefly and then released.

As occurred when the party began the suppression of the Democracy Wall movement, other CDP members organized to defend their colleagues. A letter protesting the charges against Wang Youcai was signed by fifty-three political activists and distributed to foreign journalists and then reported back into China via VOA and the Internet.[72] The letter stated that Wang's advocacy of political reforms by peaceful, rational, and nonviolent means did not constitute any crime, and that what Wang had done was exercise his freedom of association guaranteed by the constitution.[73] On the next day, 136 of Wang's colleagues signed another petition calling on the government to release him.

By December 1998, however, when the series of visits by important foreign visitors came to an end, and with the onset of 1999, a year of portentous anniversaries—the tenth anniversary of June 4 and the fiftieth anniversary of the People's Republic—that the party feared would be marked by large-scale demonstrations, China clamped down harshly on the CDP. Virtually all of the CDP's leaders were arrested. The severest sentences were meted out to the CDP leaders who had the longest and most persistent records of involvement in political activities, specifically those who had participated in and had been punished for the Democracy Wall movement and the 1989 demonstrations. For his defense Xu Wenli recruited the well-known defense lawyer Mo Shaoping. Despite Mo's argument that Xu's efforts to establish the CDP were meant to "end one-party rule by peaceful means," on December 21, 1998, Xu was sentenced to thirteen years for plotting to overthrow the government and for undermining state security.[74]

Qin Yongmin was sentenced to twelve years for organizing the CDP and for editing the *Citizens Rights Observer* newsletter and transmitting it abroad. Wang Youcai was sentenced to eleven years for being the prime mover behind the formation of the CDP, drafting its initial declaration, and sending information about it abroad. A court in Suining, Sichuan, sentenced Liu Xianbin, who had attempted to register the CDP in that province, to thirteen years in prison, a sentence equal to that of Xu Wenli.[75] Unlike some of his colleagues, Liu was unable to engage a defense counsel.[76] Lawyers had withdrawn, following pressure from the authorities, and he was not allowed to argue in his own defense. His trial on August 6, 1999, which took only four hours, demonstrated total disregard for due process. Other CDP members who were workers were also given long prison sentences. One of them, Yue Tianxiang, who was not a founding member, was sentenced to ten years for setting up an organization to protect the rights of laid-off workers.[77]

Once again, the trials of the major CDP leaders—Wang Youcai, Xu Wenli, and Qin Yongmin—revealed both how much and how little China had changed.[78] The trials took place in three different provinces barely three weeks after they had been detained in late November 1998.[79] Although theoretically they were allowed to hire lawyers to defend themselves, the speed with which they were brought to trial made it difficult for them to prepare a proper defense. This was still a change from the Mao era, when defendants were not allowed to seek legal representation, but these trials' disregard for proper procedures demonstrated that the leadership's repeated emphasis on introducing the rule of law was primarily to promote economic development and business procedures, not political and civil rights.

In fact, the party's interference in Wang Youcai's efforts to find a defense lawyer demonstrates the hollowness of the party's stress on the need for the rule of law. Wang's first lawyer, Wang Peijian, a law graduate of Peking University, was detained on July 29 when he went to copy legal documents for Wang's defense at a copy shop. All copy shops in Hangzhou were ordered not to allow the copying of any materials related to the CDP. Wang Youcai's family then contacted Wang Wenjiang, a lawyer in Liaoning. Although Wang Wenjiang had once been a CCP member in Anshan, he had quit the party and attempted to register the CDP in Anshan. When he attempted to travel to Hangzhou to defend Wang Youcai, he was physically blocked by the police. Pressure from the authorities also thwarted Wang Youcai's efforts to hire a third lawyer, and Wang ended up presenting his own defense. He argued that freedom of association, including the establishment of political parties, was the right of all citizens, as mandated by China's signing of the U.N. Covenant on Civil and Political Rights. Despite the CCP's efforts to block Wang Youcai's legal defense, more than one thousand people staged protests outside the courtroom during his trial, again a major change from the Mao era, when even family members were not informed about when such trials were taking place.[80] Among the protesters were workers and ordinary city residents as well as students from Zhejiang and Ningpo universities.

The severe sentences given the top leaders of the CDP did not deter the second level of leaders from publicly protesting the imprisonment of their colleagues. Hangzhou continued to be a center of political activity as Wu Yilong, who had spread the word about the initial effort to establish the CDP and had been expelled from the literature department of Hangzhou University, assumed leadership. Gao Hongming, a former government employee who had attempted to set up an independent labor union and had also urged a reevaluation of June 4, took over the leadership of the Beijing-Tianjin branch of the CDP after Xu Wenli was imprisoned. Moreover, as on April 5, 1976, when demonstrators used the occasion of the Qingming festival of paying respects to the dead to honor Zhou Enlai by marching to Tiananmen Square, in Hangzhou about fifty remaining activists in the outlawed CDP used the occasion of the Qingming festival in 1999 to honor the memory of those killed on June 4.[81] Splitting into two groups, the demonstrators carried wreaths that bore the message: "To those who laid down their lives for democracy and freedom."[82] Eight vans of police were waiting for them and ordered them to disperse. By mid-1999, more than 190 party members of the CDP had been arrested, with 27 remaining under detention and 30 others being held under a form of house arrest.[83] More trials in October 1999 resulted in lengthy sentences for most of the second tier of CDP leaders, who were also charged with "subverting the state." By late 1999, the public activities of the CDP had ended.

Only two leaders who continued to claim CDP membership remained at large at the start of the twenty-first century. One was He Depu of the Beijing-Tianjin branch, an establishment intellectual at CASS. The other was seventy-year-old Nie Minzhi of Zhejiang, another founding member, who had served ten years in prison as a "counterrevolutionary" during the Cultural Revolution.[84] On January 1, 2000, the two men issued a statement entitled "The New Century Declaration of the China Democracy Party," which was mailed to the Communist Party headquarters in Beijing and posted on the Internet. Like Xu Wenli's earlier statement, this declaration traced the roots of the formation of the CDP back to the 1898 Hundred Days of Reform. But this declaration also cited the Cultural Revolution as a more recent inspiration for the CDP's actions, explaining that "the devastation of the Cultural Revolution taught the Chinese people to push back."[85] It specifically singled out the 1974 big-character poster by Li-Yi-

Zhe poster entitled "Democracy and the System of Law" that "sounded the first dissent from the masses," followed by the April 5 movement. It asserted that "China Democracy Party's mission is to bring about China's transformation into a democracy and a modern society," and that for this transformation to happen, China must "abandon one party rule and allow the existence of opposition parties . . . move steadfastly towards free elections, including the election of the president." It referred to the example of Taiwan as demonstrating "[to] China and the rest of the world what can happen to a Chinese society in the process of democratization."[86]

The declaration criticized "a surface kind of stability" that currently existed in China, which it explained was "achieved under an intense political terror," while "unresolved social issues continue to build looking for the next incident to erupt." It cautioned, "Stability thus achieved is only temporary and will lead to future disturbances." Although the declaration expressed concern about the "acute" state of China's peasants, the authors devoted most of their attention to the need to establish independent trade unions, because, they said, "Labors [sic] still do not have their own identity or representation before law. Therefore, legislation of a trade union bill is urgently needed. This bill will allow the formation of free trade unions." Such legislation would create the mechanisms "whereby labor unrest will be resolved in a peaceful and lawful manner." It also referred to China's signature on the two U.N. covenants, specifically citing section 8 of the Covenant on Economic, Social, and Cultural Rights, which stipulates the rights to organize and to form national and international trade union associations. It pointed out that at a time when millions of workers have lost their jobs because of the privatization of SOEs and were demonstrating in the streets, the "China Democracy Party has pushed hard for the right to form free trade unions."[87]

In spring 2000 He Depu was expelled from CASS, and in November 2002, three days before the opening of the Sixteenth Party Congress, he was taken away in handcuffs, supposedly because he had signed a petition, along with 192 others, calling for political reform and because he had published political statements on the Internet.[88] His computer, printer, scanner, and disks were confiscated. On October 14, 2003, he was put on trial, charged with "inciting subversion of state power," and was subsequently sentenced to eight years in prison.[89] He Depu's CDP colleague Nie Minzhi, who had co-authored the January 2000 declaration, was sent to a labor re-education camp in 2001 and later died after failing to recover from a stroke he suffered in the camp. His last words are reported to have been: "Continue to work for the democracy party."[90]

It is not surprising that the CCP finally suppressed the CDP so decisively. Although at any one time the CDP never numbered more than about two hundred activists[91] and it did not appear to attract a mass following, the multiclass makeup of its membership, its nationwide organizational reach, its participation in local elections, its efforts to help laid-off workers publicize their plight, and particularly its attempts through legal procedures to establish an alternative party, were regarded by the CCP as a direct threat to its legitimacy and authority. Accompanying the suppression of the CDP, the party reemphasized its opposition to a multiparty system and the importance of maintaining the existing party-state system and its leadership over China's eight small "democratic" parties. Jiang Zemin's speech at the spring festival forum of nonparty figures on February 12, 1999, appeared to be a response to the CDP's efforts to establish an opposition party. Jiang declared that "[the] facts show that the system of multiparty cooperation and political consultation under the CCP's leadership has its own advantages and strong vitality, providing effective political guarantee for China's reform, development, and stability." Jiang insisted, as had Deng Xiaoping before him: "We should by no means copy the two-party system or the multiparty system that is practiced in Western countries. We should be firm in upholding this major political principle."[92] The CDP's efforts to establish an opposition party were the most direct challenge to China's party-state system since the 1949 revolution.

Citizenship Extends into Cyberspace despite Repression

The arrest of the CDP members in late 1998 and 1999, and the dismissal of a small number of liberal establishment intellectuals, marked the end of the liberal flowering during the final years of the twentieth century. The party's retightening of ideological controls was provoked not only by the attempt of political activists to build an opposition party, but also by the liberals' advocacy of a system of checks and balances. Those who were critical of the economic reforms but did not publicly call for political reforms were left relatively untouched. Consequently, the new left, neonationalists, and neoconservatives, whose statist views did not diverge too much from those of the leadership, continued to express their views, gain establishment appointments, and travel relatively freely abroad. In addition, a small number of establishment intellectuals continued to discuss political reforms within the party in their scholarly journals.

The End of the 1998 Beijing Spring

Ironically, the twentieth anniversary of the launching of the post-Mao reforms at the Third Plenum of the Eleventh Central Committee marked the end of the liberal flowering. On this anniversary, Jiang Zemin asserted that the issue of political reform could not be raised for another few years and that the four basic principles must be upheld.[1] Shortly before Jiang's speech, an order was issued to ban public discussion of political reform in the media. The muffling of liberal voices was reinforced by a new surge of popular nationalism sparked by the May 7, 1999, American accidental bombing of the Chinese embassy in Belgrade.

Even Jiang's intellectual adviser, Liu Ji, under whose auspices a number of controversial books had been published, was retired from his post as a vice president of CASS in the fall of 1998, supposedly in accordance with the order that those aged sixty and above were to retire. Yet the neo-Maoist Wang Renzhi, who had turned sixty-five in September 1998, still became party head of CASS with the rank of full minister, and CASS president Li Tieying, an associate of Li Peng, who was also over sixty, remained on in his position.[3] The publishing authority of Today's China Publishing House, which had published a number of the books sponsored by Liu Ji, was revoked and the director was dismissed and subjected to investigation. In addition to the banning of the two compilations of liberal essays *Political China* and *Liberation Literature,* one of the editors of *Political China,* Shi Binhai, was detained as early as September 5, 1998, on charges of personally interviewing and releasing information about disgraced party leader Zhao Ziyang. After being held for seven months, Shi was released, but he was discharged from the press agency where he worked and sent to his hometown of Shanghai. He Qinglian was reassigned to the *Shenzhen Legal Daily* research department in June 2000.[4] In 2001, fearing further punishment, she fled the country and found exile in the United States.[5]

In addition to books calling for political reforms, books recalling the abuses of the Mao era were also banned. Among them was *The Political Movement I Personally Experienced,* which contained memoirs by Li Rui and other party elders, who exposed the destructive impact of the political persecutions during the Mao era. The three-volume *Anthology of Reminiscences,* containing writings by people charged as "rightists" in the 1957–1958 anti-rightist campaign, published by Economic Daily Publishing House in September 1998, was also banned.[6] The major journal calling for political reform, *The Way,* was closed down when the State Press and Publication Administration canceled its April 1999 issue, supposedly because it contained too high a proportion of articles in the social sciences and too few in the sciences. At the same time, new regulations for the registration of NGOs were promulgated in October 1998, requiring a half-year trial period during which the new NGOs would be closely monitored to ensure they did not engage in controversial political activities.[7]

Following the arrest of the CDP leaders and the muffling of the liberal voices, the neo-Maoists, who still controlled three journals, were the next ideological group to be suppressed, particularly after they vociferously opposed Jiang Zemin's "three represents," which justified bringing more members of the new business class into the party. An article in the neo-

Maoist journal *Midstream*, for example, complained that too many private businessmen were joining the party, and that half of the party's new members in small towns were private business owners.[8] It estimated that 40 percent of the private business owners in three cities in Jiangsu had applied to join the local party branch, and asserted that "private businessmen cannot accept the party's principles and policies . . . they only want to join the party to influence the adoption and implementation of local policies." Although "they wear communist caps on their heads," the article warned, "inside they have the brains of capitalists."[9]

Deng Liqun and a number of other neo-Maoists also issued another ten-thousand-character letter, which charged that implementation of the "three represents" was a violation of party regulations that would lead to a qualitative change in the makeup of the party's membership.[10] To support their claim that Jiang was acting unconstitutionally, it charged that the "three represents" had not been debated. The letter argued: "It is a violation of party rules that a major political issue of this importance had not been discussed fully at the National People's Congress and the Central Committee and a formal decision had not been taken."[11] Seemingly in rebuttal to the neo-Maoist opposition to the entry of private entrepreneurs into the party, a commentator article released by Xinhua News Agency responded: "We cannot . . . turn Marxism into dogma and taboos and into shackles hampering people's ideological development. Marxism has the theoretical property of moving with the times." It argued that "the new historical conditions require that we continually break through the binding of certain outdated traditional concepts and structures, and we must in particular pay attention to overcoming 'leftist' ideological concepts."[12]

Yet by the start of the twenty-first century the party's efforts to rein in increasingly independent intellectuals and ideologues, and to ban their books and journals, were having a diminishing impact. China's openness to the outside world and move to the market continued to fill bookstores and bookstalls with controversial books and journals. Individuals who wished to speak out could still find a variety of platforms from which to express dissident views. Even individuals with controversial ideas and histories were able to find enough public space in which to communicate their ideas. Furthermore, despite being purged from the establishment, they were able to sustain themselves in the late 1990s by doing freelance work. Liu Ji, for example, joined a Chinese-European think tank concerned with issues of economic globalization, and he continued to be involved in political issues.[13] Despite his dismissal from CASS, Mao Yushi, together with other economists who advocated political reform along with privatization, worked relatively unhindered at the nonofficial Unirule think tank and in other private economic consultancy groups established in China's major cities.[14] Thus, unlike in other periods of repression, the move to the market and opening to the outside world made it possible for individuals and groups to continue to express dissent on political issues through a variety of means. China's more open climate, however, did not extend to political activists, such as members of the CDP who had attempted to establish an opposition party and were silenced by imprisonment.

Assertion of Political Rights in Cyberspace

China's embrace in the mid-1990s of the new communications technologies also facilitated independent political discourse and organization of political activities. The number of Internet users in China grew rapidly—reaching 94 million by the end of 2004. The number of computer users was doubling every eighteen months, surpassing the number of party members in 2002. Among China's new computer users were a small number of mostly urban, educated youth of the post-1989 generation who used computers and the Internet to criticize party policies and urge political reforms. They were called "cyber-dissidents." In addition, critical scholars in the establishment posted their work on the Internet. Initially unable to publish in scholarly journals after his dismissal from the Institute of Political Science at CASS, Liu Junning published on the Internet a newsletter, called "The Constitutionalist," that discussed political reforms. Similarly, the independent intellectual and lobbyist Cao Siyuan, who sought to delete the Marxist-Leninist verbiage from China's constitution, used the Internet to spread his ideas for constitutional reform.

The party was well aware of the political implications of the introduction of the new technologies, which by the early twenty-first century had spread from urban centers along the coast to smaller cities in the interior.[16] It intensified its use of regulations, censorship, filters, site blocking, and periodic closures of Internet cafes to control content it considered "inappropriate." A study by Harvard Law School's Berkman Center for the Internet and Society reported in December 2002 that the Web sites of major foreign media stations (CBS, ABC, NBC, the BBC, and CNN) and newspapers (the *New York Times* and *Washington Post*) were often, though not always, rendered inaccessible to Internet surfers in China.[17] The government in 2002 also imposed Internet filtering technology on search engines, such as Google and Altavista, that selectively blocked access to "subversive" information. Anyone wanting to open an Internet account had to register with the police and was monitored by the security organizations. China's Internet users nevertheless were able to circumvent these obstacles; enforcement was inconsistent, and connections could be routed through proxy servers in Hong Kong, the United States, and Europe. Thus the Internet could still provide access to multiple sources of information, and it created a virtual public space that challenged government propaganda and control of information. It became a new forum where politically dissident views were expressed and even, at times, mobilized for political action, as seen with the effort to establish the CDP.

An example of the Internet's impact on political issues was demonstrated in the case of Sun Zhigang, a graphic designer in Guangzhou who was detained by police on March 17, 2003, for not carrying proper identity papers. He died, owing to beating, three days later while in police custody. His case was picked up by the outspoken Guangdong newspaper *Southern Metropolis News,* reprinted across the country, and then posted on China's largest news portal, sina.com, and discussed throughout cyberspace. The official media, including China's prime television station CCTV, soon focused on the issue of the treatment of migrants and police brutality. For years advocates of legal reforms had been calling for an end to arbitrary detention, but nothing was done until the widespread outrage against what happened to Sun, generated by the Internet, put pressure on the government to investigate Sun's death. Three months later, in May 2003, the government abolished the system of arbitrarily taking migrants into custody.[18]

While the publicity that the Internet gave to the Sun case provoked bottom-up pressure for something to be done about the unjust treatment of undocumented migrants in China's cities, unofficial Internet groups, focused on a number of political issues, had been organizing in China since the late 1990s. As early as 1997, a group of anonymous Chinese launched an underground electronic magazine, *Tunnel,* that was distributed through electronic mail.[19] Its inaugural issue stated that its purpose was to break through government control of information. The first two issues of *Tunnel* were memorials to those killed on June 4, 1989. The third issue discussed the collapse of Communism in the Soviet Union and Eastern Europe. The fourth and fifth issues reprinted the script of the U.S. documentary film

The Gate of Heavenly Peace, which described the events leading up to June 4. *Tunnel* also carried articles written and compiled by Chinese exiles abroad. The publisher of *Tunnel* was arrested in Jiangxi in 1998, and his Web site was wiped out by a police computer program.[20]

Another online journal, *VIP Reference News* or *Large Reference News (Dacankao),* was based in the United States and distributed back to China via email. Its name was a play on the words "Reference News" *(cankao),* the name of China's state-run publication of uncensored translations of foreign news reports and internal reports for the official elite. The editors and distributors of *VIP Reference News* were a group of overseas Chinese students and scholars who sent articles on human rights, democracy, and political reform to more than 250,000 email addresses in China.[21] A Shanghai computer specialist, Lin Hai, helped collect the Chinese email addresses to which *VIP Reference News* was sent. Born in 1968 in Shanghai, Lin Hai had studied computer science at Beijing Aeronautics Technical University and then returned to Shanghai, where he set up the Zhengfang Software Company. From September 1997 to February 1998, it has been reported, he supplied *VIP Reference News* with 30,000 email addresses of Chinese computer users.[22] As a result, he was detained, was tried on December 4, 1998, and on January 20, 1999, was sentenced to two years in prison for "inciting the subversion of state sovereignty."[23] Given the charge of subversion, his sentence was relatively light. Another contributor to and recipient of *VIP Reference News* was Qi Yanchen, a freelance journalist and economist and one of the founders of the China Development Union. He also was involved in an email-distributed magazine, *Consultations,* linked to the China Development Union. Qi was arrested at his office in Hebei in September 1999 and charged with spreading "antigovernment" messages via the Internet; later he was sentenced to four years in prison.[24]

More threatening to the party than individual cyber-dissidents were groups that used the Internet to spread political ideas. Perhaps the best-known was the New Youth Study Group *(Xin Qingnian Xuehui),* whose name resonated with the May 4th movement. This group was launched in August 2000 by eight young people, brought together by their shared desire for political reform. It never had more than ten members, had no source of funding, and formed no branches in other cities.[25] But it used the Internet to circulate views discussed among its members and to disseminate relevant articles to a much wider audience. The group included Yang Zili, a computer expert who had set up his own software company; Xu Wei, a reporter and editor for *Consumer Daily* newspaper, who had graduated from Beijing Normal University with a doctorate in philosophy; Jin Haike, a geophysicist who at that time worked at the Geological Survey Institute; and Zhang Honghai, a graduate of Beijing Broadcasting Institute who had become a freelance writer after graduation.[26] Xu Wei and Jin Haike were party members. In addition to their online discussions, the group also met regularly to discuss political and social issues, especially the growing inequalities in the countryside. They visited various rural areas to observe the voting procedures used in village elections, and they helped organize free training and provided teaching materials for teachers in schools set up for children of migrants in Beijing.[27] They invited lecturers from Beijing universities to speak at their meetings about history and contemporary topics and to exchange views on political issues.

Typical of the members of the New Youth Study Group was the computer expert Yang Zili, the eldest son of poor farmers from Hebei Province. After graduating from Xi'an Communications University, Yang attended Peking University in 1997 to study for a master's degree in mechanics. While becoming a computer expert, he read the works of a variety of political thinkers, such as Vaclav Havel, Friedrich Hayek, and Samual Huntington. He was especially concerned about the rural poverty from which he had come, and he formed a group to discuss what should be done for those left behind by the economic reforms. The group also held seminars, with participants that ranged from a member of the banned CDP to individuals who expressed Marxist views.[28] Yang built a Web site that was able to run circles around the government's electronic firewalls by using overseas proxy servers. It contained essays promoting liberal democratic reforms. Despite Yang's skills, the Web site had been up and running for less than a year when Yang and the other members of his group were detained in March 2001.[29] The main focus of the Beijing procuratorate case against them was the group's writings on the Web site, specifically such articles as "Be a New Citizen, Remake China," "What Is to Be Done?"—a takeoff on Lenin's article, with the same title but with a different answer—and "China's Democracy Is Fake."[30]

At the one-day trial on September 28, 2001, the authorities claimed that these articles, as well as a number of meetings of the New Youth Study Group held at Peking University and People's University, presented a platform to overthrow the party leadership. The four were charged with "inciting subversion of state power," for setting up branches of their group across the country, publishing articles on the Internet, and building Web sites. The defendants, who spoke in their own defense, countered that their meetings had been convened in public places at universities. Moreover, Yang stated, "The task of 'liberalizing society' in no way implies an intention to subvert state power. When we speak of freedom and liberalization, we believe such changes come about through a process of reform."[31] After being detained for two years, in May 2003 journalist Xu Wei and geologist Jin Haike were each sentenced to ten years in prison and Internet engineer Yang Zili and freelance writer Zhang Honghai were each sentenced to eight years.[32] Xu Wei told the court that he had been brutally beaten and tortured with electric shocks after refusing to admit guilt.[33] Again, these heavy sentences can be attributed not only to the fact that they transmitted their political views over the Internet, but also to the fact that they had convened group discussions without first registering with the Ministry of Civil Affairs.

Once more, as happened to others imprisoned on similar charges in the post-Mao era, several of their colleagues came to their defense. The most eloquent was the writer Yu Jie, a graduate of Peking University who had been acquainted with several members of the group while at the university. Well known for his book reviews and critical essays *(zawen)*, he supported himself as a freelance writer through contract publishing and publications in Hong Kong and Taiwan.[34] Like Liu Junning and Li Shenzhi, Yu had been inspired by Peking University's early history of intellectual freedom and diversity of ideas. While still a graduate student, he had written a best-selling, controversial volume of essays, *Fire and Ice (Huo yu bing)*, published in 1998, in which he lamented the waning of the May 4 spirit of protest.[35] It was named one of the ten best books of 1998, but it was banned one year later.[36] Nevertheless, he followed it with a number of other books that contained merciless dissections of contemporary Chinese society in the style of Lu Xun. Among Yu Jie's targets were the intellectuals of the post–June 4 period, who, owing to party pressure and the temptations of China's market economy, had suppressed their criticisms and opposition. Most of these intellectuals, Yu charged, had become part of the power structure.

After graduation Yu was offered a position as a researcher at the Chinese Association of Writers, but when he showed up for work, his contract was withdrawn.[37] He fought back by bringing suit against the association and posting articles on the Internet in which he stated: "Persecution of intellectuals is nothing new in China." What had changed, Yu claimed, was that "intellectuals had new weapons with which to fight back." Though he explained that he was not optimistic about the outcome of his lawsuit, he asserted, "I believe that if every citizen stands up and fights for his rights, real democracy will come to China."[38]

In addition to using the law and the Internet to defend his own rights, Yu also used the Internet to defend the rights of the members of the New Youth Study Group after their arrest. In May 2001 he posted an essay on the Internet that not only defended the four leaders of the group, but extolled their virtues. In contrast to the conventional depiction of his generation that came of age in the post-1989 period as materialistic and consumer-oriented, Yu portrayed the members of the group as models for the younger generation. Yu wrote: "I am proud to be of the same age as these four people." As he explained, "although most seventies people [people who were born in the 1970s and entered college after June 4] gave themselves up to individualism, consumerism and meaningless play, finally there appeared very talented people like these four who are aware, who are responsible, and are willing to make sacrifices. Their appearance is a sign that the great divide that appeared after 'June 4' has already begun to quietly disappear." With Confucian resonance, Yu described the four men as "people of sterling character, clear on their own values, who empathize with the people at the lower levels of society, and willing to sacrifice themselves to create the new era." He concluded that with their example, "the very definition of 'seventies person' has shifted and changed." Yu added that "in an undemocratic country, not one of us 'citizens,' who can't really be considered citizens in the true sense of the term, [is] free.'"[39]

Others also protested the treatment of the members of the New Youth Study Group. Literary critic Liu Xiaobo, who had denounced both the government and the establishment intellectuals during the 1989 Tiananmen demonstrations and had served three years in a labor camp in the 1990s, organized a public letter that he and five others signed and sent to the Beijing Municipal Higher People's Court, demanding the immediate release of the four men.[40] This willingness to speak out and to organize support for colleagues or kindred spirits imprisoned by the party for their political views, in the face of a real threat of punishment for such actions, was yet another unprecedented change in the post-Mao period and an example of individuals' efforts to assert their political rights.

Huang Qi, a computer engineer from Chengdu, Sichuan, who trained at Peking University, also used his technical skills to assert his political rights.

He built a Web site with his wife, Zeng Li, in 1998, to help track down missing people.[41] And in 1999 he set up another Web site, which published information about what had happened to the victims of June 4, a taboo topic in the official media, as well as what happened to Uighur separatists in Xinjiang Province. Huang also called for remembrance of the victims of June 4, compensation for their families, and the release of political prisoners.[42] In 2000, on the eve of the eleventh anniversary of June 4, users posted on his Web site their own views, as opposed to those of the party, about what had happened on June 4, 1989. It soon became a site that also listed people who had disappeared into police custody, usually for their political or religious beliefs. In addition, it posted articles about human rights abuses and the activities of the Falungong. Huang's Web site was operated through a U.S.-based Internet service provider, so it was possible for the information to be updated from the United States when the Chinese authorities blocked the Chinese site.[43]

When on June 3, 2000, local police came to detain Huang Qi and his wife, visitors to Huang's Web site were able to follow his arrest as it was happening. Reporting that the Public Security Bureau had just come to summon him for interrogation, Huang posted his final message: "Thanks to all who make an effort on behalf of democracy in China. . . . Goodbye."[44] Although his wife was released three days later, Huang was charged with "subversion"; on May 9, 2003, almost two years after his trial, he was sentenced to five years in prison by the Intermediate People's Court in Chengdu on the charge of subverting state sovereignty. Huang's site was officially closed down, but it continued to operate from its U.S. server. On May 18, 2003, Huang appealed his sentence, denying that he had posted subversive materials and asserting that he had the right to speak and publish, as guaranteed in the Chinese constitution.

In reaction to the party's suppression of Huang Qi and other cyber-dissidents, on July 29, 2002, a Declaration of Citizens' Rights for the Internet was circulated online.[45] It was initiated by prominent intellectuals, lawyers, and private webmasters and gained the support of more than one thousand Web publishers and Internet users. Again, among the signers were intellectuals both in the establishment (such as Beiing Film Academy professor Hao Jian) and outside it (such as Liu Xiaobo, Yu Jie, and economist Mao Yushi) who continued to assert their right to speak and organize freely. As released by the Hong Kong Information Centre for Human Rights and Democracy, the declaration stated: "We, as Internet freelancers, personal Web site managers, persons who are concerned with Internet freedom, publish a 'Declaration of Citizens' Rights for the Internet,' so as to safeguard the legitimate rights of PRC citizens to use the Internet." The declaration defended the right to publish online by citing the U.N. Universal Declaration of Human Rights and the U.N. Covenant on Civil and Political Rights. It also demanded the freedom to put together Internet pages, with the only restriction being "'obvious and factual' slanders violating the freedom of speech, . . . pornography, and offensive and violent behavior." It emphasized that "a modern government should be based on the right of individual freedom of speech, the right of organizing associations, the right of questioning government decisions, and the right of openly criticizing the government."[46]

A fourth-year psychology student at People's University and well-known cyber-dissident, Liu Di, protested against Huang Qi's arrest in a different way. Using the online name Stainless Steel Mouse, she wrote on the Internet in a sardonic style reminiscent of the Eastern European dissidents of the 1970s and 1980s.[47] On learning of Huang Qi's arrest in June 2000, she wrote: "We could not bear to see Huang Qi alone struck by the mishap of imprisonment and ourselves remaining at large and therefore decided to surrender ourselves en masse to justice so as to show fairness." Spoofing the authorities' hypocrisy, she wrote: "Today we are all free men. We may launch a campaign to regularly act by the criteria for a free man. On such a day, everybody will say only things they want to say and do only things they want to do without regard to . . . the party. . . . Only on other days will we take part in political studies and say things contrary to our inner beliefs. I think this may after all be accepted as a path of freedom with Chinese characteristics."[48] Liu Di even ridiculed China's public security apparatus, which monitored the Internet. In an article posted on January 27, 2002, criticizing its limitless power, she asked: "Who knows what our national security people do with so much information? . . . Perhaps if the size of our national security apparatus continues to expand, it may ask all policemen on the streets to record every word uttered by pedestrians."[49]

In addition to her sardonic style, another indication of the influence of events in the former Communist countries on Liu Di's views was the appreciation she expressed for dissidents in the former Soviet Union. In a posting on July 16, 2001, she wrote: "I admire the dissidents in the former Soviet Union. They are critical not only of the horrendous crimes committed by the old totalitarian regime, but also of the abuses in today's privatization. They are perennial dissidents." She suggested, "Suppose that, for various reasons (perhaps fear of repression), these dissidents had not written the works that shook the foundations of Soviet communism. Then there would have not been the disintegration of the former Soviet Union."[50] But what had happened to the former Soviet Union was exactly what China's party leadership most feared for China.

Liu Di's description of her various activities on the Internet reveals that her views were also influenced by the discourse on various Chinese Web sites dedicated to the discussion of democracy and human rights.[51] She first began to use the Internet in 2000 by accessing it from computers in a number of universities and from Internet cafes. At first she only read articles from a Web site called Xici Hutong in Nanjing, which had a number of sites, such as Forum on Democracy, later called Democracy and Human Rights and then Democracy and Freedom Forum. When one forum would be closed down by the authorities, she would move to another one.

Liu Di registered under the name Stainless Steel Mouse in order to facilitate the downloading of articles. David Cowhig has pointed out that her Internet name was derived from a knight-errant hero of a science fiction novel, *The Stainless Steel Rat*, by Harry Harrison, published in 1961.[52] In the beginning, Liu seldom participated in the discussions, but when Yang Zili of the New Youth Study Group was detained in spring 2001, she began to speak out. She had often "roamed" the Web site of Yang Zili's group, called Garden of Thoughts Forum. When Xici's and other Web sites were closed down from June 1 through 7, during the sensitive anniversary of June 4, Liu Di and other cyber-dissidents opened a new site, Let's Come Together, and subsequently called Forum of Smoke and Rain. The participants decided they would all access it together at 8 p.m. on Fridays. Several of the participants in this Web site proposed going beyond the Internet gatherings and setting up an organization. Liu Di opposed such an action, explaining that she did not want to suffer the same fate as the New Youth Study Group; she just wanted to exchange ideas with her colleagues on the Internet. One action they did take together, however, was to donate money to Zeng Li, the wife of Huang Qi, who since her husband's detention in June 2000 had become financially destitute. The Forum of Smoke and Rain survived two months before it was closed down. Its participants then set up another site, in which they parodied the party's rhetoric, giving the Web site the name Fan Club of the People's Daily, later changed to Group of People's Daily Readers, where they poked fun at the party.

During the week of the celebration of the National Day holiday in 2001, Liu and her colleagues decided to organize an interprovincial Website gathering of people from Liaoning to Anhui. To memorialize the event, Liu Di wrote a report again spoofing the party's rhetoric, saying that "the first general convention of Freedom Party is held in Nanjing City," and posted it on a Xici forum in Nanjing. When this discussion waned, she and her colleagues moved on to other Web sites. In the process, Liu Di's identification as Stainless Steel Mouse had become "well known," and for a while Liu served as the manager of the various Web sites. On May Day 2002, when she and her colleagues were planning to hold another big Website gathering, the public security police called on several of her colleagues and the gathering was canceled. Liu Di learned that the police had also asked questions about her, and she kept silent for a while; but then she once again began posting her articles on the Internet, spoofing the authorities. When in September 2002 the university authorities informed her that the police had contacted them about her and charged that she was organizing a party with a political agenda, she stopped writing and no longer tried to access the various Web sites. Nevertheless, on November 7, 2002, Liu Di was arrested at her university. That night her apartment was ransacked by police, who confiscated a computer, floppy disks, and books.

Among the banned books taken from Liu's apartment were the prison letters of Wei Jingsheng and a book on the Tiananmen protests that had been bought at a bookstall in Beijing.[53] She also had been impressed with George Orwell's *1984* attack on totalitarianism. Her father worked in the library of the China Fine Arts Museum, and her mother, a worker, had died when Liu was fifteen.[54] Liu lived with her eighty-one-year-old grandmother, Liu Heng, who had been a senior reporter at the *People's Daily* in the early days of party rule, and who had suffered a fate similar to that of her granddaughter for defending others who were under attack. When Liu Heng refused to confess to protesting against the persecution of rightists in the 1950s, she herself was labeled a rightist and imprisoned for more than two decades. She was not rehabilitated until the 1980s. On March 7, 2003, Liu Heng called on the authorities to release her granddaughter.[55]

Again, Liu Xiaobo organized a petition to protest against Liu Di's arrest. He tried to deliver the petition, signed by 690 Chinese Internet users, to the NPC, but police prevented him from doing so.[56] Other petitions called for Liu Di's release, including one dated a year after her arrest and signed by three hundred supporters. In late November 2003, days before Premier

Wen Jiabao's trip to Germany and the United States, most likely in an effort to deflect criticism of China's human rights abuses during the visits, the government released Liu Di and two other cyber-dissidents, Li Yiban, who ran the Web site Democracy and Liberty, and Wu Yiran, a graduate of Jiaotong University in Shanghai.[57]

Despite the fact that security police were periodically posted outside her living quarters, on January 16, 2004, Liu Di posted a statement that revealed that she had again joined her colleagues in political discussions on an Internet Web site. She asserted that "the Internet has replaced the functions of 'organization' in many respects, which stimulates the integrity of Chinese society, and provides the space for the nurture of a citizenship society in China. Despite setbacks, she insisted that progress had been made and cited the examples of the government's recognition of the term *human rights* as well as the ability of "friends" to meet on the Internet. She acknowledged that "this freedom is gained by hard struggles" but that "the more we speak, the more we do, the Chinese government will be more tolerant, thus the safer we are."[58]

Among the people who had organized a petition in Liu Di's defense was a minor government official, Du Daobin, from Hubei. Like Liu Di, he had gained a following because of his commentaries on political issues on the Internet. Described as a "liberal thinker," Du had organized an online campaign to win Liu Di's release, arguing that her prolonged detention without trial was a direct violation of China's criminal procedure law.[59]

Like Liu Di, Du Daobin not only supported others who were arrested for what they said, but also was a prolific writer on the Internet. He discussed a broad range of topics, from criticism of the Propaganda Department's control over the media, which he called unconstitutional, to criticism of the harsh treatment of Falungong practitioners.[60] Most of his Internet essays protested against the party's repressive policies and called for democratic reforms. Du was detained in October 2003. Among the twenty-six essays the Public Security Bureau cited to charge him with "subverting the state," three opposed the passage of the article 23 antisubversion legislation in Hong Kong.[61] These specific essays revealed that the events in Hong Kong have an impact on China, especially among intellectuals who learn about them via the Internet and overseas radio. In fact, the struggle of the Hong Kong population against article 23 inspired some Chinese to demand freedom of expression and call for clarification of China's subversion laws.

As Du Daobin had organized efforts to defend Liu Di, a petition defending Du was made public in early November 2003, signed by fifty critical intellectuals in the establishment. Among the signatories were several of the liberals who had published articles in *Political China*, such as philosopher Xu Youyu, political scientist Liu Junning, law professor He Weifang, as well as the translator of Einstein, Xu Liangying, and the writer Yu Jie. Their petition demanded to know why Du had been arrested on charges of subverting the state merely for exercising the right to freedom of speech as protected in article 35 of China's constitution. Like the dissidents in the former Communist states of Eastern Europe and the leaders of the Democracy Wall movement, reference to the constitution continued to be a source of legitimacy for those seeking to assert their political rights to freedom of speech and association. Their petition asserted that "freedom of speech not only implies citizens' basic political rights but closely concerns the protection of other economic and civil rights and will ultimately contribute to the rejuvenation of the Chinese nation and the well-being of the broad masses of the people." It went on to say that "the words and deeds of intellectuals in their criticism of the actions of the government, the policies of the ruling party and individual leaders, even their conceptual criticism and questioning of the ruling party and the way it governs the country, all fall within the scope of freedom of speech guaranteed by the Constitution. . . . As long as a writer is not involved in seditious propaganda for concrete acts and means intended to overthrow the power of the state, he should not be charged for the 'crime of instigation to subvert the power of the state.'"[62]

On February 1, 2004, more than one hundred intellectuals, from both inside and outside the establishment, signed another joint petition, this one to the NPC and China's highest court, once again demanding clarification of the definition of freedom of speech in China's constitution and the extent to which one could legally criticize the government, specifically with reference to Du Daobin's arrest. The petition was posted on Web sites in China and overseas and asked for more signatures online, another example of the use of the Internet to mobilize support on political issues.[63] Signers of this petition included the leaders of the Tiananmen Mothers movement (such as Ding Zilin, her husband Jiang Peikun, and Jiang Qisheng), the economist Mao Yushi, and Liu Di, in addition to others who had signed the previous petition, such as Liu Junning, Xu Youyu, He Weifang, and Yu Jie.

The organizer of this petition, Liu Xiaobo, mentioned that the impetus for the petition had come from the massive Hong Kong protest on July 1, 2003, against the People's Republic's effort to pass the article 23 sedition laws, which had subsequently led to the government's suspension of the effort to pass such laws. Clearly, whether over the Internet or through radio broadcasts, information about the protests of the Hong Kong people against what they considered unfair government actions filtered through to China and influenced people seeking political rights in China. As the petition organizers explained, the Hong Kong protest demonstrated that people had to fight to achieve their rights. Liu pointed out, "Their protest taught us that we must assert our rights." Another one of the signers of the petition, Wang Yi, a legal scholar at Chengdu University, stressed that the strong reaction of the people of Hong Kong to article 23 showed that the quest for freedom was a universal desire and countered the view that people in "commercialized societies" did not care about political rights.[64]

The petition explained that "[Du's] articles merely expressed dissenting political views in a peaceful manner, which was a far cry from what constituted 'a crime of instigation to subvert the power of the state.'" Therefore, his arrest "violated the right of citizens to freedom of expression under Article 35 of the present Constitution." In addition, the petition asserted that Du's arrest ran counter to China's acceptance of international practices on the protection of human rights and its signature on the two U.N. human rights covenants.[65]

The petition also pointed out that whereas "not even the central government had accused Hong Kong citizens who opposed Article 23 legislation of 'instigating to subvert the power of the state,'" the police in Hubei had listed Du's articles criticizing article 23 as evidence of his acts of subversion. Therefore, Du's case, the petition asserted, demonstrates that the charges of subversion "are completely manipulated by an unpredictable and indeterminate political standard and not by a legal or judicial standard." If Du were found guilty, it warned, all Internet users may be charged with subversion "for discussing political affairs or publishing their personal political views on the Internet." Thus, the petition urged "people of all walks of life, especially Internet users and people writing in the Chinese language, to show concern for this case, because showing concern for Du Daobin means showing concern for ourselves." It also called on China's Supreme People's Court and the NPC to define clearly the difference between the "crime of instigation to subvert the power of the state" and freedom of expression under article 35 of the constitution, in order to end "China's judicial history of people being punished for what they have said."[66]

Although Du's family hired the defense lawyer Mo Shaoping to defend him, Mo was notified of the trial only at the last minute and was unable to get to the trial in time to defend him. On June 11, 2004, Du Daobin was found guilty of subversion and given a three-year sentence, but in a rare move of tolerance the court commuted his sentence to four years' probation.[67] Could it have been the public outcry, the numerous petitions and protests against Du's imprisonment, that spurred the court's lenient verdict against Du Daobin as well as Liu Di's early release from prison? Until these two cases, the punishment against cyber-dissidents, as epitomized in the New Youth Study Group, had been relatively severe.

The succession of the fourth generation of party leaders, led by party general secretary Hu Jintao and Premier Wen Jiabao, to power in 2002–2003 did not slow the arrests of cyber-dissidents. In fact, Amnesty International reported that the number of arrests of cyber-dissidents increased sharply. As of January 7, 2004, it recorded fifty-four people who had been detained or imprisoned for disseminating their beliefs or information over the Internet, a 60 percent increase over 2002.[68] In spring 2004, Reporters Without Borders reported that China jailed more Internet users for their expression of political views than the rest of world combined. Of the seventy-three cyber-dissidents in prison worldwide, sixty-one were in China.[69]

Despite the arrests, the Internet continued to be an outlet for views that could not be published in the official media. It also became a public space in which both established and disestablished intellectuals expressed views that could not be published in the conventional media. For example, a former journalist and professor of journalism at Peking University, Jiao Guobiao, launched a scathing attack on the Internet against the Propaganda Department (renamed the Publicity Department), which continued to be controlled by the most conservative party officials even after the dismissal of its neo-Maoists. Jiao called for abolition of the department, which he charged protected corrupt officials and covered over the darkest moments in China's history. He pointed out that "the Central Propaganda Department has become the bastion to defend the most reactionary forces, allowing them to abuse power and practice corruption at the cost of ruining the images of the party and government as well as damaging the civil development of the nation."[70] He specifically criticized the department for preventing media discussion of the petitions of ordinary citizens and their demands for back wages in the name of stability. He asked, "How is a news report going to affect social stability? Refusing to report on these issues is what will lead to social instability." He described the Propaganda Department as being "like a dark cloud hanging over the head of the Chinese news industry. It is contemptuous of all the rights and wrongs in civil society, it is the worst eroder of popular opinion about the government and the party, it is the worst eroder of support for the legality of the government and the party, and it is the secondary causal agent of disasters visited upon the needy groups in China."[71] In March 2005, Jiao was dismissed from Peking University.

Yet despite arrests, detentions, increasing surveillance, and intimidation, the cyber-dissidents continued to find ways to communicate on the Internet and express political views that challenged the party and advocated political reforms. As long as the People's Republic remained committed to an expanding market economy, openness to the outside world, and new communications technologies, it would be unable to repress completely such dissident views.

— 8 —

The Expansion of Rights Consciousness

Most of those who participated in independently organized political activities in the 1990s, whether through political discourse, organized protests, public petitions, efforts to register an opposition party, or discussion on the Internet, were somewhat isolated from the general population and were eventually suppressed. But this does not mean that their writings and activities did not have an impact on the general population. Political philosopher Michael Walzer observes that even if those involved are a "fairly small number," acting as a citizen develops one's own consciousness and also awakens others to the benefits that can be achieved by the assertion of political rights.[1] Moreover, as Kevin O'Brien explains, even if the populace at large, unlike the intellectuals and political activists involved in these efforts, does not articulate a rights consciousness in words, people act as citizens long before they may be fully conscious of or articulate their demand for political rights.[2]

One way in which people act as citizens is by participating in a group protest. In a political system without an independent judiciary or elected legislature, freedom of the press and association, an opposition party, or independent unions, one of the only ways for individuals to focus attention on their grievances is to stage protests; protests can be risky, but they do get attention. As economist Amartya Sen has repeatedly pointed out, because political and civil rights give people an opportunity to focus public attention on acute needs and to demand appropriate public action, they can help prevent economic and social disasters.[3] Sen suggests that if people had been able to act as citizens during the Mao era, they would have criticized Mao's policies and hence might have prevented the Great Leap Forward and the Cultural Revolution.[4]

Yet one of the lasting impacts of the Cultural Revolution, as Elizabeth Perry explains, was "to imbue ordinary citizens with a greater awareness of the possibilities and practices of mass protest than we might normally expect in an authoritarian regime."[5] The Democracy Wall movement exemplified such an awareness. Although the events precipitating a protest may be provoked by economic, social, or religious issues, an implicit common factor is the issue of political rights, particularly the right of assembly and association. The widespread demonstrations by different sectors of the Chinese population—workers, peasants, pensioners, migrant laborers, religious believers, and urban and rural residents protesting confiscation of their homes and land for development—that exploded all over China in the 1990s revealed through actions an increasing popular awareness of people's rights to associate and organize in order to gain their due—whether unpaid wages, pensions, and health care, more compensation for confiscated property, less official corruption, lower rural tax burdens, or freedom of religious worship.

Developing a Workers' Citizenship

The rising consciousness of rights among workers was revealed in the myriad of protests that punctuated the 1990s. Although the protests were primarily directed at achieving economic rights, they were implicitly seeking to gain political rights. The liberals in the establishment articulated this connection through their writings; the protesters, whether workers in SOEs, migrant workers, or farmers, generally did this through their actions in organizing their own groups to fight for economic rights. Toward the end of the decade, however, after China signed the U.N. Covenant on Civil and Political Rights in October 1998, a number of the demonstrators increasingly articulated the connection between the achievement of political rights and the achievement of economic rights.

Although under Mao workers in state industries were the honored heroes of the People's Republic, in the late 1990s they were becoming the relative losers in China's economic reforms, as China's bankrupt, moribund SOEs were being privatized, merged, or shutdown. A Chinese study, "China in Transition," published in 2001, revealed that almost a quarter (23 percent) of the population of China's eleven largest cities had lost their jobs in the previous two years, owing to the economic reforms. Another 16 percent in the rural areas had been put out of work. And less than two-fifths of the laid-off workers in the cities and only half in the rural areas had been able to obtain other employment.[7] Workers and retirees in many cities were left with little means of subsistence after the factories they had depended on for their livelihood, health care, housing, and pensions went bankrupt, trimmed their workforces, or privatized.

As workers lost their social security along with their jobs in the SOEs, some were emboldened to make their plight known to the authorities and to the outside world in an effort to seek redress. At times they had the assistance of a small number of marginalized intellectuals, such as members of the CDP, some of whom had themselves become workers because their past political activities had deprived them of positions in the establishment. Without institutionalized political channels through which ordinary people could express their grievances or seek redress, segments of China's population took to the streets to call attention to the growing inequalities in Chinese cities and the countryside. In the first ten months of 1995, for example, there were reports of more than twelve thousand protests and petitions to government offices.[8] The number of participants in these organized protests ranged from several people to more than ten thousand, and the frequency of protests accelerated in the late 1990s. In 1999 there were a hundred thousand protests, compared with sixty thousand only a year earlier; most of these involved workers.[9] Though their number increased, the protests generally lasted no more than a few days, and none developed into a national or even a regional movement. Usually local officials were authorized to use emergency funds to pacify the disgruntled workers and to detain the protest leaders, temporarily bringing stability. By the beginning of the twenty-first century, though, a few demonstrations did become regional and lasted for weeks.

Ordinarily, workers protesting against the closure of SOEs and local corrupt officials did not demand political rights; their major concern was to get what they believed was their due, such as unpaid wages, compensation, health care, or pensions. An early example was a protest in Chengdu, Sichuan, in mid-April 1991, when tens of thousands of workers in a private cotton mill carried out a sit-down strike at the gates of the provincial government office because their wages had been cut by 40 percent.[10] The workers protested in rotation, with a few thousand attending each day. One of their posters read: "We want neither democracy nor freedom. What we want is only payment of wages so we can buy food to eat."[11] Yet despite their disavowal of political demands, there were several efforts to establish independent workers organizations at the time. In addition to the Beijing Workers Autonomous Federation, established in May 1989, one of the first examples of an organized workers' demonstration to take place outside of Beijing occurred in late May and early June 1989 at the No. 1 Automobile Manufacturing Plant in Changchun and at nearby enterprises, in support of the students and in opposition to the military suppression. For the first time since 1949, workers marched in the streets in coalition with other classes. After June 4, the leaders of the independent labor unions were detained and treated more harshly than the student protesters; most were given prison sentences exceeding ten years, and some were executed. Despite their repression, reports of underground labor unions with memberships ranging from twenty to three hundred continued to crop up.[12] The China Free Workers Trade Union, formed in the mid-1990s, was an example of such a union.

In the second half of the 1990s, as the pace of privatization accelerated, so did the pace of worker demonstrations, still focused primarily on economic rights. In late June 1997, three state-run textile enterprises in Mianyang city in Sichuan declared bankruptcy, sparking more than a week of demonstrations in which protesters charged that local officials had embezzled unemployment funds. Demanding compensation, the protesters appealed to the government to protect their rights of subsistence.[13] When the government announced that the mayor would meet with the workers, about seven hundred workers went to the factory, but the mayor did not show up.[14] Although the authorities imposed a citywide curfew, the unrest continued until the People's Armed Police carried out a brutal crackdown in a clash with about a hundred thousand laid-off workers.[15]

Intellectuals did not play a direct role in the Mianyang protest, but several helped call attention to the strike and its underlying grievances. Though the government blocked any mention of these happenings in the official press, Li Bifeng, a former tax official in Sichuan, sought to publicize the grievances of the Mianyang textile workers as well as those of other workers.[16] During the 1989 demonstrations, Li had set up the Autonomous Youth Association of Chengdu, for which he was arrested on July 5, 1989, and sentenced to five years. After his release, he dedicated himself to fighting for workers' rights. In an open letter dated July 16, 1997, Li described the events in Mianyang and appealed to international labor organizations to back the Mianyang workers. He urged them to persuade the Chinese government to release those detained by police, to allow medical treatment for those injured in the crackdown, and to punish those officials accused of embezzling factory funds.[17] Although Li's appeal was not covered by the Chinese media, it was broadcast into China by VOA. Li was arrested in April 1998, on charges of fraud, in order to avoid attracting further international attention to the labor unrest.[18] He was subsequently sentenced to seven years in prison, primarily for leaking news of the 1997 Mianyang demonstration to the outside world.

By the late 1990s there were almost daily demonstrations of jobless workers and pensioners demanding back wages, unpaid pensions, or health benefits in front of local government headquarters. These demonstrations used such tactics as blocking roads and railways, which required a degree of advance planning and organization. In November 2000, for example, rail traffic between Shanghai and Beijing was reported to have been suspended for nearly eight hours because one thousand workers blocked a railway line in Anhui to protest layoffs and mounting back pay.[19] Some three hundred retired workers from a factory in the northeast blocked the entrance to the main office of their factory, China Third Metallurgical Construction Corporation, holding signs reading: "We Have Given Our Youth to the Chinese Communist Party, but Now We Have Been Abandoned in Our Old Age" and "We Have Asked for Help from Our Children but They Also Have Been Laid Off."[20] Another strategy was to travel to Beijing to demonstrate, to make the central authorities aware of their plight. There is no evidence, however, that these demonstrators blamed the central government or the political system for their grievances. They generally blamed the local SOEs and local corrupt officials and regarded the central government as a kind of ombudsman that could be persuaded to intervene locally on their behalf.

With little help from the official All-China Federation of Trade Unions (ACFTU), which was entrusted to carry out party policy, and despite an expectation of severe crackdowns, some workers turned to forming independent unions as a way to regain their economic rights. Several of the independent labor organizers articulated the demand for human rights and cited China's signing of the U.N. covenants as the basis for their actions. One such worker was Li Qingxi, then unemployed, who formerly worked at a health clinic attached to the Datong Coal Mining Administration in Shaanxi.[21] In early 1998 Li posted notices calling for the formation of independent trade unions, citing China's signing of the U.N. Covenant on Economic, Social, and Cultural Rights as the basis for such unionization. Although Li was quickly detained, in late January 1998 thirty sympathizers wrote to the United Nations urging his release, explaining that Li was "the first person arrested for asking for the formation of independent labour unions since China signed the convention."[22] In 1999, retired steel mill workers protesting pension cuts near the Chongqing Special Steel Factory held up posters reading: "Give Me Back My Human Rights," an indication that some workers were knowledgeable about and acquiring the language of rights consciousness.[23]

Not surprisingly, several people active in the formation of independent unions were veterans of the 1989 movement. Zhang Shanguang, for example, was a former secondary school teacher from Hunan who had been sentenced to seven years for organizing the Hunan Workers Autonomous Federation during the 1989 demonstrations. Upon his release in 1996, he had difficulty finding a job. Yet he continued his political activism and set up the Association to Protect the Rights and Interests of Laid-Off Workers.[24] He also gave interviews to the international media, specifically Radio Free Asia, about labor and peasant protests in Hunan. His campaign on behalf of workers' rights led to his arrest and a second trial, at which he was sentenced to a ten-year prison term.[25] Zhang was convicted of providing intelligence to a foreign organization because of an interview he gave to Radio Free Asia. Political activists signed an open letter demanding that he be released, and Zhang appealed his ten-year sentence by challenging the charges.[26] He rhetorically asked: "When China does not have a clear definition of secret information, how can there be a conviction on those grounds?"[27]

Another effort to establish an independent union took place in 2000 in Funing County, Jiangsu Province, where workers, led by factory electrician Cao Maobin, age forty-seven, organized themselves at a silk factory. They were owed large amounts of back pay as well as compensation for laid-off and retired workers. More than half of the workforce had been put on indefinite leave. Even though they were to receive a meager subsistence salary of 100 to 150 yuan monthly, they had not been paid for several months.[28] The ACFTU refused to help them, so on November 11, 2000, more than three hundred workers signed a petition requesting permission to form an independent union. Their leader, Cao Maobin, asserting that their purpose was not to oppose the party, stated: "We just want what has been promised us."[29] As Cao explained: "We're abiding by the country's laws and regulations, trying to ensure that they are observed."[30] Thus, like the political activists, as the workers' spokesperson, Cao used China's laws to justify their actions. The workers also used the words and deeds of China's leaders to support their demands. Referring to Jiang Zemin's speech on the fiftieth anniversary of the U.N. Universal Declaration of Human Rights in December 1998, they said: "We're acting in the spirit of Jiang Zemin's words, when he spoke about Chinese people enjoying their full entitlement of human rights."[31] They pointed out that only after protests did they sporadically receive the modest living stipends to which they were legally entitled. In December 2000, one day after he spoke to the Western media about his efforts to set up an independent union, the police took Cao from his home and put him in No. 4 Psychiatric Hospital in Yancheng, where he was forcefully drugged and detained.[32] His fellow workers at the silk factory demanded his release from the psychiatric hospital, but to no avail.[33]

Whereas most worker protests in the 1990s took place at individual factories, early in the twenty-first century there occurred a new phenomenon—coordinated joint actions. In the three months from March through May 2002, well-organized worker protests took place jointly in a number of different factories in three northeast cities—Liaoyang, Daqing, and Fushun—in China's rust belt, where thousands of laid-off workers protested nonpayment of back wages and pensions, loss of health benefits, insufficient severance pay, and widespread corruption.[34] These protests, involving thousands of workers from a number of different factories and lasting several weeks longer than any previous protests since 1989, began on March 11 in Liaoyang in Liaoning Province at the Ferro-Alloy Company. Intermittently for at least ten weeks, about two thousand laid-off (xiagang) metalworkers expressed their economic grievances and protested against endemic corruption. About fifteen thousand workers from the piston, instruments, leather, and precision tool factories in the city joined them. The protesters charged local officials with standing by while factory managers and corrupt officials had allowed the embezzlement of their wages. As in other strikes, they protested against the collusion of factory managers and local officials in stripping the factories of their assets and closing them down, thereby depriving the workers of their jobs and leaving the factories with insufficient funds to pay for the workers' medical insurance, pensions, and severance packages.

On March 20, 2002, public security officers and the People's Armed Police attacked groups of protesting workers in Liaoyang and detained three

of their elected worker representatives.[35] While the Liaoyang protests were
brought to an end, workers' protests in other northeast cities continued. In
the coal-mining city of Fushun, thousands of laid-off miners and workers
from nearby factories blocked roads and rail lines to protest their inade-
quate severance pay. More significantly, in nearby Heilongjiang Province,
in Daqing, once a Maoist model oil town, large-scale protests continued,
owing to arbitrary changes made in the severance agreement with laid-off
workers and the dismissal of the majority of workers in the local oilfields.[36]
At the same time, the local government reneged on its promise to pay the
heating bills for the retired workers in the extremely cold city and then demanded new payments from the retired workers in order to continue their
medical benefits and retirement insurance. These actions sparked the retired employees to engage in public protests.[37]

The protests in the northeast in 2002 were the most sustained and largest self-organized worker demonstrations in the post-Mao era. At the peak
of the protests, in the first half of March, thirty to fifty thousand workers
were demonstrating in the streets. Unlike in 1989, the protesters were not
demanding political rights. They were asking for economic rights—the
money that had been promised them. Nevertheless, the main leader of the
Liaoyang protest, Yao Fuxin, revealed implicitly through his actions that in
order to obtain economic rights, it was necessary to achieve political rights.
Yao, a high school graduate, spent five years in the countryside during the
Cultural Revolution, and had listened to VOA broadcasts.[38] He began organizing protests in Liaoyang as early as 1992, when he lost his job at a state-
owned steel-rolling mill. He then became the owner of a convenience
store. When his wife was forced into early retirement at the Liaoyang
Ferro-Alloy Factory and the factory stopped paying its employees and
withdrew their pensions and insurance benefits, Yao attempted to organize
an independent audit of the factory's accounts, as well as to appeal to
higher authorities.[39]

In addition to their economic grievances, the Liaoyang worker protests
were ignited by the statement of the head of the Municipal People's Congress in Liaoyang, Gong Shangwu, who at the annual meeting of the NPC
in Beijing had declared that there was "no unemployment" in Liaoyang
and that the city guaranteed a minimum living allowance of 280 yuan
monthly to those without a source of income. One of the demands of the
protesters was that Gong resign because he had failed to represent the
workers' interests. On March 18, a day after Yao was detained, more than

forty thousand workers from more than twenty factories protested against his detention. A demonstration held two days later led to the detention of three more men, who were formally charged with "gathering a crowd to disrupt social order."[40]

Although Yao's family was able to engage well-known defense lawyer Mo Shaoping,[41] the court proceedings bore little resemblance to the regularized procedures and the rule of law that the party leaders were calling for at the time. Mo was allowed to meet with Yao only five days before the hearing, with the police watching and listening on a video monitor. Moreover, the prosecution case against Yao was made available to Mo just a few days earlier. Several dozen workers attended the trial; many others who tried to attend were stopped by the police.[42] To support the charge against Yao Fuxin and another of the leaders, Xiao Yunliang, that they sought to "subvert state power and overthrow the socialist system," the indictment charged that they were members of the CDP and had participated in a ceremony to commemorate June 4. It also claimed that when the two men had heard on VOA that a branch of the CDP was being set up in the northeast, they expressed interest in joining to Wang Wenjiang, the person in charge of the northeast branch.[43] Moreover, on September 27, 1998, they attended a meeting in Anshan with several of the CDP leaders and agreed to establish a Liaoning steering committee. Yao was alleged to have served as the coordinator of the CDP in Liaoyang. On November 29, 1998, Yao met again with Wang Wenjiang in Anshan and planned to attend the first meeting of the Liaoning CDP on December 5, but it never took place because the police suppressed the CDP and arrested its leaders.

According to Yao's daughter, her father never joined the CDP, though he had expressed an interest in it, and he admitted attending an introductory meeting on September 27, 1998. Though he had wanted to work under the constitution to set up a new party, she insisted that her father had walked out of the second meeting on November 29, 1998, because he feared that the CDP would overthrow the CCP.[44] In their defense, Yao Fuxin and Xiao Yunliang insisted that they were merely exercising their internationally recognized rights of freedom of association and collective bargaining when they took to the streets with other Liaoyang workers to demand payment of wages and pensions owed them and to seek help for laid-off workers. In May 2003, more than a year after the protests, Yao and Xiao were sentenced to seven and four years, respectively, for subverting the state.[45] On the day of their sentencing, hundreds of Liaoning workers gathered to protest out-

side the court building. The two men were without legal representation because their lawyer, Mo Shaoping, was unable to attend. Based in Beijing
where the SARS epidemic was at its height, Mo would have to have been
quarantined for ten days before he could participate at the trial, and he was
not notified of the hearing date in time to fulfill the quarantine requirement. Significantly, the verdicts on Yao and Xiao were announced at the
height of the SARS epidemic, a time when international attention was focused on China's health policies rather than its human rights violations.
Later in the year their families reported that they were suffering severe
health problems in prison and were denied medical parole.[46]

Despite the fate of Yao and Xiao, the Liaoyang protests were not completely in vain. To prevent further pressure from workers, the former director of the ferro-alloy factory was formally arrested in July 2002.[47] Moreover, laid-off workers in Liaoyang continued to demand Yao's and Xiao's
release. In early November 2002, around one thousand people held a protest in front of Liaoyang city government headquarters to demand better
conditions for laid-off workers, and on the next day two hundred people demonstrated there to demand the release of the labor leaders.[48] The
persistent protests, plus the fact that Yao had expressed interest in an opposition party, though he had not joined the CDP, and had sought to engage
a well-known defense lawyer in his case, indicate that there was an extension of rights consciousness from small elite groups of students and intellectuals in the 1980s to a broader population including workers in the
1990s.

The worker protests in the northeast were also qualitatively different
from the previous protests in the 1990s, in that this was the first time so
many well-organized, laid-off workers from a number of different factories
and cities had taken to the streets simultaneously and sustained their protests for weeks rather than for days. The Liaoyang demonstrations in particular revealed a degree of organization and coordination that previous
demonstrations lacked. Clearly, the party's response indicated an awareness of the political implications of joint efforts of intellectuals and workers. Given the specter of Solidarity, the CCP tried to crush such alliances
almost immediately, and it consistently tried to diffuse any worker cohesion across occupations, industries, and regions. In comparison to its treatment of the CDP, and later the Falungong, however, the party's response
was relatively restrained toward the rank-and-file worker protesters. It imprisoned the leaders or sent them to mental institutions, but because it
feared further protests it made token payments to the striking workers, and

dismissed a number of corrupt managers and officials, in an effort to placate the workers.

Moreover, the party was not unmoved by the hardships the workers suffered on account of the privatization of the SOEs. An article in *People's Forum (Renmin luntan)* by a deputy secretary of the Labor Movement Research Society of the ACFTU acknowledged: "This action of indiscriminately selling off enterprises has brought extremely harmful effects to the reform of state-owned enterprises." The article noted that such action had "deprived the workers of their status as the masters of their enterprises, and led to social instability." Yet even though the article recognized the hardships inflicted on workers and suggested ways to ameliorate them, it blamed the unrest on "hostile forces at home and abroad that are using the name of reform with ulterior motives to undermine reform and . . . to attain their goal of toppling socialism and restoring capitalist private ownership."[49]

Expanding Farmer Citizenship

Like the workers in China's northeast, in the late 1990s farmers were also organizing their own groups to protest the economic hardships that had accompanied the economic reforms. Most farmers initially benefited from the land reform of the early 1980s, but the dissolution of the collective sector that accompanied reform induced local officials to levy all kinds of extra fees for local projects, such as road construction, irrigation, workshops, housing, schools, and medical care, that had previously been taken care of by the collective sector.[50] Although villagers began holding elections for village heads and village councils beginning in the late 1980s, and by the late 1990s most Chinese villages were holding such elections, village officials had little control over taxes. The villagers' taxes were set by the appointed leaders of the townships, the lowest extension of the formal government. In response, peasants protested against corrupt local officials, whom they charged with imposing extra fees, pocketing money allotted to peasants, and seizing their land for public works without sufficiently compensating them. Consequently, declining farm incomes along with increasing taxes and land confiscation provoked the peasant protests that sparked widespread unrest in the countryside in the 1990s. It is estimated that in 1999 in more than two thousand protests against rural authorities, most farmers were demonstrating against excessive taxation and corruption.[51]

Like the worker demonstrations in the late twentieth century (with the exception of the strikes in the northeast), the peasant protests, as described by Thomas Bernstein and Xiaobo Lu, were localized, relatively brief, uncoordinated, and limited to a single village or township area.[52] Peasants still looked to the central government as a fair arbiter of their disputes. Nevertheless, what made the peasant protests different in the post-Mao era was that in sometimes using the government's laws to justify their actions, the peasants expressed a developing sense of rights consciousness. Kevin O'Brien points out that as villagers became more aware of state laws protecting their rights, they become more emboldened to act in defense of those rights and appeal to the law and the courts to protect them against abusive officials.[53]

A prominent example of such action took place in the villages in Zizhou County, a drought-prone area several hundred miles north of Yan'an, Shaanxi Province, Mao's revolutionary base area. Farmers in Zizhou protested against local taxes in 1998 by bringing a lawsuit, based on the Administrative Litigation Law (ALL), against local township officials who had imposed higher and extra taxes. The Yulin Prefecture Intermediate Court decided in the farmers' favor and ordered local officials to reduce the total tax burden by almost half. Because such a ruling was rare, the case was given national attention in the official newspapers and on *Focus*, CCTV's investigative news magazine.[54] Nevertheless, the Yulin party branch punished the judges who delivered the verdict and imprisoned two of the villagers responsible for bringing the lawsuit. Despite that crackdown, as news of the successful lawsuit spread, farmers in other villages in Zizhou began to prepare lawsuits as well.[55]

A survey carried out by a historian at the Rural Development Institute of CASS, Yu Jianrong, reveals that in peasant-organized protests, a leader who is somewhat more educated than the average farmers usually emerges to act as spokesman.[56] Ma Wenlin, the leader of the Zizhou protest, fit this description. Born in 1942 into poverty in Lijia, Zizhou County, Ma did seasonal labor to make money in order to finish elementary and middle school. A Cultural Revolution veteran and a radical Maoist in his youth, he then passed the exam to enter the Chinese department at Shaanxi Normal University. After graduation, he taught third grade in a Yan'an middle school. He became a party member in 1985 and was selected to teach at a more prestigious middle school. In spring 1994, Ma completed the Department of Justice exam for lawyers in Yan'an and started working as a lawyer at the Yan'an Hushi Legal Service Center, where he handled hundreds of cases. He devoted himself to defending the rights of individual farmers who were involved in disputes with local officials.

When Ma returned to his home village during Spring Festival in 1997, the villagers pleaded with him to take their case. As one said of him: "He helped us . . . to use the law as a weapon to fight corruption." Even though his efforts initially had party support and received sympathetic treatment in the official *Legal Daily*, the farmers had trouble getting a hearing in the court.[57] When Ma returned again to Zizhou in April 1999, he organized a delegation of representatives from eight townships that traveled to Beijing to present a petition to the State Council demanding a reduction in taxes. As they waited for their appointment in Beijing on July 8, 1999, Beijing police detained Ma and sent him back to Shaanxi, where he was put on trial.[58] Although none of his supporters were allowed to attend the trial at the Shaanxi Provincial High Court, hundreds stood outside, listening to Ma present his own defense over a loudspeaker. In November 1999, Ma was sentenced to five years of hard labor for "disturbing social order." Subsequently some thirty thousand Shaanxi farmers signed a petition to the provincial high court calling for Ma's release. Nine local villagers were sentenced to prison for protesting Ma's conviction.[59]

In addition to the farmers' organized protests against Ma's treatment, fifteen prominent legal experts in the province called for a reopening of the case. The local media also began reporting on the case. On December 18, 1999, the Shaanxi Lawyers Association and the Shaanxi Legal Institute organized a forum on the case and issued a petition that declared that "Ma should be regarded as a hero in defending the farmers' rights, and carrying out the policies of the central government."[60] In addition, farmers gathered signatures for more petitions in support of Ma. More than ten thousand affixed their thumbprints to a document entitled "Appeal to . . . Rescue Ma Wenlin from Prison." The petition declared that "they arrest the ones who speak the truth." As one farmer observed, "Ma showed us what our rights are under the law."

As indicated in the Zizhou County case, by century's end some of the peasant protests, like the worker protests, were qualitatively different from previous efforts to call attention to grievances. These examples reveal that a number of the protests had become multiclass efforts in which intellectuals and small business owners joined with workers and farmers to deal with perceived grievances. Laws such as the ALL provided ordinary people with a vehicle to challenge local officials. Since the ALL came into force in

October 1990, more than seventy thousand such suits against officials had been dealt with by 1994; about 37 percent of the lawsuits were won by the litigants.[62] The ALL became a powerful weapon for those seeking redress from local officials.[63] For the law to work effectively, though, it would be necessary to establish an independent judiciary so that the party could not dictate the verdicts, and such an institution would require a change in the political system. Yet even under the prevailing political system, as the case of Zizhou County demonstrates, in the 1990s ordinary people, including farmers, attempted to use the law to uphold what they regarded as their legitimate rights.

Another area of increasing rights awareness developed in the protests of both rural and urban home owners in the late 1990s. These two groups protested against local governments and private developers that confiscated their homes and land for urban development and provided little, if any, compensation. An example of such a protest occurred in Xi'an in August 2003, when peasants put up posters protesting the demolition of their homes to make way for development in the area around the Big Goose Pagoda. On the walls opposite the pagoda, posters protested the confiscation. A number of the posters dealt specifically with the local situation: "Two years ago peasants lived here and their land was confiscated to beautify the area"; "Give back my land; give back my home"; and "Peasants' homes cannot be arbitrarily taken away. Without land and without homes, how can we survive?" Yet several other posters dealt with the issue of rights, such as ones that read "Oppose officials and business people joining together to take away peasant rights" and "Oppose unlawful confiscation of our land."[64] Moreover, makeshift tents topped with similar banners had been put up at the site of the demolition. Thus, at century's end, farmers, not only through their actions but also through their words, were learning to use the language of human rights against oppressive local officials, tax collectors, and officials confiscating their land, just as middle-class dwellers were doing in China's urban centers.[65]

The Chinese government was acutely aware of the potential threat of worker and peasant protests. The report *2000–2001: Studies of Contradiction within the People under New Conditions*,[66] drawn up under the auspices of Politburo member and adviser to Jiang Zemin, Zeng Qinghong, and based on research in eleven provinces, acknowledged that as SOEs closed down and subsidies to farmers were removed in order for China to join the World Trade Organization, social unrest could grow and worsen.[67]

Admitting that ordinary Chinese showed a willingness to express their grievances, the report stated that China's institutions, such as its "incomplete" legal system and "backward" social welfare structure, were unable to deal with these protests. Two days after the report was released, the editors of one of China's most daring newspapers, *Southern Weekend,* were removed precisely because they had reported on rising local protests and anger in the rural areas.

Dorothy Solinger, in her book *Contesting Citizenship in Urban China,* describes an increasing rights consciousness among farmers who migrate to the cities in search of better lives.[68] Evidence of this developing consciousness among migrant workers was displayed on a banner in the dusty industrial town of Tangxia, in Zhejiang Province, about 250 miles south of Shanghai, where farmers had migrated in search of jobs: the banner, hanging over a main road, read: "Protect the Rights of Migrant Workers!" The walls outside the mostly privately owned factories were papered with posters echoing similar messages. In response to the migrant workers' demands, local officials experimented by setting up the Tangxia Migrant Workers' Assembly to represent the migrants' interests, help resolve disputes, and manage the thousands of migrants coming from the countryside. But the party stopped the experiment because it feared that such an organization had the potential to become an independent labor movement.[69] Nevertheless, in 2001 a number of municipal governments established "rights-defending" organizations that mediated labor disputes between enterprises and migrant workers and helped implement local laws and regulations to safeguard the legitimate rights and interests of workers.[70]

The Right of Meditation and Religious Belief: The Falungong

As groups of workers and farmers sought to regain their economic rights and achieve political rights in the 1990s, religious groups tried to assert their right to worship and meditate as they wished. In so doing, through their actions they also were trying to assert their political rights. With the loosening of controls in the post-Mao period, a number of unorthodox groups within China's traditional popular religions and Christian evangelical groups, which were not recognized by the state, attempted to fill the spiritual void left by the bankruptcy of Marxism-Leninism and Mao Zedong Thought and party-approved religious practice. In addition, in the 1990s there was a resurgence of China's traditional *qigong* exercises and meditation movements, which, in the post-Mao era and especially after June 4, the party encouraged as an expression of a genuine Chinese spirit and a symbol of national pride.

One of the most controversial nonorthodox groups to emerge was the Falungong (Wheel of Law), which combined Buddhist-Daoist beliefs and traditional exercises. Like the groups of farmers calling for reduced taxes, laid-off workers demanding back wages and benefits, and migrant workers demanding better working conditions, the Falungong sought the right to associate and assemble in order to practice their exercises and meditate together. Its charismatic founder, Li Hongzhi, a former soldier from the rust-belt northeast, born in a town in Jilin Province in 1952, was exposed to the teachings of *qigong* at age four and studied various forms of traditional exercises. In 1991 Li left his job at the Changchun Grain and Oil Supply Commune, and in 1992 he founded his own school of *qigong*, called Falungong. In December 1995 Li published the book *Zhuan Falun*, printed by the government-run publisher China Broadcasting and Television Publishing House. The book was listed as a best seller in the *Beijing Youth Daily* in January 1996.[71] Given the official tolerance of *qigong* in the early 1990s and the establishment of a national *qigong* association with its own bureaucracy, Li's activities initially met with the party's approval. On May 12, 1992, Li officially registered his Falungong with the Qigong Research Association of China, under the direction of the All-China Sports Federation, which awarded him an honorary certificate on August 31, 1993, for providing free healing and rehabilitation treatments. In the same year, Li also received the title *Most Acclaimed Qigong Master*. In the mid-1990s, he lectured to large audiences, published books, and sold videos and audio-cassettes, from which he received financial support.

In addition to its exercises, the Falungong also advocated "truthfulness, benevolence, and forbearance" and condemned drinking, smoking, and homosexuality. Elements of Li Hongzhi's teachings suggested that those who believed in the Falungong might attain supernatural powers, such as the ability to levitate and travel through space and time. Li also predicted the end of the world for those who did not believe in his teachings. Beginning in 1996, however, officials periodically attacked the Falungong, and on July 24, 1996, the China News Publication Office issued a nationwide circular banning the distribution of all Falungong publications.[72] In November 1996 the Ministry of Public Security retracted the Falungong's registration, charging that under the pretext of popularizing *qigong*, Li

Hongzhi was engaging in a cult of the individual, raking in money, and threatening social stability. In 1998 Li emigrated to New York; from there he communicated with his followers in China over the Internet.[73] Despite the loss of their registration and the exile of their leader, Falungong groups continued to practice and grow.

A specific appeal of the Falungong was that it addressed the loss of health care caused by the near collapse of the state-sponsored medical system that accompanied China's market reforms. As clinics were made to pay for themselves, they became increasingly out of reach for those not engaged in the market economy. Li Hongzhi's teachings provided a broad range of traditional healing techniques, martial arts, and meditation that supposedly protected from disease. They were especially appealing to those who had lost their health care with the privatization of SOEs. Li had developed five simple exercises. Four were performed standing and involved stretching various parts of the body and moving the arms in circular motions around the body. The fifth was performed sitting in a lotus position and focusing the mind in meditation on a visualized wheel, spinning within the core of the body. Along with meditation and breathing techniques, the exercises supposedly harnessed the *qi* (internal energies) to strengthen the mind and body. These exercises embodied the traditional Chinese beliefs that the human body and mind are integrated and that through exercises one can achieve mental and physical well-being and harmony with the universe.

Besides providing a practical alternative to privatized health care, Falungong appealed to people who had a sense of powerlessness in the face of increasing change and modernity. Not only did it address the ideological and spiritual void left after the Cultural Revolution, but it also rejected the materialism and consumer frenzy accompanying China's move to the market in favor of a more spiritual way of life. Its ability to attract followers in the millions revealed that Deng Xiaoping's message "To get rich is glorious" did not appeal to everyone. Unlike the participants in the independently organized political groups, the Falungong had a far more diverse and broad social following, with people of all ages, ranging from well-educated young scientists, party members, and middle-aged housewives to retired workers and poor farmers. However, it appealed primarily to laid-off workers who had lost their social security and health care benefits and to those who felt alienated or were suffering from the economic reforms.

The Falungong had a pyramidal, decentralized organization, with Li

Hongzhi at the top. By the late 1990s the official media reported the establishment of thirty-nine provincial-level "general guidance stations" and more than twenty-eight thousand practice sites, mostly in urban parks and public places, which were organized and coordinated through the use of the new communication technologies.[74] What distinguished the Falungong from other popular meditation groups was its leaders' adeptness in using these technologies—the Internet, CDs, text messages on mobile phones, and electronic pagers—to mobilize and activate a mass base. These technologies helped it establish and multiply networks to disseminate its teachings to thousands of tutors, who led daily group exercises in parks and other public spaces.[75] Even when their Internet sites were blocked, Falungong believers found ways to communicate through overseas proxy servers, telephones, and other technologies.

Though in early 1997 the Public Security Bureau began a nationwide investigation, the campaign against the Falungong began in earnest when a seventy-three-year-old Marxist physicist, He Zuoxiu, who for years had crusaded to popularize science and combat superstition and who was active in the China Atheists Association, became directly involved. One of He's students was committed to a mental institution in spring 1998 for practicing Falungong. Insisting on meditating, the student had refused to eat or drink. When Beijing television came to film a report on He's institute on May 11, 1998, He took the opportunity to criticize the Falungong for what had happened to his student. The day after the show aired, half a dozen Falungong adherents showed up at He's apartment to argue with him, while several others picketed outside the Beijing television station. By early June the number of protesters engaged in a peaceful, orderly demonstration had grown to more than two thousand.

Despite the pickets, He Zouxiu continued his crusade against the Falungong, writing a short commentary in the Tianjin College of Education's *Youth Reader* entitled "I Do Not Agree with Youth Practicing Qigong," in which he referred disparagingly to the Falungong and Li Hongzhi. From April 18 to April 24, 1999, protesters gathered at the journal's office at the Tianjin College of Education and related government agencies.[76] When they were dispersed, they moved to the gate of the Tianjin Municipal Party Committee to lodge their protest. Their efforts climaxed on April 25, 1999, when they moved their protest to Zhongnanhai, the central party-state headquarters in Beijing, where more than ten thousand practitioners from all over the country, but mainly from Tianjin and Hebei, began to arrive before dawn. They displayed no banners, nor did they chant any slogans. They sat silently in orderly rows while designated speakers spoke on their behalf. Their only demand was a meeting with Prime Minister Zhu Rongji. At 8:15 a.m., Zhu met with their representatives, who made three requests: release the Falungong practitioners arrested in Tianjin, provide their organization with a more tolerant environment, and allow them to publish books. They also asked that they be able to "conduct activities openly and legally."[77] By dusk, Tianjin had released all the detained Falungong practitioners, and the Zhongnanhai demonstrators quietly dispersed. But the CCP still did not recognize the Falungong as a legitimate organization, which was one of the demands of its representatives. Even though Zhu Rongji had dealt flexibly with the immediate sit-in, Jiang Zemin subsequently clamped down harshly on the Falungong and similar organizations, outlawing all "evil cults" in July 1999. The party leadership was particularly concerned because the Falungong had been able to mobilize such a well-organized demonstration in front of Zhongnanhai without being detected in advance by the public security apparatus or by party grassroots organizations.

Although its adherents sought the right to assemble, meditate, and do their exercises, the Falungong did not specifically demand any political rights. Once again, it was not the ideas that they propounded, but rather the methods they used to express their ideas, that directly challenged the party's authority. The party regarded public space as the sphere for the exercise of state power; the Falungong used public space, including the space in front of the party-state's central headquarters, as a legitimate place in which to meditate and demand that it be recognized. Even more threatening to the party than the existence of a nationwide organization outside the party's control was the Falungong's ability, using the new telecommunications technologies, to mobilize large-scale collective action to defend its interests, undetected by the party. Their movement was unprecedented in the history of the People's Republic in terms of the size of its independent organization and its ability to organize protests. In some ways the Falungong posed a greater threat to the party than the 1989 student demonstrations, because its followers were mostly ordinary urban dwellers, particularly workers, who had formerly been among the party's strongest supporters, and it was held together largely by a common set of values and activities that the party deemed unacceptable.

Equally threatening to the party's authority was the fact that the beliefs and actions of the Falungong resonated with movements in Chinese history that had challenged previous political regimes and upset social stability. Several scholars have described the traditional Chinese ideas implicit in Falungong actions and beliefs—specifically its view that the existing world is corrupt and doomed to end and that only by participating in a spiritual movement can one bring about a new order. Thus, the Falungong resonated with China's historical religious sectarian movements, such as the Yellow Turbans, Red Eyebrows, White Lotus, Taipings, and Boxers, all of which had mobilized thousands of followers in organized protests that threatened and ultimately led to the overthrow of the existing regimes.[78]

Central Committee Document No. 13, issued on July 20, 1999, outlawed the Falungong and other heterodox *qigong* cults and banned their activities, and on July 22, 1999, the Ministry of Civil Affairs specifically banned the Falungong. Adherents responded by engaging in a form of civil disobedience. They attempted to practice their slow-motion exercises in Beijing, primarily in Tiananmen Square, directly across from the portrait of Mao Zedong that hangs over the entrance to the Forbidden City. These actions became almost daily occurrences, as adherents arrived in the square and tried to unfurl their banners and either stand or sit to meditate in small groups in a well-organized manner.[79] They did not shout slogans, parade in the streets, or stop traffic. The police quickly detained them by hauling them away in waiting vans, so their protests were small and short-lived. Those who refused to renounce their beliefs were expelled from schools or fired from their jobs. Neighborhood committees and work units were ordered to collect Falungong books, posters, and audiotapes and destroy them.[80]

With its practitioners faced with fines, detentions, loss of jobs, banishment to labor camps and prisons, and torture under questioning, the Falungong's attempts at group exercises in public squares waned in 2002. However, they continued to practice their exercises, in private or underground, like the millions of Protestant and Roman Catholic adherents who met secretly for prayer sessions, Bible study, and services in house churches rather than in the officially sanctioned "patriotic" churches, which required their believers to pledge their highest loyalty to the state. On October 31, 1999, a new anti-cult law was passed, specifying prison terms of three to seven years for cult members who "disrupt public order" and distribute publications.[81] At the same time, the party imposed heavy penalties on Falungong leaders, especially on high party officials whose membership in the Falungong the party found most threatening. On December 26, 1999, Li Chang, a former official at the Ministry of Public Security, was sentenced to eighteen years in prison, and a former Railways Ministry official, Wang Zhiwen, was sentenced to sixteen years in prison for practicing Falungong.[82]

Although the Falungong did not talk about rights, their persistent efforts, under threat of punishment, to practice their exercises together in public were an assertion of the right to associate and assemble. Among their official critics were those who urged them to try other methods to achieve their rights. One such critic was a vice president of the Shanghai Academy of Social Sciences, Shen Guoming, who, while criticizing the Falungong for protesting in front of government headquarters, urged that "Chinese citizens should realize their rights according to legal processes, and not by doing whatever they want to do."[83] Similarly, Xia Yong, deputy director of the Institute of Political Science of CASS, condemned the Falungong for using superstition to defraud practitioners of money and for illegally assembling and disturbing the public order.[84] He urged: "We should pay attention to handling things according to law, and solving legal problems though judicial channels."[85] Yet despite the establishment scholar's advice that the Falungong should use legal procedures to win their right to assemble, Chinese lawyers were intimidated from defending Falungong members. The party ordered that any lawyer who was asked by Falungong members to defend them "must write a report about the request and apply for special permission from judicial authorities."[86] On November 26, 1999, the *People's Daily* carried a commentator's article that condemned the Falungong, not only because the group was opposed to science and rationality, but also because it was a political organization that sought to undermine the party-state. It called the fight against the Falungong "a serious ideological and political struggle."[87]

The campaign against the Falungong extended to other meditation groups as well. One such group, called Zhong Gong, also claimed to heal illnesses through its breathing exercises, enabling practitioners to develop extrasensory abilities. Zhong Gong, established in 1988, had attracted twenty million adherents and boasted eighteen thousand teachers. The Public Security Bureau closed its main training center in central Shaanxi in December 1999. Like the Falungong, Zhong Gong members resorted to civil disobedience in the face of government repression. They sent an open letter to the NPC, accusing Jiang Zemin of illegally ignoring the group's lawful registration, and called on the NPC to investigate. They also demanded an apology from the government and the return of the group's legal documents and funds that had been confiscated.[88]

The Zhong Gong, the Falungong practitioners, and other meditation groups not only engaged in civil disobedience, but also attempted to use other political institutions, such as the NPC, to redress their grievances. With the explanation that they were using what they called their constitutional rights to petition the government, the Falungong tried to register complaints against the government's July 22, 1999, ban and urged the NPC in its March 2000 meeting to engage in a fair and public debate on the ban.[89] They also called for the release of Falungong practitioners who had been imprisoned for their beliefs. Likewise, the Chinese Evangelistic Fellowship petitioned the NPC to protect the religious freedom of its members and retract the label of "evil cult."[90] In addition, the Falungong internationalized their protest when, at the opening of the annual session of the U.N. Commission on Human Rights in Geneva in 2000, they sent followers to plead with the Commission to help them achieve the freedom to practice their beliefs, as guaranteed in the Chinese constitution.[91]

On the second anniversary of the Falungong's protest in front of Zhongnanhai there was no sign of a large protest.[92] Falungong followers were reduced to using television signals to interrupt official television programming with brief video demonstrations of their exercises.[93] They also used international phone calls and mobile phone text messaging to spread their beliefs. By late 2001, after thousands of detentions and intense media criticism, the campaign of intimidation and imprisonment had finally suppressed the movement's public gatherings and protests. However, the issues of attaining the right to assemble and practice one's beliefs and filling the spiritual void left by the collapse of the Communist ideology remained unresolved.

Thus, in addition to the impact of China's accelerating movement to the market and opening to the outside world, by the century's end the sense of rights consciousness among a small number of people involved in political movements had spread to an ever-growing number of Chinese beyond intellectual and elite circles. *Outlook (Liaowang)* magazine, published by Xinhua News Agency, reported that more than three million people had participated in protests in 2003. This was a 14.4 percent increase from 2002.[94] The variety of the groups that were expressing a rights consciousness through words as well as through actions—workers, farmers, migrants, evicted home owners, and religious believers and practitioners—revealed that rights consciousness was developing beyond the veterans of the Cultural Revolution, Democracy Wall, and the 1989 demonstrations, and beyond the intellectual elites, the Tiananmen Mothers, the Peace Charter group, and the CDP, to the population at large.

Epilogue

Redefinition of Chinese Citizenship on the Eve of the Twenty-first Century

Until the late twentieth century, most Chinese who had articulated their desire for political rights and sought to achieve them were from the intellectual and political elites. Their efforts began during the 1898 Hundred Days of Reform and continued, on and off, during the first half of the twentieth century until interrupted by the 1949 Communist revolution and the rule of Mao Zedong (1949–1976), and then resumed in the last two decades of the twentieth century. As we have seen, in the 1980s and 1990s those elites were joined by disestablished and marginalized intellectuals, who had been forced out of the establishment because of their earlier political activities, and by a small number of workers and owners of small businesses. And by the century's end, rights consciousness was spreading to other social groups—workers, farmers, migrant workers, religious believers, and evicted home owners—in part because the disestablished intellectuals were participating in the wider community, and in part because these groups themselves were gradually developing a new political consciousness and new strategies, expressed not only in their actions but also in their words.

Still, virtually everyone in China remained unprotected by institutions or laws. In fact, the fourth generation of Communist Party leaders—a technocratic elite under the leadership of party general secretary Hu Jintao and prime minister Wen Jiabao, who took over the leadership from Jiang Zemin in 2002–2003—reinvigorated the repression of dissident intellectuals, particularly independent or "public" intellectuals. This younger generation of CCP leaders was more concerned than the Jiang administration had been with alleviating the inequalities, especially for farmers, produced by the economic reforms. But they suppressed the very people who tried to draw attention to China's growing inequalities and sought to restrict the public space for political discourse that had opened up during Jiang's later years.

While Hu Jintao's government expressed concern for the peasants, it suppressed the expressions of concern and criticisms of the peasants' impoverishment that it had not officially approved. This can be seen in its treatment of the book *A Survey of Chinese Peasants* (2004), written by Chen Guidi and Wu Chuntao, based on their interviews with farmers in the poor province of Anhui over several years.[1] The authors, a husband-and-wife team, both born in the countryside, described the land seizures in which developers took rural residents' land without giving them adequate compensation, the imposition of unfair taxes by local officials, and the lack of recourse available to farmers to right these wrongs. The book vividly depicted the increasing impoverishment of peasants that the new generation of leaders had declared it sought to alleviate. Most important, the book revealed the official abuses of power that the new leadership feared would eventually undermine the party's hold on power and sought to remedy. Even so, just a month after its February 2004 publication the book was banned, though it continued to be sold on China's black market.

By the fall of 2004, Hu Jintao's crackdown on unofficial critics of party policies spread to other independent "public" intellectuals. Ironically, the crackdown began after the September 2004 publication of an article entitled "Fifty Influential Public Intellectuals" in *Southern Personalities Weekly* (*Nanfang renwu zhoukan*), a periodical that was connected to the daring Guangzhou Southern Media Group, which also published *Southern Weekend*. In an accompanying commentary, the *Weekly* praised public intellectuals, defined as intellectuals who speak out publicly on political issues. It pointed out that "this is the time when China is facing the most problems in its unprecedented transformation, and when it most needs public intellectuals to be on the scene and to speak out."[2] Although the article's list of fifty included intellectuals in a variety of professions—writers, artists, film directors, cartoonists, lawyers, and environmentalists—and a number of overseas Chinese intellectuals, the intellectuals who in the 1990s had called for political reforms, freedom of speech and association, and greater political participation stood out.

On November 23 an article in Shanghai's *Liberation Daily* (*Jiefang ribao*) attacked the concept of public intellectuals, claiming that such intellectuals' independence "drives a wedge" between the intellectuals and the party and the intellectuals and the masses.[3] It insisted that China's intellectuals belong to the working class, under the leadership of the party, and cannot be independent. Moreover, it called the concept a foreign import. The idea of a public intellectual in fact was not alien to China, as seen in the obligation of the Confucian literati to criticize, no matter what the consequences, leaders who did not live up to the highest ideals. It is also seen in the demands of intellectuals in the early decades of the twentieth century for wide-ranging political reforms and in their efforts to organize groups to work to achieve those reforms. Nevertheless, the *Liberation Daily* article was reprinted in the party's official newspaper, the *People's Daily,* giving the party's official imprimatur to the criticism of public intellectuals.

Shortly thereafter, the party detained several well-known public intellectuals. In December 2004 the writers Yu Jie and Liu Xiaobo, among others who personified public intellectuals, were taken into custody. In October their independent chapter of PEN had given an award to writer Zhang Yihe for her memoir *The Past Is Not Like (Dissipating) Smoke* about the party's 1957 anti-rightist campaign against intellectuals, which even the Deng Xiaoping leadership had denounced in the 1980s. Though the book was banned, it continued to be sold on street corners and circulated widely in pirated copies. Political theorist Zhang Zuhua, who attended the PEN ceremony where the award was presented, was also detained. The three were all criticized for articles they had published in overseas journals, which found their way back to China via the Internet. Although the three were later released, their detention was a warning to other public intellectuals.

Along with the detention of a number of well-known independent intellectuals and the negative characterization of public intellectuals in the *People's Daily,* Hu Jintao's government tightened controls over the media. Reports on the growing protests against corruption, abusive officials, and property confiscation were banned from the media. The journal *Strategy and Management,* a monthly that had been an outlet for intellectuals of a more liberal persuasion—such as Li Rui, a party elder, and Liu Junning— was closed down. Chen Min, the chief editorial writer for the monthly magazine *China Reform,* was detained. Using the pen name Xiao Shu (Smiling Sichuanese), Chen had declared in one of his commentaries that a natural gas explosion in December 2003 in Chongqing, which killed several hundred people, demonstrated that the government lacked concern for human lives.[4] *China Reform* had also published many articles on the plight of the peasants. Even the editor in chief of the *China Youth Daily,* which was the newspaper under Hu Jintao's Communist Youth League power base and had been very aggressive in exposing official corruption, was detained.

Unlike suppressions during the Mao period, however, when millions were harshly persecuted for the acts of a small number, in the post-Mao period the crackdown on public intellectuals and the media did not reach far beyond the accused and their immediate families. Moreover, though some establishment intellectuals lost their jobs and some were briefly detained, they were able to find other jobs and outlets for their views in China's expanding market economy. The government continued to arrest political activists, but gone were the zealous campaigns of denunciation, coerced mass participation, and forced confessions of the Mao era. And the individuals who were persecuted and imprisoned were not completely silenced after their release. Some still tried to function as citizens, either on their own or with others, and they continued to express their political views in nonestablishment publications, on the Internet, and in organized demonstrations. In addition, writings that were officially banned were still sold on the streets and distributed over the Internet.

There were also differences between the advocates of political rights in the 1990s and their predecessors in the post-Mao 1980s. It was not so much that the former were imbued with a different political consciousness, but that they used different political strategies to express their ideas. Unlike their Marxist humanist predecessors of the 1980s and earlier, most activists in the 1990s came to believe that creating political change in China would require more than just educating the people ideologically.[5] Rather, they believed, it would be necessary to establish new institutions to make possible a system of checks and balances. As a result, they adopted a more activist approach, through independent publications, organized debates, petitions, or group mobilization, and they were willing to risk their jobs and to work outside the political and intellectual establishments to achieve their goals. At times they joined with members of other social groups and drew them into their political activities.

The institutional guarantors of citizenship that Western political thought takes to be necessary for the exercise of political rights, such as freedom of expression and association guaranteed by laws, an independent judiciary, and an elected legislature, did not yet exist in China. The difficulty in establishing such institutions was due not only to the continuing dominance of the Leninist party-state, but also to the fact that China had not yet developed an independent middle class, a bourgeoisie, to support such institutions. Most of China's growing business and professional communities in the late twentieth century were co-opted into the official establishment. Yet, as we have seen, though they were unprotected by institutions and laws, various individuals and groups in the post-Mao era contested the policies of China's authoritarian government and attempted to assert their political rights.

Unquestionably, the behavior and beliefs of most of these individuals and groups in the late twentieth century had much in common with both the Confucian literati and the establishment intellectuals of the People's Republic. Like their predecessors, they remonstrated with the leaders to change their political ways; they continued to see themselves as members of a vanguard that spoke for others and told the truth; and they sought to work within the prevailing structure to achieve their aims. Yet, unlike the Confucian literati of the late Qing dynasty and Marxist humanists in the 1980s, a significant number of intellectuals, both establishment and marginalized, in the 1990s rejected the need for official and political patronage and sought to build an independent base for their actions. Like their Eastern European counterparts in the 1970s and 1980s, they were willing to work both inside and outside the party and the intellectual establishment to influence and challenge the entrenched regime.

Unlike the Eastern Europeans, however, the Chinese in the last decades of the twentieth century were unable to bring down the Leninist party-state and establish new political institutions. China's party-state was stronger than the Eastern European party-states had been before their fall, in spite of the fact that the party in China had been decimated in the Cultural Revolution, and despite the loosening up and devolution of party power that accompanied China's economic reforms. China's party-state was not affected by Mikhail Gorbachev's efforts to reform the Soviet political system, which had also weakened the party-states of Eastern Europe. And in contrast to the economic reforms in the former Soviet Union, which initially caused great distress to the Soviet population, China's economic reforms of the post-Mao period were able to improve the livelihood of most of the population, thereby retaining the legitimacy of the party despite the resultant increasing inequalities and rampant corruption. Furthermore, unlike the Eastern European intellectuals and even the May 4 activists in the 1920s and 1930s, China's political activists did not link up with the emerging merchant class and workers in political action until after the June 4 crackdown; and even then, only a small number of disestablished and marginal intellectuals joined forces with other social groups. Therefore, they did not have the broad-based social support enjoyed by their Eastern European counterparts that might have helped them succeed at bringing down the party-state.

The formation of what B. Michael Frolic has called a "community of rational self-directing individuals who can elevate their private interests to a consideration of the greater public good" has been a rare occurrence in the People's Republic.[6] Yet, as we have seen, a growing number of Chinese citizens in the last two decades of the twentieth century tried to form such a community, by forming independent groups that took initiatives and attempted to assert their political rights. They sought to hold the state publicly responsible for its officially recognized commitments in both domestic and international affairs. Although they still lived under an authoritarian party-state and were eventually suppressed, they made a contribution to the process by which Chinese subjects on the eve of the twenty-first century were beginning to act like citizens.

Some of these groups, such as SERI and the CDP, came close to creating truly independent political organizations. But without any laws to protect them, and without the backing of a broad social base or a robust civil society as had developed in Eastern Europe in the 1970s, they could not function openly for very long. In their actions these groups in late twentieth-century China resembled more the dissident groups in the former Soviet Union than Solidarity in Poland or Charter 77 in Czechoslovakia, both of which directly challenged the party-state. Like their Soviet counterparts, the Chinese political activists were relatively few in number and had only limited contacts with other social classes. Moreover, there was no developed civil society to support them. Also like the Soviet activists, for the most part they too were silenced, put in prison camps, or exiled.

The Soviet activists had tried to build some coalitions with workers and other social groups, but they had been unable to organize politically and publicly until the late 1980s, when the Gorbachev government, just before the fall of the Soviet Union, allowed the formation of a nascent civil society. If China's party-state unravels like the former Soviet Union did, will the politically active groups in China that are demanding political reforms also be as bereft of intellectual and political leadership as the Russian groups were with the collapse of the Soviet Union? Unlike its post-Confucian East Asian neighbors, China has not allowed the organization of independent political groups that could assume leadership, if and when the party-state collapses.

Yet in other ways, China in the early twenty-first century is very different from the former Soviet Union and closer to its post-Confucian East Asian neighbors. It is much more open and connected to the outside world, especially economically, than the Soviet Union ever was. Chinese intellectuals and professionals are in regular contact with their international colleagues. True, Chinese political culture, in which the intellectuals' highest calling is to enter government service, is so deeply embedded that most intellectuals are likely to continue to work in the political and economic establishments and to plead with the regime to reform itself. However, there now exists a minority within the Cultural Revolution and 1989 generations, and a small number of the post–June 4 generation—specifically the cyber-dissidents—who have come to believe that they can help their country more by being independent of the party-state and by joining together with other groups to bring about change.

Under Mao's totalitarian controls such activity was impossible. Under the authoritarian rule of the post-Mao era, the veterans of both the Cultural Revolution and June 4 have been able to exert pressure and assert their political and economic rights, however briefly, despite the risks of harsh penalties. Whether such actions can prevent disasters comparable to those of the Mao period, as Amartya Sen has suggested, is hard to know. What is clear is that China's government will have to respond to potentially severe social unrest and pressures building up from below—from workers, farmers, migrants, religious believers, and displaced home owners—who are dissatisfied with their present lot and are gradually acquiring a consciousness of political rights.

Comparison with Taiwan

Even more relevant to China's future political development than the Soviet and East European experiences may be a comparison with Taiwan. Like China, Taiwan also had a Leninist party-state, albeit a more loosely controlled party-state than the People's Republic, before its democratization in the late 1980s.[7] Taiwan's transition to democracy was characterized by dynamic economic growth for several decades, fueled by private businesses, which never had been eliminated, and the formation of a middle class, which constituted the core of a nascent civil society, prior to the lifting of authoritarian rule in 1987. Taiwan also had competitive local elections, decreasing government control over the media, and budding political organizations. Unlike Russia's precipitous shift from party-state rule to anarchic

democracy, change in Taiwan was gradual as one-party rule successively allowed more freedom of expression and permitted small opposition groups,
the *dangwai,* to contest first in local and then, in December 1986, in national elections.

Will China's move to the market, opening to the outside world, and burgeoning civic groups lead its one party-state to devolve into a pluralistic,
democratic political system as occurred in Taiwan? Most of the grassroots
groups that articulated demands for political reform in Taiwan were led
by dissident intellectuals, journalists, and students, who then linked up
with other social classes.[8] The grassroots political efforts by disestablished
or marginalized intellectuals in conjunction with other developing social
groups in China in the 1990s do have some similarities with those in Taiwan. However, in Taiwan the impetus for political reform came from *both*
above and below. Chiang Kai-shek's son, Chiang Ching-kuo, decided to
recognize an opposition party and a free press in 1986–1988, as the grassroots political changes that had been under way in Taiwan since the 1950s
precipitated Taiwan's democratization.

Still, Taiwan's democratization was an evolutionary process that did not
always move in a straight line. The Kuomintang repressed, sometimes violently, domestic pressures for political change from the very beginning of
its rule in 1947. These pressures intensified in the late 1950s but were repressed again in the early 1960s. When they resurfaced in the 1970s, they
were less effectively repressed until they finally were successful in the late
1980s. International pressure, especially American pressure, also played a
role in pushing Taiwan toward building democratic institutions, including
multiparty elections. As in other post-Confucian societies, Taiwan's gradual, relatively peaceful, though erratic, transition from authoritarian to
democratic government since the 1950s also evolved from its economic
growth, the communications revolution, the emergence of a more diverse,
pluralistic society, and the development of an urban middle class, coupled
with domestic political changes such as village elections, empowerment of
local assemblies, the formation of NGOs, the development of a modern legal system, and the beginnings of interest-based politics.

Taiwan's political development, like that in South Korea and Japan,
demonstrates that post-Confucian societies have no cultural values that in-
trinsically prevent them from becoming democratic. Some of the political
reforms in China, such as the local elections and the efforts to establish
legal procedures, are reminiscent of early steps toward democracy in Tai-

wan. Similarly, there are in China, as there were in Taiwan, a small number of businesspeople who are willing to fund independent political journals, symposia, and political think tanks. Generally, however, in China the emerging business community has not yet linked up with those engaged in independent political activities. Moreover, Taiwan experienced liberalization of the political system prior to its lifting of authoritarian rule. There has been a loosening of controls over personal life in China, but only a slight liberalization of the political system. Still, China faces mounting internal pressure from various social forces adversely affected by the economic reforms and from increasingly independent political and intellectual groups, as well as international pressure to live up to its international human rights commitments.

Another major difference between the People's Republic and Taiwan is in their tolerance for opposition parties. The People's Republic has banned the formation of opposition parties. In contrast, prior to the democratization of its political system, Taiwan gradually came to tolerate the participation of small parties that presented themselves as alternatives to the Kuomintang in local elections, and then in national elections. In time these parties became increasingly well organized. Even though the Kuomintang tried to constrain their activities and at times suppressed them, they existed as channels through which a political opposition could participate in the political system. In place of disruptive protests and demonstrations, they provided a legitimate outlet for the expression of grievances. The Kuomintang's tolerance of the gradual expansion of independently organized political activity helped bring about Taiwan's peaceful democratic transition.

Contrary to the warnings of China's party leaders, the Taiwan experience demonstrates that the transition to democracy need not lead to instability and chaos. And contrary to the views of some establishment intellectuals in the People's Republic, the Taiwan example shows that the development of a democratic culture need not precede democratization. Rather, the Taiwan case shows that democratization develops by building institutions that help create a democratic political culture. Although at the start of the twenty-first century there is more political debate and there are more diverse intellectual groups in the People's Republic, and China's new leadership under Hu Jintao and Wen Jiabao is talking about intra-party democracy, the party's prohibition against independent political groups and its denunciation of public intellectuals might make a gradual transition to democracy or any other major political reform more difficult than in Taiwan. As a much larger polity, with a more deeply entrenched and stronger Leninist party-state structure, China may take much longer than the forty years it took Taiwan to democratize.

The Role of Citizenship in China's Future

Even though the internal and external forces pushing for political reforms in the People's Republic have been periodically repressed, they have not been silenced. It is not completely unrealistic to expect that some form of democracy will emerge in the People's Republic in the early decades of the twenty-first century. It might evolve from the grassroots level if elections are allowed to move up from the village to the township, county, and eventually the provincial and then the national levels, and if the NPC becomes more assertive and the media more free. China's budding civil society may also develop from the various social forces that in time could act as a counterweight, rather than a complement, to the state and lead to organized political groups. Institutionally, the dissolution of the party-state began in the late 1980s when former party general secretary Zhao Ziyang and his advisers started to separate the party from the state by eliminating the party committees from state organs, factories, and schools. Those efforts were aborted after the June 4 crackdown and Jiang Zemin's ascension to power. But a study by the Central Party School in 2002 reported that political reform topped the list of concerns of mid- and high-ranking cadres, who specifically designated the separation of party and government functions, followed by expanding democracy in the party, as keys to effective political reform.[9]

Thus, in the last decade of the twentieth century China witnessed a growing consciousness of citizenship and several organized efforts to assert political rights, both by ordinary people as well as by intellectuals. These developments do not necessarily imply movement toward democracy, but they are prerequisites for the establishment of a democratic political system. Democracy depends on the desire of organized citizens to participate in the political process in order to hold the political authority accountable for its actions and to improve the public good. There can be citizenship without democracy, but there cannot be democracy without citizen participation. Therefore it would be wrong to discount the impact of the various efforts to assert political rights in late twentieth-century China because they were quickly suppressed and the institutions they sought to build have not yet been established. Despite their failure and the relatively small number of people involved, these actions signify the beginnings of a genuine change in the relationship between China's population and the state in the post-Mao era.

Though they were suppressed, those who attempted to act as citizens in China in the 1980s and 1990s, whether they advocated liberal democracy or organized pressure from below to move the government toward political change, have had a profound influence. For independent political actors and groups to continue to survive or develop, they will need much more support from Chinese society than they had in the last two decades of the twentieth century, and they will need laws to protect their political activities if they are to have an impact on policy making. Nevertheless, the transition from comrade to citizen in the People's Republic of China has begun.

Notes

Index

Notes

Abbreviations

FBIS   Foreign Broadcast Information Service

JPRS   Joint Publications Research Service

Introduction

1. Xinhua News Agency, Mar. 17, 2003, in BBC monitoring Asia Pacific-Political, Mar. 17, 2003.

2. Xinhua News Agency, Dec. 15, 2003, in BBC monitoring Asia Pacific-Political, Dec. 15, 2003.

3. Benjamin L. Read, "Revitalizing the State's Urban 'Nerve Tips,'" *China Quarterly*, no. 163 (Sept. 2000), pp. 806–820.

4. Barrett McCormick is writing a book with Liu Qing on reforms in the Chinese media; see Yuezhi Zhao, "Underdogs, Lapdogs and Watchdogs," in Edward Gu and Merle Goldman, eds., *Chinese Intellectuals between State and Market* (London: RoutledgeCurzon, 2004), pp. 43–74.

5. Murray Scot Tanner, *The Politics of Lawmaking in Post-Mao China: Institutions, Processes, and Democratic Prospects* (New York: Oxford University Press, 1999).

6. Elisabeth Rosenthal, "China Leader Steps Down, but Not Out of the Picture," *New York Times*, Mar. 16, 2003, p. 8.

7. Tony Saich, "Negotiating the State: The Development of Social Organizations in China," *China Quarterly*, no. 161 (Mar. 2000), pp. 124–141.

8. John Pomfret, "China Orders Halt to Debate on Reforms," *Washington Post*, Aug. 27, 2003, p. A1; Robert J. Saiget, "China Political Reform Honeymoon Over, Scholars Say," Agence France-Presse, Oct. 12, 2003.

9. Carol Lee Hamrin and Timothy Cheek, eds., *China's Establishment Intellectuals* (Armonk, N.Y.: M. E. Sharpe, 1986).

10. Merle Goldman, *Sowing the Seeds of Democracy in China* (Cambridge, Mass.: Harvard University Press, 1994); Joseph Fewsmith, *Dilemmas of Reform in China* (Armonk, N.Y.: M. E. Sharpe, 1994).

11. Richard Posner, *Public Intellectuals: A Study of Decline* (Cambridge, Mass.: Harvard University Press, 2001).

12. Anthropologist Adam Yuet Chau in a personal communication suggests the use of the term *cohort*.

13. Ezra F. Vogel, "From Friendship to Comradeship: The Change in Personal Relations in Communist China," *China Quarterly,* no. 21 (Jan.–Mar. 1965), pp. 54–55; for a discussion of individual dissent in the Mao era, see Merle Goldman, *Literary Dissent in Communist China* (Cambridge, Mass.: Harvard University Press, 1967).

14. Frederick Teiwes, "Establishment and Consolidation of the New Regime," in Roderick MacFarquhar and John K. Fairbank, eds., *The Cambridge History of China,* vol. 14, *The People's Republic,* part 1, *The Emergence of Revolutionary China 1949–1965* (New York: Cambridge University Press, 1987), p. 139.

15. Goldman, *Sowing the Seeds.*

16. T. H. Marshall, *Citizenship and Social Class* (Cambridge: Cambridge University Press, 1950); idem, *Class, Citizenship, and Social Development* (Garden City, N.Y.: Doubleday, 1964).

17. Catherine Keyser, *Professionalizing Research in Post-Mao China* (Armonk, N.Y.: M. E. Sharpe, 2003).

18. Geremie R. Barmé and Gloria Davies, "Have We Been Noticed Yet? Intellectual Contestation and the Chinese Web," in Gu and Goldman, *Chinese Intellectuals between State and Market,* pp. 75–108.

19. Merle Goldman and Elizabeth Perry, "Introduction: Political Citizenship in Modern China," in Merle Goldman and Elizabeth Perry, eds., *Changing Meanings of Citizenship in Modern China* (Cambridge, Mass.: Harvard University Press, 2002), p. 10.

20. Teresa Wright, "Intellectuals and the Politics of Protest: The Case of the China Democracy Party," in Gu and Goldman, *Chinese Intellectuals between State and Market,* pp. 158–180.

21. Elizabeth Perry, in a personal communication.

22. Andrew J. Nathan, *Chinese Democracy* (New York: Knopf, 1985), p. 49.

23. Ibid., p. 127.

24. Roger R. Thompson, *China's Local Councils in the Age of Constitutional Reform, 1898–1911* (Cambridge, Mass.: Council on East Asian Studies, Harvard University, 1995).

25. Joshua A. Fogel and Peter G. Zarrow, eds., *Imagining the People: Chinese Intellectuals and the Concept of Citizenship, 1890–1920* (Armonk, N.Y.: M. E. Sharpe, 1997), pp. 4–6.

26. Ibid., pp. 20, 19, 25.

27. Ibid., p. 29.

28. Robert Culp, "Articulating Citizenship: Civic Education and Student Poli-

tics in Southeast China, 1912–37" (Ph.D. diss., Cornell University, 1999), pp. 1–28.

29. Don C. Price, "From Civil Society to Party Government: Models of the Citizen's Role in the Late Qing," in Fogel and Zarrow, *Imagining the People*, pp. 159–160.

30. Goldman, *Sowing the Seeds.*

31. Liu Xiaobo, "Modern Chinese Intellectuals and Politics—Part V," *Cheng Ming* (Hong Kong), no. 143 (Sept. 1989), pp. 88–90, translation in JPRS-CAR-90-006, Jan. 25, 1990, p. 72.

32. Liu Xiaobo, "Contemporary Chinese Intellectuals and Politics," *Cheng Ming* (Hong Kong), no. 141 (July 1989), pp. 74–77, translation in JPRS-CAR-89-107, Oct. 31, 1989, p. 53.

33. Liu Xiaobo, "China's Contemporary Intellectuals and Politics," *Cheng Ming* (Hong Kong), no. 146 (Dec. 1989), pp. 53–55, translation in JPRS-CAR-90-020, Mar. 14, 1990, p. 62.

34. Ibid.

35. Liu Xiaobo, "Contemporary Chinese Intellectuals and Politics, Part XIII," *Cheng Ming* (Hong Kong), no. 156 (Sept. 1990), pp. 56–58, translation in JPRS-CAR-91-001, Jan. 8, 1991, p. 60.

36. Ibid., pp. 60, 61.

37. Liu Xiaobo, "Contemporary Chinese Intellectuals and Politics, Part VI," *Cheng Ming* (Hong Kong), no. 144 (Oct. 1989), pp. 68–70, translation in JPRS-CAR-90-011, Feb. 12, 1990, p. 8.

38. Seymour Martin Lipset, "Some Social Requisites of Democracy: Economic Development and Political Legitimacy," *American Political Science Review*, vol. 53, no. 1 (Mar. 1959), pp. 69–105.

39. Bruce Dickson, *Red Capitalists in China: The Party, Private Entrepreneurs, and Political Change* (New York: Cambridge University Press, 2003).

40. Wang Renzhi, "On Opposing Bourgeois Liberalization," *Qiushi*, no. 3 (Feb. 15, 1990), translation in FBIS-CHI-90-037, Feb. 23, 1990, p. 15.

41. Jürgen Habermas, *The Structural Transformation of the Public Sphere: An Inquiry into a Category of Bourgeois Society,* trans. Thomas Burger, with the assistance of Frederick Lawrence (Cambridge, Mass.: MIT Press, 1989), pp. 31–43.

42. Mary Backus Rankin, "Some Observations on a Chinese Public Sphere," *Modern China*, vol. 19, no. 2 (Apr. 1993), p. 160.

43. Ibid.

44. Ibid., pp. 160–162.

45. William T. Rowe, *Hankow: Conflict and Community in a Chinese City, 1796–1895* (Stanford: Stanford University Press, 1989).

46. David Strand, *Rickshaw Beijing: City People and Politics in the 1920s* (Berkeley: University of California Press, 1989).

47. William T. Rowe, "The Problem of 'Civil Society' in Late Imperial China," *Modern China*, vol. 19, no. 2 (Apr. 1993), p. 142.

48. Edward Gu and Merle Goldman, "Introduction: The Transformation of the Relationship between Chinese Intellectuals and the State," in Gu and Goldman, *Chinese Intellectuals between State and Market*, p. 9.

49. Habermas, *Structural Transformation*, p. 231, quoted in ibid.

50. Marina Svensson, *The Chinese Conception of Human Rights: The Debate on Human Rights in China, 1898–1949* (Lund, Sweden: Lund University, 1996), pp. 154–155.

51. "China's Internet Population Hits 94 Million, but Growth Is Slowing," Agence France-Presse (Hong Kong), Jan. 19, 2005.

52. Michael Chase and James Mulvenon, *You've Got Dissent! Chinese Dissident Use of the Internet and Beijing's Counter Strategies* (Santa Monica: Rand, 2002).

53. Wright, "Intellectuals and the Politics of Protest."

54. Murray Scot Tanner, "China Rethinks Unrest," *Washington Quarterly* (Summer 2004), pp. 137–156.

55. David Strand, "Protest in Beijing: Civil Society and Public Sphere in China," *Problems of Communism*, vol. 39, no. 3 (May–Jun. 1990), p. 2.

56. Timothy Brook, "Auto-Organization in Chinese Society," in Timothy Brook and B. Michael Frolic, eds., *Civil Society in China* (Armonk, N.Y.: M. E. Sharpe, 1997), pp. 44–45.

57. Ibid., p. 29.

58. B. Michael Frolic, "State-Led Civil Society," in Brook and Frolic, *Civil Society in China*, pp. 48–49.

59. Heath B. Chamberlain, "Civil Society with Chinese Characteristics?" *China Journal*, no. 39 (Jan. 1998), pp. 70–71.

60. Steven Mufson, "Fragile Civil Society Takes Root in Chinese Reform," *Washington Post*, Jun. 4, 1996, p. A13.

61. Andrew G. Walder, *Popular Protest in the 1989 Democracy Movement* (Hong Kong: Institute of Asia-Pacific Studies, Chinese University of Hong Kong, 1992).

62. Frolic, "State-led Civil Society," pp. 46–47.

1. Democracy Wall

1. Martin King Whyte, "Prospects for Democratization in China," *Problems of Communism*, vol. 41, no. 3 (May–June 1992), p. 65.

2. Wei Jingsheng, *The Courage to Stand Alone: Letters from Prison and Other Writings*, ed. Kristina M. Torgeson (New York: Viking, 1997).

3. Guobin Yang, "The Liminal Effects of Social Movements: Red Guards and the

Transformation of Identity," *Sociological Forum,* vol. 15, no. 3 (Sept. 2000), p. 393.

4. Wang Juntao, interview with the author, Cambridge, Mass., 1994.

5. Xia Tianyang, "Idealism and Pragmatism Clash in Cultural Revolution Generation," *Beijing qingnian bao,* Apr. 6, 1995, p. 4, translation in FBIS-CHI-95-116, June 16, 1995, p. 39.

6. Sebastian Heilmann, *Turning Away from the Cultural Revolution: Political Grass-Roots Activism in the Mid-Seventies* (Stockholm: Center for Pacific Asia Studies, Stockholm University, 1996), p. 30.

7. Ibid., pp. 31–32.

8. Ba Jin, *Random Thoughts* (Hong Kong: Joint Publications, 1984), p. xvi.

9. Ibid., pp. xvi, 103, 76.

10. Gregor Benton and Alan Hunter, eds., *Wild Lily, Prairie Fire* (Princeton: Princeton University Press, 1995), pp. 19–20.

11. Marina Svensson, *The Chinese Conception of Human Rights: The Debate on Human Rights in China, 1898–1949* (Lund, Sweden: Lund University, 1996), pp. 295–296.

12. Roger Garside, *Coming Alive: China after Mao* (New York: McGraw-Hill, 1981), pp. 223–225.

13. Yan Hong, "An Account of Democracy Wall in Beijing," *Reference News for the Masses,* no. 3 (Feb. 1979), p. 2, translation in *Chinese Law and Government,* vol. 13, nos. 3–4 (Fall/Winter 1980–1981), pp. 97–105.

14. Garside, *Coming Alive,* p. 212.

15. Andrew J. Nathan, *Chinese Democracy* (New York: Alfred A. Knopf, 1985), p. 107.

16. "Fervently Support the Publication of the Article 'Long Live the People' on December 21, 1978," translation in *Chinese Law and Government,* vol. 14, no. 3 (Fall 1981), p. 19.

17. "Democracy Wall Prisoners," *Asia Watch,* vol. 5, no. 6 (Mar. 28, 1993), p. 7.

18. Benton and Hunter, *Wild Lily, Prairie Fire,* p. 239.

19. Xu Wenli, interview on *The Connection,* WBUR (Boston), Jan. 13, 2003.

20. "An Interview with Xu Wenli," translation in *Chinese Law and Government,* vol. 13, nos. 3–4 (Fall/Winter 1980–1981), p. 131.

21. Benton and Hunter, *Wild Lily, Prairie Fire,* p. 189.

22. "Democracy Wall Prisoners," p. 8.

23. Claude Widor, ed., *Documents on the Chinese Democratic Movement, 1978–1980,* 2 vols. (Hong Kong: Observer, 1981, 1984).

24. Lu Lin, "Inauguration and Suspension of the Journal," translation in *Chinese Law and Government,* vol. 13, nos. 3–4 (Fall/Winter 1980–1981), p. 159.

25. Merle Goldman, *Sowing the Seeds of Democracy in China* (Cambridge, Mass.: Harvard University Press, 1994).

26. Garside, *Coming Alive*, p. 243.

27. On intellectuals' debates about rights during the early twentieth century, see Marina Svennson, "A Hundred Year Long Debate," *China Rights Forum* (Spring 1999), pp. 20–25.

28. "Introducing April Fifth Forum," translation in *Chinese Law and Government*, vol. 13, nos. 3–4 (Fall/Winter 1980–1981), pp. 30–31.

29. "Introducing Seek Truth Journal," translation in *Chinese Law and Government*, vol. 13, nos. 3–4 (Fall/Winter 1980–1981), pp. 32–33.

30. "Introducing Spring of Peking," translation in *Chinese Law and Government*, vol. 13, nos. 3–4 (Fall/Winter 1980–1981), pp. 37–38.

31. "Announcement Soliciting Contributions by China Human Rights [Journal]," translation in *Chinese Law and Government*, vol. 13, nos. 3–4 (Fall/Winter 1980–1981), p. 61.

32. Garside, *Coming Alive*, p. 431.

33. Widor, *Documents on the Chinese Democratic Movement*, vol. 1, p. 421.

34. Ibid., pp. 421–422.

35. Garside, *Coming Alive*, p. 434.

36. Ibid., p. 228.

37. "Interview with Xu Wenli," p. 138.

38. "Queries on Vice-Premier Deng Xiaoping's Answers to Questions Raised by U.S. Newsmen," translation in *Chinese Law and Government*, vol. 14, no. 3 (Fall 1981), p. 17.

39. Ming Di, "Democracy in the Show Window," translation in *Chinese Law and Government*, vol. 14, no. 3 (Fall 1981), p. 112.

40. "Interview with Xu Wenli," pp. 138, 134, 135.

41. Wang Juntao, interview with the author, Cambridge, Mass., 1994.

42. George Black and Robin Munro, *Black Hands of Beijing: Lives of Defiance in China's Democratic Movement* (New York: John Wiley, 1993), pp. 5–20.

43. Ibid., pp. 33–36.

44. "Students of the No. 1 Branch School of Beijing Teachers' College Won a Victory in Their Strike," *Beijing zhichun*, no. 3 (Feb. 1979), translation in *Chinese Law and Government*, vol. 13, nos. 3–4 (Fall/Winter 1980–1981), pp. 127–128.

45. Garside, *Coming Alive*, pp. 219, 227–228.

46. Benton and Hunter, *Wild Lily, Prairie Fire*, p. 229.

47. "Dissident Tells It All," in T. C. Chang, C. F. Chen, and Y. T. Lin, comps., *Catalog of Chinese Underground Literatures* (Taipei: Institute of Current China Studies, 1982), vol. 2, p. 230.

48. Isabella Stasi Castriota Scanderbeg, "Forgotten Champion of the Outcasts," *China Rights Forum* (Fall 1998), p. 44.

49. Law Research Group, China Human Rights League, "What Actually Hap-

pened in Fu Yuehua's Case," translation in *Chinese Law and Government,* vol. 14, no. 3 (Fall 1981), pp. 81–87.

50. "Joint Statement by Seven Journals," *Tansuo* (Jan. 1979), translation in *Chinese Law and Government,* vol. 13, nos. 3–4 (Fall/Winter 1980–1981), pp. 74–75.

51. Deng Xiaoping, "Uphold the Four Cardinal Principles," in *Selected Works, 1975–1982* (Beijing: Foreign Languages Press, 1984), pp. 182, 183.

52. Benton and Hunter, *Wild Lily, Prairie Fire,* p. 246.

53. Ibid., p. 240.

54. Black and Munro, *Black Hands of Beijing,* p. 52; Widor, *Documents on the Chinese Democratic Movement,* vol. 2, pp. 75–76.

55. Black and Munro, *Black Hands of Beijing,* p. 53.

56. Benton and Hunter, *Wild Lily, Prairie Fire,* p. 262.

57. Ibid., p. 229.

58. Yan Jiaqi, *Toward a Democratic China: The Intellectual Autobiography of Yan Jiaqi,* trans. David S. K. Hong and Denis C. Mair (Honolulu: University of Hawaii Press, 1992), p. 43.

2. The Establishment of an Independent Political Organization in the 1980s

1. See Zhidong Hao, *Intellectuals at a Crossroads* (Albany: State University of New York Press, 2003).

2. "China: Defense Statement of Chen Ziming," *Asia Watch,* vol. 4, no. 18 (June 10, 1992), p. 7.

3. Ibid.

4. George Black and Robin Munro, *Black Hands of Beijing: Lives of Defiance in China's Democracy Movement* (New York: John Wiley, 1993), pp. 82, 93; "Rough Justice in Beijing," *News from Asia Watch* (Jan. 17, 1991), p. 21.

5. Black and Munro, *Black Hands of Beijing,* p. 55.

6. Wang Juntao, interview with the author, Cambridge, Mass., 1994.

7. During his first four months in prison after the 1989 demonstrations, Chen wrote a manuscript of 250,000 characters, later published as *Chen Ziming fansi shinian gaige* [Reflection on Ten Years of Reform] (Hong Kong: Dangdai yuekan, 1992), p. 510.

8. Ibid., pp. 506, 507, 508–509.

9. Ibid., pp. 511, 512, 513.

10. Kung Po, "Summary of the Student Election Campaign at Beijing University," *Cheng Ming* (Hong Kong), no. 41 (Apr. 1981), pp. 87–90, translation in JPRS 78012, *China Report: Political, Sociological, and Military Affairs,* no. 189 (May 6, 1981), pp. 81–89.

11. Wang Juntao, interview with the author, Cambridge, Mass., 1994.

12. Hu Ping et al., eds., *Kaituo: Beida xueyun wenxian* [Opening Up: Documents on the Student Movement at Peking University] (Hong Kong: Tianyuan shuwu, 1990), p. 84.

13. Ibid., pp. 85, 87.

14. Ibid.

15. Ibid., pp. 108, 109.

16. Jian Jun, "Yijiubalingnian Beida jingxuan fengchao" [The Storm of the 1980 Elections at Peking University], *Zhongguo zhichun* [China Spring], no. 84 (May 1990), p. 32.

17. Ibid., pp. 33, 34.

18. Wang Juntao, "Election Manifesto," in "Rough Justice in Beijing," p. 12.

19. Wang Juntao, interview with the author, Cambridge, Mass., 1994.

20. "Rough Justice in Beijing," p. 20.

21. Wang Juntao, interview with the author, Cambridge, Mass., 1994.

22. "China: Defense Statement of Chen Ziming," p. 9.

23. For more discussion on the 1989 Tiananmen demonstrations, see Merle Goldman, *Sowing the Seeds of Democracy in China* (Cambridge, Mass.: Harvard University Press, 1994), pp. 303–337.

24. Black and Munro, *Black Hands of Beijing*, p. 178.

25. Ibid., p. 222.

26. Ibid., p. 193.

27. "Declaration of the Capital Liaison Group, May 25, 1989," in "Rough Justice in Beijing," p. 30.

28. Black and Munro, *Black Hands of Beijing*, p. 223.

29. Ibid., p. 230.

30. Ibid., p. 223.

31. Wang Juntao, interview with the author, Cambridge, Mass., 1994.

32. The term *zone of indifference,* to refer to a situation in a totalitarian regime whereby "political power on its own volition does not try to penetrate or control," appears in the introduction to Tang Tsou's *The Cultural Revolution and Post-Mao Reforms: A Historical Perspective* (Chicago: University of Chicago Press, 1986), p. xxiv.

3. The Emergence of Unofficial Political Movements in the 1990s

1. Ding Zilin, "Hardship Years," trans. Sophie Beach, *China Rights Forum* (Summer/Fall 2000), p. 27.

2. "Wu Zuguang Calls for Reversal of Verdict on June 4 Incident," *Sing Tao Jih Pao* (Hong Kong), Mar. 14, 1997, p. A4, translation in FBIS-CHI-97-073, Mar. 17, 1997.

3. Ding Zilin, "Documenting Death—Reflections after Ten Years," *http://www.hrichina.org/june4–10yr/death.htm*.

4. Ibid..

5. Ding Zilin, interview with Rebecca Mackinnon, CNN bureau chief, early spring 1999, *http://edition.cnn.com/WORLD/asiapcf/9906/02/tiananmen/Mackinnon/ding.zilin.html*.

6. Cecile Kung, "Chen Ziming's Mother Plans Protest March," *Hong Kong Standard*, Oct. 18, 1995, p. 7, in FBIS-CHI-95-201, Oct. 18, 1995, p. 23; Amy Liu, "Chen Ziming's Wife Arrested after Protest," *Hong Kong Standard*, Oct. 23, 1995, p. 6, in FBIS-CHI-95-204, Oct. 23, 1995, pp. 19–20.

7. Geoffrey Crothall and John Kohut, "Students Hold Silent Protest to Remember Dead," *South China Morning Post*, June 4, 1994, p. 8, in FBIS-CHI-94-108, June 6, 1994, p. 16.

8. Agence France-Presse, May 29, 1996, translation in FBIS-CHI-96-104, May 30, 1996.

9. Benjamin Kang Lim, "Relatives of 1989 Tiananmen Victims Oppose Li Peng," Reuters, Feb. 15, 1998.

10. "Calls for a Rights-Centered Citizens Movement," *China Rights Forum* (Spring 1999), p. 4.

11. "Declaration on Civil Rights and Freedom," *China Rights Forum* (Spring 1999), pp. 5, 7, 8, 9.

12. "Declaration on Civil Rights and Social Justice," *China Rights Forum* (Spring 1999), p. 10.

13. Ibid., p. 11.

14. Ibid., p. 13.

15. "Jiang Qisheng: Arrested for Keeping the June Fourth Spirit Alive," *China Rights Forum* (Fall 1999), p. 9.

16. Ding Zilin, "Persistence Above All," trans. Victi Ho, *China Rights Forum*, no. 2 (2002), p. 48.

17. "Jiang Qisheng," p. 9.

18. "A Procedural Nightmare: Jiang Qisheng on Trial," *China Rights Forum* (Winter 1999–2000), p. 12.

19. Daniel Kwan, "Democracy Activists Apply to Stage Rally," *South China Morning Post*, May 20, 1999.

20. "Former Tiananmen Student Leader amongst Chinese Dissidents Arrested," Agence France-Presse, July 17, 1999.

21. Jiang Qisheng, "My Statement of Defense," *China Rights Forum* (Spring 2001), pp. 27–28.

22. "For Mr. Mo, Court Win Can Mean Jail," *The Age* (Australia), Jan. 20, 2003, *http://www.theage.com.au/articles/2003*.

23. Mo Shaoping, "Statement of Defense," *China Rights Forum* (Spring 2001), pp. 28–29, 58.

24. Ibid.

25. "Support the Tiananmen Mothers," *China Rights Forum* (Summer/Fall 2000), p. 12.

26. Ding Zilin, "Hardship Years," p. 27.

27. "China Detains 2 Dissidents Ahead of Anniversary," Associated Press, June 2, 2002.

28. "Mothers Urge Beijing to Clear the Names of Tiananmen Victims," Agence France-Presse, June 4, 2002.

29. John Schrecker, *The Chinese Revolution in Historical Perspective,* 2nd ed. (Westport, Conn.: Praeger, 2004), pp. 145–148.

30. Merle Goldman, *China's Intellectuals: Advise and Dissent* (Cambridge, Mass.: Harvard University Press, 1981).

31. "Text of the Peace Charter," *Human Rights Watch: Asia,* vol. 6, no. 2 (Mar. 11, 1994), pp. 15–17.

32. Qin Yongming, "Peace Charter (Draft)," *Lien Ho Pao* (Taipei), Nov. 16–18, 1993, translation in JPRS-CAR-94-004, Jan. 13, 1994, p. 1.

33. Dan Biers, "Dissidents Seek 'Peace Charter' for Non-Violent Political Change," Associated Press, Nov. 15, 1993.

34. Agence France-Presse, Oct. 11, 1994, translation in FBIS-CHI-94-196, Oct. 11, 1994, p. 40.

35. Chan Wai-fong, "Shanghai Rejects Legal Status for Human Rights Group," *South China Morning Post,* Apr. 12, 1994, in FBIS-CHI-94-070, Apr. 12, 1994, p. 39.

36. Chen Ching, "Dissident Ma Shaohua's Book Discussing Causes for Drastic Changes in Eastern Europe Banned," *Ming Pao* (Hong Kong), Nov. 29, 1993, p. A10, translation in BBC Summary of World Broadcasts, FE/1868/G, Dec. 10, 1993.

37. Geoffrey Crothall and Willy Wo-Lap Lam, "Dissident Bao Ge Explains Aims of Signature Campaign," *South China Morning Post,* Mar. 30, 1994, pp. 1, 10, in FBIS-CHI-94-061, Mar. 30, 1994, pp. 20–21.

38. "Police Arrest Dissident as Hosokawa Arrives in Shanghai," Associated Press, Mar. 21, 1994.

39. "Shanghai Dissident Yang Zhou Sentenced to Three Years," Agence France-Presse, Oct. 11, 1994, translation in FBIS-CHI-94-196, Oct. 11, 1994, pp. 40–41.

40. Daniel Kwan, "Jiang Zemin: Dissidents' League 'Biggest Threat,'" *South China Morning Post,* Mar. 27, 1995, pp. 1, 7, in FBIS-CHI-95-058, Mar. 27, 1995, p. 23.

41. Willy Wo-Lap Lam, "State Blocks Petition Signature Campaign," *South China Morning Post,* Mar. 8, 1994, p. 8, in FBIS-CHI-94-045, Mar. 8, 1994, pp. 14–15.

42. "League for the Protection of the Rights of the Working People of the People's Republic of China," *Human Rights Watch: Asia,* vol. 6, no. 2 (Mar. 11, 1994), p. 10.

43. Cary Huang, "Major Cities to Ban Petitions, Gatherings," *Hong Kong Standard,* Oct. 17, 1994, p. 1, in FBIS-CHI-94-200, Oct. 17, 1994, p. 45.

44. John Kohut, "Dissident Wang Dan Rests after Interview Session," *South China Morning Post,* Feb. 19, 1993, p. 12, in FBIS-CHI-93-032, Feb. 19, 1993, p. 11.

45. Wang Dan, "An Open Letter to My Friends at Home and Abroad Who Showed Their Concern for Me," *Ming Pao* (Hong Kong), Mar. 4, 1993, p. 66, translation in FBIS-CHI-93-041, Mar. 4, 1993, p. 9.

46. Willy Wo-Lap Lam, "Wang Makes a Living as Freelance Writer," *South China Morning Post,* July 3, 1993, p. 8.

47. Agence France-Presse, Dec. 7, 1994, translation in FBIS-CHI-94-235, Dec. 7, 1994, pp. 14–15.

48. Willy Wo-Lap Lam, "Dissidents Sign Protest Letter on Wang Dan," *South China Morning Post,* Dec. 9, 1994, p. 11, in FBIS-CHI-94-237, Dec. 9, 1994, p. 10.

49. Patrick Tyler, "U.S. Rights Official Meets with Leading Chinese Dissident," *New York Times,* Feb. 28, 1994, p. 2; Patrick Tyler, "China Says It Holds Dissident to Check 'New Crimes,'" *New York Times,* Apr. 5, 1994, p. 6.

50. "Full Text of the Verdict on the Wei Jingsheng Case," *Ming Pao* (Hong Kong), Dec. 16, 1995, translation in BBC Summary of World Broadcasts, Part 3, Asia-Pacific, FE/D2489/G, Dec. 17, 1995.

51. Kyodo News Agency, Mar. 17, 1993, translation in FBIS-CHI-93-050, Mar. 17, 1993, pp. 38–39.

52. Xu Liangying, "Chinese Physicists' Sense of Social Responsibility," speech prepared for the conference "Physicists in the Postwar Political Arena: Comparative Perspectives," University of California, Berkeley, Jan. 22–24, 1998.

53. Xu Liangying, "Reflections on the Occasion of the Tenth Anniversary of June Fourth," *China Rights Forum* (Summer 1999), pp. 46–47.

54. Ibid., pp. 46–47, 49.

55. Editorial Report, "Official Journal Closed for Publishing Pro-Democracy Articles," BBC Summary of World Broadcasts, FE/1581/B2, Jan. 8, 1993.

56. Ibid.

57. *Weilai yu fazhan,* no. 5 (Oct. 5, 1992), pp. 7–9, translation in FBIS-CHI-93-005, Jan. 8, 1993, p. 17.

58. Ibid., p. 18.

59. Ibid., p. 19.

60. Editorial Report, "Official Journal Closed."

61. Willy Wo-Lap Lam, "Intellectuals Throw Down Gauntlet; Alarm at Challenge to Leaders," *South China Morning Post,* Mar. 11, 1994, p. 1.

62. Patrick Tyler, "7 Chinese Intellectuals Appeal for End to Political Repression," *New York Times,* Mar. 11, 1994, p. 1; "'Climbing a Tree to Catch a Fish,'" *New York Times,* Mar. 11, 1994, p. 10.

63. "Climbing a Tree to Catch a Fish," p. 10.

64. Ibid.

65. China News Agency, Sept. 14, 1994, in FBIS-CHI-94-183, Sept. 21, 1994, p. 77.

66. Patrick Tyler, "12 Intellectuals Petition China on Corruption," *New York Times,* Feb. 26, 1995, p. 1.

67. The full text of the petition of Feb. 25, 1995, is in *Lien Ho Pao* (Taipei), Feb. 27, 1995, translation in FBIS-CHI-95-040, Mar. 1, 1995, pp. 16–18.

68. Yang Qingjuan, "Exercise Modern Social Control to Curtail Corruption," *Shehui,* Nov. 1994, pp. 30–33, translation in FBIS-CHI-95-017, Jan. 26, 1995, p. 11.

69. The full text of the petition is in *Lien Ho Pao* (Taipei), May 18, 1995, p. 10, translation in FBIS-CHI-95-086, May 18, 1995, p. 13.

70. Ibid., p. 14.

71. Patrick Tyler, "China Arrests Prodemocracy Petitioner," *New York Times,* May 20, 1995, p. 4.

72. Ibid.

4. Ideological Diversity Challenges the Party

1. Feng Chongyi, "The Party-State, Liberalism and Social Democracy: The Debate on China's Future," in Edward Gu and Merle Goldman, eds., *Chinese Intellectuals between State and Market* (London: RoutledgeCurzon, 2004), pp. 223–260.

2. Indira A. R. Lakshman, "China's Reforms Turn Costly," *Boston Globe,* July 22, 2002, p. A9. *Shehui lanpi shu 2002 nian: Zhongguo shehui xingshi: fenxi yu yuce* [Blue Book of Chinese Society, 2002: Analysis of the Chinese Social Situation, Its Prospects] (Beijing: Shehui kexue wenxian chubanshe, 2002).

3. Perry Link, " The Anaconda in the Chandelier: Censorship in China Today," *New York Review of Books,* Apr. 11, 2002.

4. *Cheng Ming* (Hong Kong), no. 175, May 1, 1992, translation in FBIS-CHI-92-084, Apr. 30, 1992, pp. 15–16.

5. Li Ren, "The Division of Marxism into Factions Is Essentially a Repudiation of Marxism," *Zhenli de zhuiqiu,* Nov. 11, 1995, pp. 26–30, translation in FBIS-CHI-96-036, Feb. 22, 1996, pp. 14–17.

6. Ibid., p. 16.

7. Li Chongfu, "A Firm Belief Should Be Based on a Scientific World Outlook,"

Renmin ribao, Dec. 12, 1990, p. 5, translation in FBIS-CHI-90-248, Dec. 26, 1990, p. 32.

8. Gu Jinping, "Carry Forward the Tradition of Studying Marxism Initiated by Mao Zedong," *Renmin ribao,* Dec. 26, 1990, p. 5, translation in FBIS-CHI-90-250, Dec. 28, 1990, p. 31.

9. *Dangdai sichao,* Apr. 20, 1991, quoted in Wen Yu, ed., *Zhongguo "zuo" huo* [China's Leftist Scourge] (Beijing: Chaohua chubanshe, 1993), p. 531.

10. *Zhenli de zhuiqiu,* July 11, 1991, quoted in Wen Yu, *Zhongguo "zuo" huo,* p. 532.

11. Reprinted in *Lishi de chaoliu* [*Historical Trends*] (Beijing: Zhongguo renmin daxue chubanshe, 1992), p. 151.

12. Ibid., p. 152.

13. Geremie Barmé, *In the Red: On Contemporary Chinese Culture* (New York: Columbia University Press, 1999).

14. Wang Renzhi, "On Opposing Bourgeois Liberalization," *Qiushi,* no. 3, Feb. 16, 1990, translation in FBIS-CHI-90-037, Feb. 23, 1990, p. 12.

15. Joseph Fewsmith, *China since Tiananmen: The Politics of Transition* (New York: Cambridge University Press, 2001), p. 45.

16. Willy Wo-Lap Lam, "Deng Xiaoping Bars Leftists from Top Posts," *South China Morning Post,* Jan. 4, 1992, p. 8, in FBIS-CHI-92-003, Jan. 6, 1992, p. 25; John Kohut and Willy Wo-Lap Lam, "Politburo Session Upholds 'Deng Xiaoping Line,'" *South China Morning Post,* Mar. 13, 1992, pp. 1, 10, in FBIS-CHI-92-050, Mar. 13, 1992, p. 18.

17. Nan Ping, "Jiang Zemin Was Challenged at the 14th Party Congress," *Cheng Ming* (Hong Kong), no. 182, Dec. 1, 1992, pp. 24–26, translation in FBIS-CHI-92-236, Dec. 8, 1992, p. 26.

18. "Talks in Wuchang, Shenzhen, Zhuhai and Shanghai," Jan. 18–Feb. 21, 1992, in Deng Xiaoping, *Selected Works, vol. 3 (1982–1992)* (Beijing: Foreign Languages Press, 1994), p. 363.

19. Bruce Dickson, email correspondence, July 7, 2002. See Bruce Dickson, *Red Capitalists in China: The Party, Private Entrepreneurs, and Political Change* (New York: Cambridge University Press, 2003), pp. 89–115.

20. Qin Liufang, "No Equivocation Possible about the Class Character of Private Enterprise Owners," *Zhenli de zhuiqiu,* Nov. 11, 1994, pp. 21–33, translation in FBIS-CHI-95-009, Jan. 13, 1995, p. 18.

21. Ibid., p. 19.

22. Jiang Nanchun, "What Is Causing Our Corruption," *Zhenli de zhuiqiu,* no. 10, Oct. 11, 1995, pp. 23–26, translation in FBIS-CHI-95-235, Dec. 7, 1995, p. 31.

23. Ibid., p. 32.

24. Ma Jian, "The Marxist Line of Party Building Must be Upheld," *Zhenli de zhuiqiu,* Sept. 11, 1996, pp. 30–33, translation in FBIS-CHI-96-222, Nov. 18, 1996, p. 1.

25. Ibid., pp. 1, 2, 5.

26. Wen Di, "Was It a Failure of Marxism or the Bankruptcy of Revisionism," *Dangdai sichao,* no. 6, Dec. 20, 1996, pp. 52–59, translation in FBIS-CHI-97-028, Feb. 12, 1997, p. 3.

27. Zhou Hao, "The Core of Politics—Political Direction and Political Stance," *Zhenli de zhuiqiu,* no. 3, Mar. 1996, pp. 7–11, translation in FBIS-CHI-96-143, July 24, 1996, p. 19.

28. Ibid., p. 21.

29. *Zhenli de zhuiqiu,* no. 15, Dec. 11, 1996, pp. 5–13, translation in BBC Summary of World Broadcasts, FE-D2838, Feb. 8, 1997, pp. G/2–3.

30. Ibid., p. G/4.

31. Fewsmith, *China since Tiananmen,* pp. 169–179. Also see Feng Chen, "An Unfinished Battle in China: The Leftist Criticism of the Reform and the Third Thought Emancipation," *China Quarterly,* no. 158 (June 1999), pp. 447–467.

32. Xing Bensi, "Never Waver in Upholding Marxism," *Renmin ribao,* June 6, 1996, p. 9, translation in FBIS-CHI-96-130, July 5, 1996, pp. 25–27.

33. Ibid., pp. 27, 28.

34. Willy Wo-Lap Lam, "Jiang Accuses Leftists of Exploiting Anxieties," *South China Morning Post,* July 31, 1997, p. 11.

35. Zhou Yonghao, Chen Yongzhang, and Hou Xiaoli, "Public Ownership as Mainstay and Enthusiasm of Working Class as Masters," *Dangdai sichao,* no. 3, June 20, 1997, pp. 17–22, translation in FBIS-CHI-97-251, Sept. 9, 1997, p. 1.

36. Gong Pu, "Where Uprightness Exists, Evil Cannot Interfere," *Dangdai sichao,* no. 3, June 20, 1997, pp. 35–38, translation in FBIS-CHI-97-251, Sept. 9, 1997, pp. 2–3.

37. Qu Zhihong and Wang Li, "The Source of the Undercurrent in Publishing Circles," Xinhua News Agency, Aug. 26, 1993, in FBIS-CHI-93-178, Sept. 16, 1993, p. 17.

38. *Lishi de chaoliu,* p. 17.

39. Ibid., pp. 20, 21.

40. Ibid., pp. 143–157.

41. Ibid., p. 149.

42. Lu Ming-Sheng, "Inside Story of How 'Historical Trends' Was Banned," *Cheng Ming* (Hong Kong), no. 177, July 1, 1992, pp. 33–34, translation in FBIS-CHI-92-130, July 7, 1992, p. 19.

43. Ibid., p. 21.

44. William Alford, "Double-Edged Swords Cut Both Ways: Law and Legitimacy in the People's Republic of China," *Daedalus*, vol. 122, no. 2 (Spring 1993), p. 58.

45. "Editor Sues University Leaders over Book Ban," Agence France-Presse, June 15, 1992, translation in FBIS-CHI-92-116, June 16, 1992, p. 16.

46. "'Historical Trends' Symposium Hears Warning of 'Anti-Rightism,'" *Ming Pao* (Hong Kong), June 15, 1992, translation in BBC Summary of World Broadcasts, FE/1410/B2, June 18, 1992.

47. Published in Taiyuan by Shuhai chubanshe in October 1992.

48. Lin Tsui-feng, "Chief Editor of Memorandum on Guarding against 'Leftism' Supports Deng Xiaoping's Thinking on Reform," *Ming Pao* (Hong Kong), Dec. 30, 1992, p. 7, translation in FBIS-CHI-93-002, Jan. 5, 1993, p. 17.

49. John Kohut, "China Notebook," *South China Morning Post*, Jan. 3, 1993, p. 13, in FBIS-CHI-93-002, Jan. 5, 1993, p. 17.

50. Zhao Shilin, ed., *Fang "zuo" beiwanglu* [Memorandum against "Leftism"] (Taiyuan: Shuhai chubanshe, 1992), p. 81.

51. Hu Jiwei (p. 84) Tang Dacheng (p. 124), and Sun Changjiang (pp. 102–103), ibid.

52. William Brent, "Book Attacking Hardline Marxism Reportedly Banned," Agence France-Presse, Dec. 9, 1992, translation in FBIS-CHI-92-237, Dec. 9, 1992, p. 16.

53. China News Agency, Oct. 27, 1992, in FBIS-CHI-92-209, Oct. 28, 1992, p. 25.

54. "Highlights of Banned Book on 'Disaster of Leftism'" (Hong Kong, n.p.), translation in FBIS-CHI-93-143, July 28, 1993, p. 16.

55. Ibid., p. 17.

56. Ibid.

57. Wen Yu, *Zhongguo "zuo" huo*, p. 541.

58. Ibid., p. 513.

59. Pan Chunliang and Yan Changgui, "China Must Be Vigilant When It Comes to Rightists, but the Important Thing Is to Guard against 'Leftists' and Study Comrade Deng Xiaoping's Discussions on the Anti-deviation Struggle," *Shehui kexue* (Shanghai), no. 5, May 15, 1994, pp. 7–11, translation in JPRS-CAR-94-045, Aug. 19, 1994, pp. 4–5, 6.

60. "Study Volume 3 of Selected Works of Deng Xiaoping, Promote the Building of a Socialist Democracy and Legal System," *Fazhi ribao*, Nov. 4, 1993, p. 1, translation in FBIS-CHI-93-222, Nov. 19, 1993, p. 37.

61. Sheryl WuDunn, "Bootleg Tape of Aide's Jab Is Hit in China," *New York Times*, May 31, 1992, p. 7.

62. Xinhua News Agency, June 14, 1992, in FBIS-CHI-92-115, June 15, 1992, p. 23.

63. Liu Xiangzhi, "On 'Leftism' and 'Rightism,'" *Jiefang ribao*, July 29, 1992, p. 6, translation in FBIS-CHI-92-153, Aug. 7, 1992, p. 14.

64. Willy Wo-Lap Lam, "Deng Expresses 'Anger' over Mao Celebrations," *South China Morning Post*, Jan. 12, 1994, p. 1, in FBIS-CHI-94-008, Jan. 12, 1994, p. 11.

65. Lo Ping and Li Tzu-ching, "Celebrities Oppose Mao Cult," *Cheng Ming* (Hong Kong), no. 192, Oct. 1, 1993, pp. 14–15, translation in FBIS-CHI-93-192, Oct. 6, 1993, p. 25.

66. Xinhua News Agency, Dec. 26, 1993, in FBIS-CHI-93-246, Dec. 27, 1993, p. 27.

67. Fewsmith, *China since Tiananmen*, pp. 75–156.

68. Ibid., pp. 145–151. Also see Fewsmith's review of *Disanshi yanjing kan Zhongguo* in *Journal of Contemporary China*, no. 7 (Fall 1994), pp. 100–104.

69. Lo Ping, "Will Beijing's Climate Change Very Soon?—Wan Li's View on Relaxation and the Book *Looking at China with a Third Eye*," *Cheng Ming* (Hong Kong), no. 203, Sept. 1, 1994, pp. 7–10, translation in FBIS-CHI-94-176, Sept. 12, 1994, p. 37.

70. "Former Cultural Minister Wang Meng Says 'Third Eye' Is a Strange Book," *Ming Pao* (Hong Kong), Sept. 25, 1994, p. 11, translation in FBIS-CHI-94-186, Sept. 26, 1994, p. 31.

71. Talk at the Fairbank Center by Tang Zhengyu, one of the authors of *China Can Say No*, Harvard University, July 1996.

72. Xiao Gongqin, "'Cultural Threat' Groundless," *China Daily*, Nov. 20, 1996, p. 4.

73. Cheung Yue-ching, "Authorities Change Attitude towards Book 'China Can Say No,'" *Ming Pao* (Hong Kong), Dec. 10, 1996, p. A12, translation in BBC Summary of World Broadcasts, FE/D2794/G, Dec. 13, 1996.

74. Talk at Fairbank Center by Cui Zhiyuan, Harvard University, Apr. 2, 2003.

75. Ibid.

76. *Yazhou zhoukan* [Asiaweek] (Hong Kong), May 26, 1996, p. 47.

77. Xinhua News Agency, Dec. 20, 2003, in FBIS-CHI-2003-1220, Dec. 22, 2003.

78. Wang Hui, *China's New Order* (Cambridge, Mass.: Harvard University Press, 2003), pp. 141–187.

79. Ibid., p. 145.

80. Ibid., p. 159.

81. Ibid., pp. 167, 180.

82. Ibid., pp. 186, 187.

83. Ibid., p. 178.

84. Susan Lawrence, "A Celebrity Critic," *Far Eastern Economic Review*, Oct. 22, 1998, p. 13.

85. Perry Link and Liu Binyan, "A Great Leap Backward," *New York Review of Books*, Oct. 8, 1998, p. 22.

86. Lawrence, "A Celebrity Critic," p. 14.

87. Link and Liu, "A Great Leap Backward," p. 23.

88. Seth Faison, "Shenzhen Journal: Hot-Selling Book Lights a Fire under the Chinese," *New York Times*, Nov. 6, 1998, p. 4.

89. Lawrence, "A Celebrity Critic," p. 13.

90. Link and Liu, "A Great Leap Backward," p. 20.

91. Ibid., pp. 21, 22.

92. Qin Hui, "Introduction: Social Justice and the Scholarly Community," in "China's Descent into a Quagmire by He Qinglian," ed. Lawrence Sullivan, *The Chinese Economy*, vol. 33, no. 3 (May–June 2000), p. 21.

93. He Qinglian, "A Socialist Free Lunch," chapter 1 in ibid., pp. 32, 41.

94. Ibid., p. 40.

95. Ibid., pp. 40–41, 49.

96. Ibid., p. 51.

97. He Qinglian, "Conflict of Interest—Differing Voices," *Huaxia wenzhai* (May 2003), translated by Kevin McCready.

98. Ibid.

99. James Kynge, "Policy Agents Fail to Silence Chinese Critic," *Financial Times*, July 17, 2000, p. 8.

5. The Flowering of Liberalism, 1997–1998

1. Su Shaozhi, *Zhongguo dalu zhengzhi tizhi gaige yanjiu* [Research on Mainland China's Political System Reform] (Taipei: Zhongguo wenhua daxue chubanshe, 2001), p. 182.

2. Jiang Zemin, "Hold High the Great Banner of Deng Xiaoping Theory for an All-Round Advancement of the Cause of Building Socialism with Chinese Characteristics into the 21st Century," *Beijing Review*, vol. 40, no. 40 (Oct. 6–12, 1997), pp. 16–18.

3. Ibid., p. 24.

4. Ibid., pp. 25, 24.

5. Willy Wo-Lap Lam, "Politburo to Be Voted in for First Time: Leap Forward for 'Inner-Party Democracy,'" *South China Morning Post*, Sept. 15, 1997.

6. Willy Wo-Lap Lam, "Congress in Grip of Frantic Poll Lobbying," *South China Morning Post*, Sept. 17, 1997.

7. Wang Huning, "Continue to Promote Political Structural Reform," *Renmin ribao*, Nov. 13, 1997, translation in FBIS-CHI-97-317, Nov. 18, 1997.

8. Tian Baichun, "Why Is It That Developing Socialist Democratic Politics Is Our Party's Consistent Goal?" *Qiushi*, no. 20, Oct. 16, 1997, pp. 45–46, translation in FBIS-CHI-98-051, Feb. 16, 1998.

9. Ibid.

10. Li Maoguan, "Party Leadership Emphasized in Building Socialist Politics with Chinese Characteristics," *Qiushi*, no. 24, Dec. 16, 1997, pp. 15–19, translation in FBIS-CHI-98-043, Feb. 15, 1998.

11. Ibid.

12. Jorge Svartzman, "Chinese Economist Relaunches Democracy Debate," Agence France-Presse, Aug. 6, 1997.

13. Jasper Becker, "The Academic Who Dared to Urge Change," *South China Morning Post*, Aug. 11, 1997, p. 9.

14. Ibid.

15. Shang Dewen, "Certain Questions and Fundamental Policies in Regard to China's Political System Reform," unpublished paper.

16. Ibid., p. 2.

17. Ibid., p. 4.

18. Ted Plafker, "Scholar Renews Call for Reforms," *South China Morning Post*, Oct. 30, 1997, p. 10.

19. Jasper Becker, "Academic Unveils Blueprint for Democracy," *South China Morning Post*, Aug. 6, 1997, p. 9.

20. Svartzman, "Chinese Economist Relaunches Democracy Debate."

21. Shang Dewen, "Certain Questions," p. 5.

22. Jasper Becker, "Professor Urges 'Democracy Zones' Trial," *South China Morning Post*, July 25, 1998, p. 7.

23. Pamela Pun, "Guangzhou Economist: 'Political Reform Is Indispensable,'" *Hong Kong Standard*, Aug. 13, 1997, p. 6, in FBIS-CHI-97-225, Aug. 14, 1997.

24. Ibid.

25. "China: Economist Says Market Economy Calls for Political Reform," Zhongguo xinwen she, Feb. 19, 1998, in FBIS-CHI-98-056, Mar. 4, 1998.

26. Ibid.

27. Chan Yee-hon, "Swift Reform Urged," *South China Morning Post*, May 19, 1998, p. 10.

28. Fong Tak-ho, "Liberal Icon and Jiang Zemin Critic Dies," *South China Morning Post*, Apr. 23, 2003, p. 4.

29. Liu Junning, "Farewell to a Courageous Thinker," *Asian Wall Street Journal*, May 14, 2003.

30. Reprinted in Qiu Shi, ed., *Jiefang wenxuan 1978–1998* [Liberation Literature 1978–1998] (Beijing: Jingji ribao chubanshe, 1998), pp. 1003, 1004 (rule of law), 1005 (rights of citizens).

31. Li Shenzhi, "Cong genbenshang shenhua gaige de sixiang" [Fundamentally Deepen Reform Thought]. Reprinted in Qiu Shi, *Jiefang wenxuan 1978–1998*, pp. 1237, 1239, 1240.

32. http://www.china-review.com/

33. Ibid.

34. "Ziyouzhuyi, dengjia guanxi he renquan." Reprinted in Mao Yushi, *Shui fang'ai womende zhifu?* [Who Bars Us from Getting Rich?] (Guangzhou: Guangdong jingji chubanshe, 1999), pp. 399–403.

35. Steven Mufson, "Debate Blossoms in Beijing Spring: Open Discussions of Reform Spread to Universities, Media," *Washington Post*, Apr. 19, 1998, p. A1.

36. Li Rui, "Accept Historic Lessons, Strengthen Inner-Party Democracy—Thoughts and Views on Guarding against 'Leftist Tendencies,'" *Gaige* (Chongqing), no. 1, Jan. 20, 1998, pp. 75–81, translation in FBIS-CHI-98-191, July 13, 1998.

37. Wang Yan, "Cujin shehui zhengzhi shenghuo de fazhihua," reprinted in Qiu Shi, *Jiefang wenxuan 1978–1998*, pp. 1160–1163.

38. "PRC State Council Official on Pace of Government Reform," Xinhua News Agency, May 12, 2000, in FBIS-CHI-2000-0512, May 15, 2000.

39. Wang Yan, "Cujin shehui zhengzhi shenghuo de fazhihua," p. 1160.

40. Ibid., pp. 1160–1163, 1161.

41. Ibid., pp. 1161, 1162, 1163.

42. Hu Weixi, "Sixiang ziyou yu minzhu zhengzhi," reprinted in Qiu Shi, *Jiefang wenxuan 1978–1998*, pp. 1173–1175.

43. Dong Yuyu and Shi, Binhai, eds., *Zhengzhi Zhongguo: Mianxiang xin tizhi xuanze de shidai* (Beijing: Jinri Zhongguo chubanshe, 1998); Qiu Shi, *Jiefang wenxuan 1978–1998*.

44. Bruce Dickson, *Red Capitalists in China: The Party, Private Entrepreneurs, and Prospects for Political Change* (New York: Cambridge University Press, 2003), pp. 106–107.

45. Hsia Wen-szu, "Intellectual Circles Should Be Kang Youwei and Liang Qichao and Promote Reforms—'Political China' and 'Current Political Situation Symposium' Urge Political Reforms," *Kaifang* (Hong Kong), no. 141, Sept. 3, 1998, pp. 11–13, translation in FBIS-CHI-98-254, Sept. 14, 1998.

46. Erik Eckholm, "After Signing Rights Pact, China Begins a Crackdown," *New York Times*, Oct. 27, 1998, p. 3.

47. Jiang Ping, "Zhengzhi tizhi gaige buneng huanxing," in Dong and Shi, *Zhengzhi Zhongguo*, pp. 1, 2.

48. Yu Keping, "Zouchu 'zhengzhi gaige—shehui wending' de liangnan jingdi," in Dong and Shi, *Zhengzhi Zhongguo*, pp. 49–53.

49. Ibid., pp. 50, 51, 52, 53.

50. Yu Keping, "Quanli zhengzhi, haishi gongyi zhengzhi" [Politics of Rights or Politics of Public Interests], in Dong and Shi, *Zhengzhi Zhongguo*, p. 284.

51. Dong Yuyu, "Tongguo zhengzhi tizhi gaige de fazhi zhilu," in Dong and Shi, *Zhengzhi Zhongguo*, pp. 60, 61, 62, 65, 66, 67, 68.

52. Zhang Ximing, "Xinwen fazhi yu shehui fazhan," in Dong and Shi, *Zhengzhi Zhongguo*, pp. 124–128.

53. Ibid., pp. 126, 128.

54. Ma Licheng, "Xinwen jiandu bu xing 'zi,'" in Dong and Shi, *Zhengzhi Zhongguo*, pp. 129–131.

55. Ibid., pp. 130, 131.

56. Zhu Huaxin, "Caogen minzhu," in Dong and Shi, *Zhengzhi Zhongguo*, pp. 352, 364, 353.

57. Wang Huning, "Jixu tuijin zhengzhi tizhi gaige," in Dong and Shi, *Zhengzhi Zhongguo*, pp. 15–18.

58. Ibid., pp. 16, 18.

59. Huang Zhong, "Zhengzhi tizhi gaige buneng zai wang hou tui: Zhonggong zhongyang dangxiao jiaoshou Wang Guixiu da wen lu" [Political Reform Can No Longer Be Delayed: An Interview with Prof. Wang Guixiu of the Central Party School], in Dong and Shi, *Zhengzhi Zhongguo*, pp. 288–292.

60. Ibid., pp. 290, 291.

61. Wang Guixiu, "'Youxuan zhi lu': Zhengzhi tizhi gaige bixu yu jingji tizhi gaige xiangshe yin" [The Best Choice: Political System Reform and Economic System Reform Should Take Place in Coordination with One Another], in Dong and Shi, *Zhengzhi Zhongguo*, pp. 293, 295, 299, 300.

62. Wang Guixiu, "Political System Reform Is a Great New Revolution," *Gongren ribao*, Mar. 25, 1998, pp. 1, 2, translated in FBIS-CHI-98-236, Aug. 24, 1998, p. 5.

63. Liu Junning, interview with the author, Cambridge, Mass., Oct. 19, 2001.

64. Qiu Shi, *Jiefang wenxuan 1978–1998*, p. 1135.

65. Liu Junning, interview with the author, Cambridge, Mass., Oct. 5, 2000.

66. Liu Junning, "Caichanquan de baozhang yu youxian zhengfu," in Qiu Shi, *Jiefang wenxuan 1978–1998*, p. 1169, 1170, 1171.

67. Ibid., p. 1172.

68. Liu Junning, "'Xuanba shehui' yu 'xuanju shehui,'" in Qiu Shi, *Jiefang wenxuan 1978–1998*, pp. 1157–1159.

69. Ibid., pp. 1158, 1159.

70. Liu Junning, "Chanquan baohu yu youxian zhengfu," in Qiu Shi, *Jiefang wenxuan 1978–1998*, pp. 40–48.

71. Ibid., pp. 41, 42, 43.

72. For the text of the speeches, see Bai Shazhou, *Jiang Zemin bianfa* [Jiang Zemin's Political Reform] (Hong Kong: Mingjing chubanshe, 1998), appendix, pp. 229–272.

73. Ibid., pp. 241, 252.

74. Ibid., pp. 241, 250, 251, 253.

75. Ibid., pp. 254, 255, 256, 262.

76. Ma Licheng and Ling Zhijun, *Jiaofeng* [Crossed Swords] (Beijing: Jinri Zhongguo chubanshe, 1998), p. 424.

77. Special Dispatch, "New Book by Jiang Zemin's Think-Tanker Criticizes Deng Liqun's Leftist Trend of Thought," *Ming Pao* (Hong Kong), Mar. 16, 1998, p. A11, translation in FBIS-CHI-98-075, Mar. 17, 1998.

78. Ma and Ling, *Jiaofeng,* p. 424.

79. "Some 150,000 Copies of 'Jiaofeng,' which Criticizes Ultra-Leftist Forces, Sold in One Month," *Ming Pao* (Hong Kong), Apr. 20, 1998, p. A10, translation in FBIS-CHI-98-110, Apr. 21, 1998.

80. Susan Lawrence, "War of Words," *Far Eastern Economic Review,* May 6, 1999, p. 27.

81. Peng Jianpu, "Two Reform Views Cross Swords," *Dangdai sichao,* Oct. 20, 1998, pp. 51–58, translation in FBIS-CHI-98-356, Dec. 23, 1998.

82. Ibid.

83. Li Ming, "Cross of Swords Caused by the Book 'Jiaofeng,'" *Ta Kung Pao* (Hong Kong), May 15, 1998, p. A4, translation in FBIS-CHI-98-135, May 18, 1998.

84. Vivien Pik-kwan Chan, "Editor Sues in Battle with Crossed Swords," *South China Morning Post,* June 25, 1998, p. 9.

85. Yeh Hung-yen, "Authors of the Book 'Crossing Swords' Sued over Copyright Infringement, Beijing Intermediate Court Conducts Open Trial," *Ta Kung Pao* (Hong Kong), Nov. 27, 1998, p. A3, translation in FBIS-CHI-98-334, Dec. 1, 1998.

86. Ibid.

87. Charles Hutzler, "Communist Ideologue Goes to Court in Sign of Progress in China," Associated Press, Jan. 19, 1999.

88. "Controversial Book Finds Publisher in China's South," *Ta Kung Pao* (Hong Kong), Jan. 1, 1999, p. A2, translation in BBC Summary of World Broadcasts, Part 3, Asia-Pacific, FE/D3435G, Jan. 18, 1999.

89. Liu Junning, *Beida chuantong yu jindai Zhongguo: Ziyouzhuyi de xiansheng* [Peking University's Tradition and Modern China: The Harbinger of Liberalism] (Beijing: Zhongguo renshi chubanshe, 1998).

90. Ibid., pp. 2, 4, 5.

91. Ibid., pp. 4, 6.

92. Liu Junning, interview with the author, Cambridge, Mass., 2001.

93. "Shui zai zhanling daxuesheng de sixiang zhendi?" *Zhongliu,* no. 4 (2000), pp. 42–44.

94. Ibid., p. 42.

95. Josephine Ma, "Scholars Placed on Publishing Blacklist," *South China Morning Post,* Dec. 16, 2000.

96. Liu Junning, "Lun jingji zhidu zai xianfa zhong de diwei" [China's Route to Constitutional Governance: On Economic Institutions' Position in the Constitution] *Zhanlue yu guanli* [Strategy and Management], no. 5, 2003, pp. 109–117.

97. Li Shenzhi, "Fifty Years of Storms and Disturbances: Soliloquy on National Day Evening," translation in *China Perspectives* (Nov.–Dec. 2000), pp. 5–12.

98. Ibid., pp. 5, 6, 7.

99. Ibid., pp. 7, 8.

100. Ibid., p. 9.

101. Ibid., pp. 9, 10.

102. Ibid., pp. 10, 12.

6. The Establishment of an Alternative Political Party

1. Bureau of Democracy, Human Rights, and Labor, U.S. Department of State, *1999 Country Reports on Human Rights Practices*, Feb. 25, 2000, *http://www.state.gov/www/global/human_rights/1999_hrp_report/china.html* (accessed Jan. 2, 2004).

2. Tony Saich, "Negotiating the State: The Development of Social Organizations in China," *China Quarterly*, no. 161 (Mar. 2000), pp. 124–141.

3. Fang Jue, "Articulating Dissent from Within," *China Rights Forum* (Spring 1998), *http://iso.hrichina.org/iso/article.adp?article_id=52&category_id=26* (accessed Jan. 2, 2004).

4. Fang Jue, "Put Political Reform Back on the Agenda: A Call from Inside the System," *China Rights Forum* (Spring 1998), *http://iso.hrichina.org/iso/article.adp?article_id=52&category_id=26* (accessed Jan. 2, 2004).

5. Ibid.

6. Ibid.

7. Ibid.

8. John Pomfret, "Reform Hot Topic of Group in Beijing: Open Debate Grows as Jiang Eases Grip," *Washington Post*, Sept. 13, 1998, p. A37.

9. "AFP: PRC Activists Hold Discussion Group," Dec. 12, 1998, translation in FBIS-CHI-98-346, Dec. 15, 1998.

10. Ibid.

11. "Intellectuals' Union Meets in Beijing," *Singtao jih pao* (Hong Kong), Oct. 7, 1998, p. A5, translation in BBC Summary of World Broadcasts, Part 3, Asia-Pacific, FE/D3353/G, Oct. 9, 1998.

12. "Nipped in the Bud: The Suppression of the China Democracy Party," *Human Rights Watch*, vol. 12, no. 5 (Sept. 2000), *http:// www.hrw.org/reports/2000/china* (accessed Jan. 3, 2004).

13. Cai Jiquan, "An Jun: Prisoner Profile," *China Rights Forum* (Spring 2001), back cover.

14. Ibid.

15. "After UN Vote, Chinese Activist Sentenced to Prison," Associated Press, Apr. 19, 2000.

16. Ibid.

17. "China to Improve Management over Ngos," *Xinhua News Agency*, Nov. 23, 1998.

18. Ibid.; David Lague, "Lobbies Come Under Fire in Beijing," *Sydney Morning Herald*, Nov. 27, 1998, p. 12.

19. "Nipped in the Bud."

20. Teresa Wright, "The China Democracy Party and the Politics of Protest in the 1980s–1990s," *China Quarterly*, no. 172 (Dec. 2002), p. 910.

21. Ibid., pp. 922, 923.

22. Cai Jiquan, "Wang Youcai," *Human Rights Forum* (Winter 1999–2000), back cover.

23. "Nipped in the Bud."

24. Ibid.

25. Wang Youcai, interview with the author, Cambridge, Mass., Apr. 30, 2004.

26. Jan Van der Made, "The Rise and Fall of the China Democracy Party," *China Rights Forum* (Winter 2000–2001), p. 30.

27. Ibid.

28. Wang Youcai, "Ruhe zujian quanguoxing gongkai fandui dang" [How to Organize a National Open Opposition Party], *Beijing zhichun*, no. 65 (Oct. 1998), p. 42.

29. "Nipped in the Bud."

30. Wright, "The China Democracy Party," p. 912.

31. Beatrice Laroche, "Qin Yongmin," *China Rights Forum* (Spring 1999), back cover.

32. Erik Eckholm, "Chinese Dissident Refuses to Leave for Exile in the U.S.," *New York Times*, Jan. 15, 1998, p. A6.

33. "Liu Xianbin: Imprisoned for Advocating Democracy," *China Rights Forum* (Winter 1999–2000), p. 8.

34. Liu Xianbin, "Lessons of the Modern Democracy Movement," *China Rights Forum* (Winter 1999–2000), p. 10.

35. Ibid., pp. 9, 10.

36. "Two Chinese Pro-democracy Activists Jailed for 10 and Six Years," *Agence France-Presse*, Jan. 3, 2000.

37. "Nipped in the Bud"; Willy Wo-Lap Lam, "Why Party Fears Voice of Opposition," *South China Morning Post*, Sept. 23, 1998, p. 19.

38. "Nipped in the Bud."

39. Van der Made, "Rise and Fall," p. 32.

40. "Chinese Press Give Low-key Coverage on Signing of UN Rights Covenant," *Agence France-Presse*, Oct. 6, 1998; "Nipped in the Bud."

41. "Nipped in the Bud."

42. Van der Made, "Rise and Fall," p. 33.

43. Xu Wenli, "Democratic Movement in China," *Issue Papers on China* (Washington, D.C.: China Strategic Institute), no. 43, Dec. 3, 1998, p. 1.

44. Ibid., pp. 1, 2.

45. Ibid., pp. 2, 3.

46. Ibid., pp. 4, 5.

47. "Nipped in the Bud."

48. "What Did Xu Wenli Actually Say?" *China Labour Bulletin,* no. 45 (Jan.–Feb. 1999), *http://www.china-labour.org.hk* (accessed Jan. 14, 2004).

49. Cindy Sui, "China Defends Move to Ban Free Trade Unions despite Ratifying UN Pact," Agence France-Presse, Mar. 1, 2001.

50. Erik Eckholm, "Chinese Democracy Campaigners Push for Free Labor Unions," *New York Times,* Dec. 23, 1997, p. A3.

51. Jasper Becker, "Police Thwart Celebrations for Rights Pact," *South China Morning Post,* Dec. 11, 1998, p. 9.

52. "Nipped in the Bud"; "Veteran Dissident Calls for Human Rights Body inside China," Agence France-Presse, Mar. 20, 1998.

53. "Jiu shenqing jianli 'Zhongguo renquan guancha' shiyi zhi zhonggong zhongyang, guowuyuan, renda, shi xie bing Rineiwa lianheguo renquan weiyuanhui gongkai xin" [Open Letter to Apply for the Establishment of 'China Human Rights Watch' Addressed to the Central Committee, State Council, NPC, CPPCC, and the U.N. Human Rights Commission in Geneva], *Zhongguo zhichun,* no. 175 (1998), p. 31.

54. "Jiu shenqing chuban minban qikan 'Gongmin luntan' zhi zhonggong zhongyang, guowuyuan, renda, zhi xie bing lianheguo renquan weiyuanhui gongkai xin" [Open Letter to Apply for Permission to Publish the "Citizens' Rights Observer' Addressed to the Central Committee, State Council, NPC, CPPCC, and the U.N. Human Rights Commission], *Zhongguo zhichun,* no. 175 (1998), p. 32.

55. "200 Workers Stage Protest in Central China over Wage Cut," Agence France-Presse, Oct. 14, 1998.

56. "Chinese Authorities Allow Dissident to Stand for Village Election," Agence France-Presse, Oct. 28, 1998.

57. Jervina Lao, "China Releases Another Dissident ahead of UN Rights Meeting," Agence France-Presse, Mar. 19, 1999.

58. H. Asher Bolande, "Activists Defy Chinese Election Practices, Insist on Legal Right to Run," Agence France-Presse, Jan. 7, 1998.

59. Ibid.; "Chinese Dissident Freed," Agence France-Presse, Feb. 22, 1998.

60. "Chinese Dissident Arrested: Rights Group," Agence France-Presse, Apr. 6, 1998.

61. Ibid.

62. "Chinese Activists Appeal for Help in Standing in Local Elections," Agence

France-Presse, Oct. 14, 1998; "Three Chinese Activists to Stand in Local Elections," Agence France-Presse, Sept. 21, 1998.

63. "Three Chinese Activists to Stand."

64. Ibid.

65. Kai Peter Yu, "Dissident Candidates in Protest over Intimidation," *South China Morning Post,* Sept. 26, 1998, p. 7.

66. "Would-be Dissident Candidate Booted in Beijing Vote," Associated Press, Nov. 24, 1998.

67. Ibid.

68. Reuters, "Enthusiasm but Little Choice in Local Ballot," *South China Morning Post Internet Edition,* Dec. 16, 1998.

69. "Nipped in the Bud."

70. Ibid.

71. "China Releases Shandong Opposition Party Activist," Agence France-Presse, Oct. 7, 1998.

72. "Open Letter Demands Release of Democracy Activist," Central News Agency (Taipei), Aug. 9, 1998, translation in BBC Summary of World Broadcasts, Part 3, Asia-Pacific, FE/D3302/G, Aug. 11, 1998.

73. Ibid.

74. Van der Made, "Rise and Fall," p. 34.

75. Elaine Kurtenbach, "Chinese Dissident Sentenced to 13 Years in Prison for Subversion," Associated Press, Aug. 6, 1999.

76. Ibid.

77. "Four Opposition Party Members Detained in Southwest China," Agence France-Presse, July 7, 1999; "Harsh Sentences for China Democracy Party in Renewed Crackdown," Agence France-Presse, Aug. 6, 1999.

78. "Abusing Rights according to Law," *China Rights Forum* (Winter 1999–2000), p. 5.

79. Ibid., p. 6.

80. Cai, "Wang Youcai."

81. Luisetta Mudie, "Chinese Dissidents Step Up Protests during Festival of the Dead," Agence France-Presse, Apr. 4, 1999.

82. Ibid.

83. "Report: Two More Chinese Dissidents Detained, Two Others Missing," Associated Press, June 28, 1999.

84. "The New Century Declaration of China Democracy Party: Brief Introduction," *China Affairs,* vol. 1, no. 1 (Spring 2000), *http://www.chinaaffairs.org/ english/01/01tcdp.htm* (accessed Jan. 14, 2003); "The Three Big Thoughts," *The Economist,* June 17, 2000; "Veteran Chinese Pro-democracy Fighter Nie Dies," Agence France-Presse, Oct. 7, 2001.

85. "New Century Declaration."

86. Ibid.

87. Ibid.

88. "No Word on Leading Dissident Arrested before China's Party Congress," Agence France-Presse, Nov. 22, 2002.

89. "Long-Time Democracy Campaigner He Depu Goes on Trial in China for Subversion," Agence France-Presse, Oct. 14, 2003; Robert J. Saiget, "Leading Chinese Democracy Activist Gets Eight Years for Subversion," Agence France-Presse, Nov. 6, 2003.

90. "Veteran Chinese Pro-democracy Fighter."

91. "Nipped in the Bud."

92. "Chinese President's Spring Festival Address Affirms Viability of Political System," Xinhua News Agency, Feb. 12, 1999, in BBC Summary of World Broadcasts, Part 3, Asia-Pacific, FE/D3460/G, Feb. 16, 1999.

7. Citizenship Extends into Cyberspace despite Repression

1. Jasper Becker, "Jiang Rejects Political Reform," *South China Morning Post*, Dec. 19, 1998, p. 1.

2. James Kynge, "Economic Ill Wind Blows China's Dissidents No Good," *Financial Times*, Dec. 28, 1998, p. 4.

3. "One Academy, Two Systems," *Far Eastern Economic Review*, Oct. 29, 1998, p. 8.

4. James Kynge, "Police Agents Fail to Silence Chinese Critic," *Financial Times*, July 17, 2000, p. 8.

5. Vivien Pik-Kwan Chan and Fong Tak-ho, "Chinese Writer Flees to US," *South China Morning Post*, June 20, 2001, p. 1.

6. Xia Wensi, "Ding Guangen Challenges Zhu Rongji," *Kaifang* (Hong Kong), Dec. 3, 1998, pp. 10–13, translation in FBIS-CHI-98-346, Dec. 12, 1998.

7. Vivien Pik-Kwan Chan, "'Problem' Social Groups Reined In: Trial Periods Planned," *South China Morning Post*, Nov. 25, 1998, p. 7.

8. Jasper Becker, "Capitalists Infiltrating Party, Article Warns," *South China Morning Post*, July 14, 2000.

9. Ibid.

10. Mark O'Neill, "Changing Party Rules a Risky Business," *South China Morning Post*, Aug. 13, 2001, p. 3.

11. "Japan's Asahi Obtains Document Criticizing Jiang Zemin's CPC Anniversary," *Asahi Shimbun*, Aug. 1, 2001, translation in FBIS-CHI-2001-0801, Aug. 1, 2001.

12. Commentator, "The Building of Ideological Style Is in Primary Position," Xinhua News Agency, Oct. 8, 2001, in FBIS-CHI-2001-1008, Oct. 9, 2001.

13. Zhao Haiyan and Dong Huifeng, "Liu Ji Says Economic Globalization Should Be a Common Banner of the People of the World," Zhongguo xinwen she, June 16, 2000, in FBIS-CHI-2000-0616, June 29, 2000.

14. Ian Johnson and Matt Forney, "Beijing Attempts to Silence Academics," *Asian Wall Street Journal,* Apr. 7, 2000.

15. "China's Internet Population Hits 94 Million, but Growth Is Slowing," Agence France-Presse (Hong Kong), Jan. 19, 2005; Philip Pan, "Webmaster Finds Gaps in China's Net," *Washington Post,* May 24, 2004, p. A1; Xiao Qiang, "The Great Leap Online That Is Stirring China," *International Herald Tribune,* Aug. 6, 2004, p. 7.

16. Guo Liang, *Surveying Internet Usage and Impact in Twelve Chinese Cities,* CASS, 2003.

17. Sam Allis, "Net Sites Blocked by China Go from Expected to Bizarre," *Boston Globe,* Dec. 5, 2002, p. D2.

18. Xiao Qiang, "The Great Leap Online That Is Stirring China."

19. "Tunnel Vision On-line," *South China Morning Post,* July 22, 1997.

20. "China to Try Entrepreneur in New Internet Crackdown," Associated Press, July 29, 1998.

21. Erik Eckholm, "A Trial Will Test China's Grip on the Internet," *New York Times,* Nov. 16, 1998, p. A7.

22. John Pomfret, "Chinese Sentenced in Internet Case," *Washington Post,* Jan. 21, 1999, p. A19.

23. Ibid.

24. "Reporters sans Frontieres Condemns Arrest of Chinese Intellectual," Agence France-Presse, Sept. 4, 1999.

25. Philip Pan, "Study Group Is Crushed in China's Grip," *Washington Post,* Apr. 23, 2004, p. A1.

26. Cai Jiquan, "Case File: Punishing Youthful Enthusiasm," *China Rights Forum* (Fall 2001), pp. 10, 40.

27. Ibid., p. 10.

28. Pan, "Study Group Is Crushed."

29. Elaine Kurtenbach, "China Renews Crackdown on Cyber-Dissent," Associated Press, Apr. 19, 2001.

30. "China Sentences Four Dissidents to Up to Ten Years for Subversion in Internet Dissent Case," Associated Press, May 28, 2003.

31. Cai, "Case File," p. 40.

32. Elisabeth Rosenthal, "4 Chinese Sentenced for Political Discussions," *New York Times,* May 30, 2003, p. A9.

33. Peter Harmsen, "China Jails Four Internet Dissidents as Crackdown Intensifies," Agence France-Presse, May 29, 2003.

34. Geremie Barmé, *In the Red: On Contemporary Chinese Culture* (New York:

Columbia University Press, 1999), p. 351; Yu Jie, interview with the author, Cambridge, Mass., July 2003.

35. Barmé, *In the Red,* pp. 351–352.

36. Verna Yu, "Crusader Vows to Fight On," *South China Morning Post,* July 31, 2003, p. 14.

37. Ibid.

38. Yu Jie, "Fight for China," *Asiaweek,* Nov. 24, 2000, p. 47.

39. "Yu Jie on Beijing University Student Arrests," essay posted on the Internet, 2001, *http://www.usembassy-china.org.cn/sandt/yujie-arrests.html,* translated by David Cowhig.

40. "Chinese Dissidents Demand Release of Four Charged with Subversion," Agence France-Presse, Feb. 9, 2002.

41. Jasper Becker, "Dotcoms 'Should Protest at Web-Creator's Arrest,'" *South China Morning Post,* June 28, 2000, p. 7.

42. Verna Yu, "Webmaster Given Five Years for Publishing Essays," *South China Morning Post,* May 19, 2003, p. 4. Huang's second Web site was *www.6-4tianwang.com.*

43. "China Shuts Down Political Website, Arrests Founder," Agence France-Presse, June 7, 2000.

44. Human Rights Watch, "China: Foreign Companies Should Protest Internet Detention," June 26, 2000.

45. "Chinese Scholars Issue Declaration of Rights of Internet Users," Information Centre for Human Rights and Democracy (Hong Kong), translation in BBC Monitoring Asia Pacific–Political, July 31, 2002. The text of the declaration is available at *http://www.worldofradio.com/dxld2123.txt* (accessed Feb. 10, 2005).

46. Ibid.

47. "Amnesty Urges Release of 22-year-old Jailed for Internet Essays," Agence France-Presse, Dec. 12, 2002.

48. Special Dispatch, "Beijing Undergraduate Liu Di Suspectedly Arrested for Mocking Politics on Internet," *Ming Pao* (Hong Kong), Dec. 9, 2002, translation FBIS-CHI-2002–1209, Dec. 11, 2002.

49. Pei Minxin's translation of Liu Di's writing, "The Powerful Voice of a Mouse," *Washington Post Outlook,* Dec. 7, 2003, p. B2.

50. Ibid.

51. *http://www.mzyzy.org/bbs/dispbbs.asp?boardID=2&replyID=5639&ID=2163 &skin=1* (accessed Jan. 16, 2004).

52. David Cowhig, personal communication with the author, Feb. 22, 2004.

53. Robert J. Saiget, "For Chinese Internet Dissident, Protest Runs in Family," Agence France-Presse, Dec. 15, 2002.

54. Jim Yardley, "A Chinese Bookworm Raises Her Voice in Cyberspace," *New York Times,* July 24, 2004.

55. "Grandmother Petitions Jailing of 'Cause Célèbre' Chinese Internet Activist," Agence France-Presse, Mar. 7, 2003.

56. Ibid.

57. Jim Yardley, "China Frees 3 'Cyber Dissidents,'" *New York Times,* Dec. 1, 2003, p. 3.

58. *http://www.mzyzy.org/bbs/dispbbs.asp?boardID=2&replyID=5639&ID=2163 &skin=1* (accessed Jan. 16, 2004).

59. Leu Siew Ying, "Loosen Control of Internet, Schroeder Urges Mainland," *South China Morning Post,* Dec. 4, 2003, p. 6; "China: CPJ Condemns Arrest of Internet Essayist," Committee to Protect Journalists, Nov. 3, 2002, letter to Hu Jintao, *http://www.cpj.org/protests/03ltrs/China03nov03pl.html* (accessed Jan. 14, 2004).

60. "China: CPJ Condemns Arrest."

61. "Website Carries Petition Letter by 103 People Calling for Release of PRC Dissidents," at *http://www.hkhkhk.com/main/messages/6610.html,* translation in FBIS-CHI-2004-0202, Feb. 4, 2004.

62. Ibid.

63. Jim Yardley and Chris Buckley, "Chinese Reformers Petition for Review of Subversion Law," *New York Times,* Feb. 1, 2004.

64. Nailene Chou Wiest, "Hong Kong Protest Encourages Activists on Mainland," *South China Morning Post,* Feb. 3, 2004.

65. "Website Carries Petition Letter."

66. Ibid.

67. Agence France-Presse, June 11, 2004.

68. Amnesty International, "Controls Tighten as Internet Activism Grows," Jan. 28, 2004, p. 1.

69. Reporters sans frontières, *http://www.rsf.org/rubrique.php3?id_rubrique=19.* Pointed out to the author by Yu Maochun, U.S. Naval Academy, May 3, 2004.

70. "Chinese Academic Levels Rare Criticism at China's Propaganda Machinery," Agence France-Presse, May 5, 2004.

71. "Declaration of the Campaign against the Central Propaganda Department," at *http://zonaeuropa.com/20040505_2.htm.*

8. The Expansion of Rights Consciousness

1. Michael Walzer, "Citizenship," in Terence Ball, James Farr, and Russell L. Hanson, eds., *Political Innovation and Conceptual Change* (New York: Cambridge University Press, 1989), p. 211.

2. Kevin J. O'Brien, "Villagers, Elections, and Citizenship," in Merle Goldman and Elizabeth Perry, eds., *Changing Meanings of Citizenship in Modern China* (Cambridge, Mass.: Harvard University Press, 2002), pp. 225–229.

3. Amartya Sen, "Democracy as a Universal Value," *Journal of Democracy,* vol. 10, no. 3 (July 1999), pp. 3–17.

4. Ibid., pp. 8–9.

5. Elizabeth J. Perry, "'To Rebel Is Justified': Cultural Revolution Influences on Contemporary Chinese Protest," in Law Kam-yee, ed., *The Chinese Cultural Revolution Reconsidered* (New York: Palgrave, 2003), p. 266.

6. Vivien Pik-Kwan Chan, "23 Percent in Cities 'Lose Jobs as Reforms Bite,'" *South China Morning Post,* Jan. 31, 2001.

7. Ibid.

8. Teresa Poole, "Peking Starts to Panic as Chinese Workers Get the Union Habit," *The Independent* (London), Mar. 5, 1996, p. 9.

9. "Five Hundred Steel Workers Protest over Fear of Job Loss," Agence France-Presse, Sept. 28, 2000.

10. "'Pai Hsing' Reports Sichuan Mill Strike in April," translation in BBC Summary of World Broadcasts, Part 3, Asia-Pacific, FE/1108/B2/1, June 26, 1991.

11. Ibid.

12. Willy Wo-Lap Lam, "Crackdown on 'Clandestine' Workers' Groups Noted," *South China Morning Post,* Dec. 13, 1991, pp. 1, 15, in FBIS-CHI-91-240, Dec. 13, 1991, p. 18.

13. Elaine Kurtenbach, "Huge Protest by Laid Off Chinese Factory Workers," Associated Press, July 17, 1997.

14. "Demonstration 'Ringleaders' Arrested," *South China Morning Post,* July 19, 1997, p. 10.

15. "Hundreds Injured in China Labor Riots," United Press International, July 17, 1997.

16. "Chinese Dissident on the Run after Revealing Workers Protest," Agence France-Presse, Aug. 8, 1997.

17. Trevor Marshallsea, "Workers' Protest Violently Put Down in SW China," *Asia Pulse,* July 17, 1997.

18. "Police Arrest Chinese Activist on Fraud Charges," Agence France-Presse, Apr. 15, 1998.

19. Josephine Ma, "Key Rail Line Blocked by Irate Workers," *South China Morning Post,* Nov. 30, 2000.

20. "Chinese Pensioners Demonstrated for Their Money," Agence France-Presse, Apr. 18, 1998.

21. Lorien Holland, "Pressure Mounts on China to Release Trade Union Activist," Agence France-Presse, Jan. 19, 1998.

22. "Chinese Dissident Calls on Beijing to Ratify UN Rights Convention," Agence France-Presse, Feb. 1, 1998.

23. "2,000 Chinese Protest Pension Cuts," Agence France-Presse, Dec. 9, 1999.

24. "Zhang Shanguang: Labour Activist Who Touched a Raw Nerve," Agence France-Presse, Dec. 27, 1998.

25. Erik Eckholm, "In Drive on Dissidents, China Gives 4th Severe Sentence in Week," *New York Times,* Dec. 28, 1998, p. 9.

26. "Chinese Labor Organizer to Appeal 10-Year Sentence," Associated Press, Jan. 14, 1999.

27. "Jailed Dissident Calls for Re-trial," Agence France-Presse, Jan. 14, 1999.

28. John Pomfret, "Leaders of Independent Chinese Labor Union Fear Crackdown," *Washington Post,* Dec. 15, 2000, p. A30.

29. Ibid.

30. Erik Eckholm, "Silk Workers in Standoff with Beijing over Union," *New York Times,* Dec. 15, 2000, p. 6.

31. Ibid.

32. Christopher Bodeen, "Chinese Union Organizer Being Doped under Detention," Associated Press, Dec. 17, 2000.

33. Agence France-Presse, "Workers Demand Release of Chinese Unionist from Mental Asylum," Dec. 17, 2000, translation in FBIS-CHI-2000-1217, Dec. 20, 2000.

34. "Paying the Price: Worker Unrest in Northeast China," *Human Rights Watch,* vol. 14, no. 6 (Aug. 2002), p. 2.

35. Philip P. Pan, "Three Chinese Workers: Jail, Betrayal and Fear," *Washington Post,* Dec. 28, 2002, p. A1.

36. "Armed Troops Seal Off Northeast China Oil Town to Stop Protests," Agence France-Presse, Mar. 21, 2002.

37. Erik Eckholm, "Leaner Factories, Fewer Workers Bring More Labor Unrest to China," *New York Times,* Mar. 19, 2002, p. A1.

38. Pan, "Three Chinese Workers."

39. Joseph Chaney, "Yao Fuxin: Prisoner Profile," *China Rights Forum,* no. 2 (2002), back cover.

40. Ibid.

41. Hamish Mcdonald, "For Mr. Mo, Court Win Can Mean Jail," *The Age* (Melbourne), Jan. 20, 2003, p. 10.

42. Philip P. Pan, "China Tries Labor Leaders amid Protest," *Washington Post,* Jan. 16, 2003, p. A14.

43. City People's Procuratorate of Liaoyang, Liaoning Province, "Indictment of Yao Fuxin and Xiao Yunliang in Liaoyang, China," *Human Rights News* (New York), *http://www.hrw.org/press/2003/02/chinaindictment.htm* (accessed Jan. 15, 2004).

44. Ibid.

45. Audra Ang, "Chinese Activists Sentenced to Prison on Subversion Charges," Associated Press, May 9, 2003.

46. "Chinese Labor Leaders Refused Medical Parole Despite Severe Illness," Agence France-Presse, Hong Kong, Dec 20, 2003.

47. "Chinese Factory Boss Arrested, but Labor Leaders Remain in Jail," Agence France-Presse, July 31, 2002.

48. "China Workers Threaten Protest in Beijing during Congress," Agence France-Presse, Nov. 5, 2002.

49. Li Yonghai, "How Could We Reform State-owned Enterprises by Simply 'Selling Them Off?'" *Renmin luntan*, no. 12, Dec. 15, 1998, pp. 8–11, translation in FBIS-CHI-99-009, Jan. 12, 1999.

50. Thomas Bernstein and Xiaobo Lu, *Taxation without Representation in Contemporary Rural China* (New York: Cambridge University Press, 2003).

51. Willy Wo-Lap Lam, "Sowing Seeds of Rural Discontent," *South China Morning Post*, Feb. 9, 2000.

52. Bernstein and Lu, *Taxation without Representation*, pp. 116–165.

53. Kevin J. O'Brien, "Rightful Resistance," *World Politics*, 49 (October 1996), pp. 31–55.

54. Jasper Becker, "Might vs. Right," *China Rights Forum* (Spring 2000), pp. 4–9.

55. Ibid., pp. 5, 6.

56. Yu Jianrong, "Nongmin you zuzhi kangzheng jiqi zhengzhi fengxian" [Organizational Struggle of Rural Residents and Its Political Risk: A Survey of County H in Hunan Province], *Zhanlue yu guanli*, no. 3 (2003), pp. 1–16.

57. Cai Jiquan, "Ma Wenlin: Prisoner Profile," *China Rights Forum*, no. 1 (2002), back cover.

58. Becker, "Might vs. Right," pp. 6, 8–9.

59. "Around 30,000 Farmers Petition Jailing of Chinese Lawyer," Agence France-Presse, Aug. 11, 2000.

60. "More than 30,000 Villages in Shaanxi Province Protest Lawyer's Sentence," Information Centre for Human Rights and Democracy (Hong Kong), Aug. 11, 2000, in BBC Summary of World Broadcasts, Part 3, Asia-Pacific, FE/D3918/G, Aug. 14, 2000.

61. Becker, "Might vs. Right," p. 9. For a much more detailed account of Ma Wenlin's activities, see Ian Johnson, *Wild Grass* (New York: Pantheon, 2004), pp. 11–86.

62. "Report Says Citizen's Legal Protection Increasing," Xinhua News Agency, July 12, 1994, in FBIS-CHI-94-133, July 12, 1994, p. 19.

63. Minxin Pei, "Citizens v. Mandarins: Administrative Litigation in China," *China Quarterly*, no. 152 (Dec. 1997), pp. 832–862.

64. Personal observations of wall posters in Xi'an, Aug. 10, 2003.

65. Yu Jianrong, of the Chinese Academy of Social Sciences, lecture at Fairbank Center, Harvard University, Dec. 4, 2003.

66. Zhonggong zhongyang zuzhibu ketizu, *Zhongguo diaocha baogao: 2000–2001 xinxing shixia renmin neibu maodun yanjiu* (Beijing: Zhongyang bianyi chubanshe, 2001).

67. Robert Marquand, "China Airs Its Dirty Laundry, a Bit," *Christian Science Monitor*, June 8, 2001, p. 6.

68. Dorothy J. Solinger, *Contesting Citizenship in Urban China: Peasant Migrants, the State, and the Logic of the Market* (Berkeley: University of California Press, 1999).

69. Philip Pan, "When Workers Organize, China's Party-Run Unions Resist," *Washington Post*, Oct. 15, 2002, p. A11.

70. Ibid.

71. "The Truth Behind the April 25 Incident" (abridged version), at *http://www.faluninfo.net/Special Topics/april25abridged.html*.

72. Ibid.

73. Craig Smith, "In a Chinese Battle, the Web Is Mightier Than the State," *Wall Street Journal*, Sept. 9, 1999, p. B1.

74. Seth Faison, "Ex-General, Member of Banned Sect, Confesses 'Mistakes,' China Says," *New York Times*, July 31, 1999, p. A5.

75. Ibid.

76. "The Truth behind the April 25 Incident."

77. Ibid.

78. Jian Xu, "Body, Discourse, and the Cultural Politics of Contemporary Chinese Qigong," *Journal of Asian Studies*, vol. 58, no. 4 (Nov. 1999), pp. 961–991; Nancy H. Chen, "Falungong: Cultivating Qi and the Body Politic," *Harvard Asia Pacific Review* (Winter 2000), p. 47.

79. Elisabeth Rosenthal, "China Admits Banned Sect Is Continuing Its Protest," *New York Times*, Apr. 21, 2000, p. A9.

80. Chen, "Falungong," p. 48.

81. Erik Eckholm, "China Enacts Tough Law to Undercut Banned Cult," *New York Times*, Oct. 31, 1999, p. 11.

82. Erik Eckholm, "China Sentences 4 in Spiritual Group to Long Jail Time," *New York Times*, Dec. 27, 1999, p. A1.

83. "Shanghai Legal Scholars Slam Falun Gong," Xinhua News Agency, Aug. 9, 1999.

84. "CASS Official Xia Yong on Falungong, Rule of Law," Zhongguo xinwen she, Aug. 3, 1999, in FBIS-CHI-1999-0824, Aug. 25, 1999.

85. Ibid.

86. "PRC Lawyers Ordered Not to Defend Falungong Members," Agence France-Presse, Aug. 24, 1999, translation in FBIS-CHI-1999-0824, Aug. 25, 1999.

87. "People's Daily Urges Continued Fight against Falungong," Xinhua News Agency, Nov. 25, 1999, in FBIS-CHI-1999-1125, Nov. 26, 1999.

88. "Qigong Sect Calls for Release of Leaders," Information Centre of Human Rights and Democratic Movement in China (Hong Kong), Mar. 13, 2000, in

BBC Summary of World Broadcasts, Part 3, Asia-Pacific, FE/D3789/G, Mar. 15, 2000.

89. "PRC Security Continues Falungong Clampdown at NPC Conclusion," Agence France-Presse, Mar. 15, 2000, translation in FBIS-CHI-2000-0315, Mar. 16, 2000.

90. "PRC Detains 16 Christians as 'Evil Cult' Members," Agence France-Presse, Mar. 13, 2000, translation in FBIS-CHI-2000-0313, Mar. 14, 2000.

91. "Agency Mocks Falun Gong's Presence for UN Human Rights Session," Xinhua News Agency, Mar. 27, 2000, in BBC Summary of World Broadcasts, Part 3, Asia-Pacific, FE/D3804/G, Apr. 1, 2000.

92. "Falun Gong Members Arrested in Beijing," United Press International, Apr. 25, 2001.

93. Christopher Bodeen, "Falun Gong Hijacks Television Broadcasts on Outskirts of Beijing to Air Protest Video," Associated Press, Sept. 5, 2002.

94. Josephine Ma, "Three Million Took Part in Surging Protests Last Year," *South China Morning Post*, June 8, 2004, p. 5.

Epilogue

1. Chen Guidi and Chun Tao, *Zhongguo nongmin diaocha* [A Survey of Chinese Peasants] (Beijing: Renmin wenxue chubanshe, 2004).

2. "Intellectuals in China under Fire Again," *The Economist*, Dec. 9, 2004.

3. David A. Kelly, "The Importance of Being Public: Gagging China's Thinkers," *China Review* (London), no. 31 (Winter 2004–2005), pp. 28–37.

4. "Chief Editor of Pro-Reform Chinese Magazine Released after Questioning," Agence France-Presse, Dec. 22, 2004, translation in FBIS-CHI-2004–1222, Dec. 23, 2004.

5. On their Marxist humanist predecessors, see Merle Goldman, *Sowing the Seeds of Democracy in China* (Cambridge, Mass.: Harvard University Press, 1994).

6. B. Michael Frolic, "State-Led Civil Society," in Timothy Brook and B. Michael Frolic, eds., *Civil Society in China* (Armonk, N.Y.: M. E. Sharpe, 1997), p. 52.

7. Bruce J. Dickson, *Democratization in China and Taiwan: The Adaptability of Leninist Parties* (Oxford: Clarendon Press; New York: Oxford University Press, 1997), chap. 1.

8. Tun-jen Cheng and Stephan Haggard, "Regime Transformation in Taiwan: Theoretical and Comparative Perspectives," in Tun-jen Cheng and Stephan Haggard, eds., *Political Change in Taiwan* (Boulder: Lynne Rienner, 1992), pp. 3–4.

9. Vivien Pik-kwan Chan, "Political Reform Cadres' Main Aim," *South China Morning Post*, Feb. 6, 2002.

Index

Administrative Litigation Law (ALL), 212, 213–214

Administrative reform, 130, 139, 145

Advocacy groups, 22, 166

AIDS, 2

Alford, William, 110

All-China Federation of Trade Unions (ACFTU), 62, 205

Anti-rightist campaign, 55, 57, 65, 70, 84, 92–93, 112, 136, 138, 159, 184, 195, 226; purge of rightists, 89, 134

April 5 Forum journal, 33, 34, 37, 44, 46, 53, 173; editorial board, 48, 49

April 5 movement (1976), 27–28, 31, 34, 41, 53, 75, 168, 180, 181

Arrest and imprisonment of dissenters, 3, 8, 41, 44, 46, 48, 67, 74, 81–84, 90, 91, 147, 165, 169, 171, 172–173, 190, 192, 227; torture of prisoners, 45, 190, 220; demands for release of prisoners, 71, 75, 77, 86, 93, 191, 195, 196, 197, 199, 210, 213, 219; house arrest conditions, 85, 93, 176, 180; in Democracy Wall movement, 106, 178; in the CDP, 175, 178–179, 180, 184, 186, 209; of Tiananmen demonstrations (1989), 176, 178; for Internet dissent, 188, 195; of rightists, 195; of student protesters, 204; of workers, 205, 206, 209; health problems in prisons, 210. *See also* Detainment of dissenters; Political prisoners

Association to Protect the Rights and Interests of Laid-Off Workers, 206

Associations and organizations, 21; in the post-Mao era, 2, 12; as threat to the regime, 3, 6, 10, 16; professional, 5; persecution of, 6, 16, 18, 19–20, 22–23; grassroots, 7, 9, 43; independent or autonomous, 11, 12, 21, 51, 57, 66–67, 229; of entrepreneurs, 15; unofficial, 16, 83; human rights, 18; political patronage of, 21, 51, 52; registration of, 22, 82, 161, 162, 190, 221–222; political, 22–23, 51; outside the control of the state, 60; international human rights, 163; political reform discussions by, 166; of migrant workers, 215. *See also* Constitutional rights and freedoms: association; Disestablished intellectuals; Establishment intellectuals

Ba Jin, 28, 114

Ban on books, 110, 111–113, 117, 118, 126, 138, 184, 185, 190, 195, 225, 226

Bao Ge, 81–82

Bao Zunxin, 84, 91

BBC, 18, 79, 133, 157

Beijing Social and Economic Research Institute (SERI), 9, 22, 53, 59, 62, 64, 67, 161, 229; discussions at, 23–24, 165; publishing arm of, 60; and student demonstrations, 61; police raid on offices, 64; repression of, 68

Beijing Spring journal, 34, 37, 38, 41, 49, 60; group formed around, 40, 47, 51–52, 53, 54, 70; advocacy of unofficial strikes, 41–42

Beijing Student Autonomous Federation, 74

Beijing Workers Autonomous Federation (BWAF), 24, 62–64, 82, 204

Berkman Center for the Internet and Society, 186–187